Y0-BEE-179

# "What Happen"

# "What Happen"

## A Folk-History of
## Costa Rica's Talamanca Coast

by Paula Palmer

Previous editions: 1979 & 1993
This newly-designed edition printed 2005

© Copyright 2005 by Paula Palmer
   All rights reserved.
   ISBN 0-9705678-3-9

Design: Zona Creativa, S.A.
Maps: Jimmy Socash
Woodcut prints: Deirdre Hyde
Word processing: Ana Ruth Tortós
Proofreading: Frankie Henry, Mina Johnson

Published by Distribuidores Zona Tropical, S.A.
S.J.O. 1948
P.O. Box 025216
Miami, FL  33102-5216
www.zonatropical.net

*For the children of the Talamanca Coast*

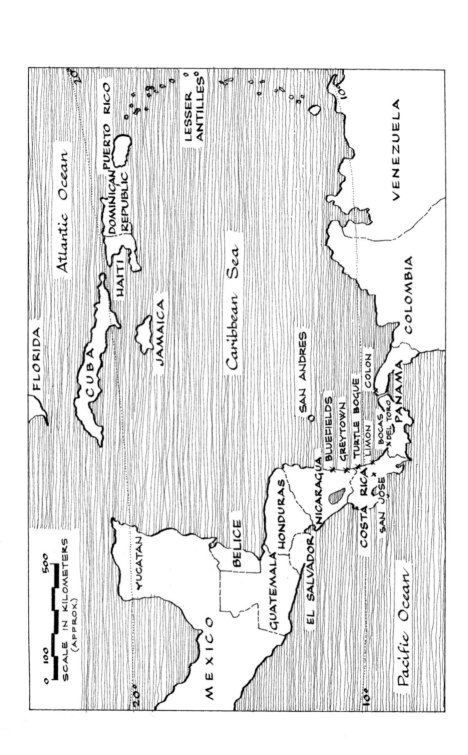

# Contents

In 1985, Talamanca high school children honored Miss Eudora "Sis" Matthews and Mr. Thomas Bethel for their life-long contributions to the development of the coastal communities. Miss "Sis" died in 1993 at age 99; Mr. Bethel died in 1986 at age 116.

# Introduction to the 2005 Edition

Twenty-five years have passed since "*What Happen*" was first published. Now the book not only tells history, it has a history of its own. This is its fifth printing in English, and—thanks to my new publisher Zona Tropical and designer Zona Creativa—it has a great new look.

I'm very pleased that this new printing will bring "*What Happen*" to a whole new generation (so different from earlier ones) on the Talamanca coast, and to thousands of visitors from countries all around the world. In the busy tourist towns of Cahuita, Puerto Viejo and Manzanillo, you have to look beyond your immediate impressions to see the villages described in the pages of "*What Happen*." The Afro-Caribbean communities are still there, albeit in the shadows of Italian restaurants, noisy shops and streets jammed with cars and tourists. Caribbean culture lends its unique rhythm and flavor to tourism on the Talamanca coast, where everyone enjoys calypsos, rice-and-beans and plantain tarts. But the homogenous culture and community of the Afro-Caribbean villages described in "*What Happen*" is gone forever, replaced by a vibrant and sometimes conflictive mix. Now people of many cultures, languages and nationalities are having an impact on the coast's development, and they all have a stake in Talamanca's future.

I wrote "*What Happen*" in 1977, before the coastal villages had electricity and telephones; a trip by bus to San José (via Turrialba) took a whole day. As I recount in the Author's Preface, my intention at that time was to convert the coast's oral history into a permanent record for its people. Most of the original thousand copies of the book are in the homes of my neighbors and former students in Cahuita and Puerto Viejo. During the 1980s, there were two additional printings of the same text in English, and I updated the chronicle through 1986 for a Spanish edition published by the Costa Rican Ministry of Culture under the title, "*Wa'apin Man*."

In 1993, we brought out a revised, expanded edition in English, but I resisted the impulse to add new material to bring the history up to date. I decided at that time to let "*What Happen*" be "*What Happen*," to let it be history, let it get old. Some day I might write a new book—the sequel—or perhaps someone else will. But for now, "*What Happen*" remains set in 1977, the year I wrote it. References in the text to "today" should be understood as 1977.

I did, however, add new material to the 1993 version, which is also included in this 2005 edition. I incorporated some new photographs and Deirdre Hyde's wonderful woodcut prints which first appeared in the 1986 Spanish edition. I also added to the original text some lengthy narratives

11

from interviews I conducted between 1979 and 1983. These add richness and depth to several chapters of "*What Happen*," for example: Mr. Paul Rodman's thoughtful account of growing up in the Sixaola Division banana plantations of the United Fruit Company (Chapter 10); Miss Daisy Lewis' memories of her star performances on the stage of the UNIA's Liberty Hall in Puerto Viejo (Chapter 12); Mr. Clinton Bennett's description of black people's struggle to obtain Costa Rican citizenship, and the rewards of political participation beginning in the 1950's (Chapters 12 and 13); and Mr. Alphaeus Buchanan's reflections on the meaning of black culture and identity in a rapidly changing world (Chapter 13).

Throughout the text I made editorial changes to correct errors, clarify meanings, improve style and give additional information. One error I was eager to correct is the spelling of Old Harbor. The North American spelling is historically inaccurate, since this name was given to the village by British subjects—pirates first, and later Jamaican immigrants. So in the 1993 and 2005 editions it is Old Harbour.

I am obliged to update one item in this 2005 edition—the list of Collaborators—in order to honor the 39 people who have died since they told me their stories of life on the Talamanca Coast. I remember each of them with much affection, and I am very glad they are alive in this book and in the imaginations of those who read their words here.

To all of the people who spent hours talking with me about their lives, their skills, their struggles and their dreams, I give my love and respect as well as my thanks. Listening to their stories filled me with wonder, warmed me with compassion, rocked me with laughter, rewarded me with precious moments, fond relationships and rich memories. It has been a pleasure to serve as the vehicle through which their stories can be told.

For their inspiration and assistance in bringing "*What Happen*" to life, I am forever grateful to Winston Lindo, Eulalia Bernard, Quince Duncan, Marcy Devine, Barney Hopewell, Eduardo Zúñiga and Mel Baker. Arnold Hanbelamt and Bob Bernthal made lasting contributions to Costa Rican history with the photographs they took in the 1970s, and Bill Bernthal put many hours of careful work into cleaning and scanning the negatives for this new printing. I owe this new edition of "*What Happen*" to John McCuen and Marc Roegiers at Zona Tropical, who rescued the book from being out of print. For their enduring friendships that make me feel forever at home on the Talamanca Coast, I am especially grateful to Laura Wilson and her family, Waltraud Barthels and Mauricio Salazar, Danny Hayling, Juanita Sánchez, Gloria Mayorga, María Eugenia Murillo and María Eugenia Bozzoli.

Paula Palmer
November 2004

# Author's Preface

(1979 Edition)

This book records the history of Costa Rica's Talamanca Coast, south of Puerto Limón, as the folks of the coast remember it.

Records exist of the exploration of this area by the Spanish conquistadores in the Sixteenth Century, of their observations of the indigenous peoples, their search for gold, their attempts at colonization and evangelism. But although the Spanish claimed the Talamanca region, they neither controlled it nor settled it. They drove the Indians farther into the mountains and largely ignored the immigrants who made their ways north from Panama (then part of Colombia), south from Nicaragua, and west from the Caribbean islands to make the Talamanca Coast their home. This book is the story of those immigrants, the English-speaking Afro-Caribbean people, who came here to stay.

They came first as fishermen and then as farmers. They traded with Indian groups in the high Talamanca mountains and merchants in their home ports of Bocas del Toro, Panama, and Greytown, Nicaragua, until later the Port of Limón offered them a market for their products. They brought seeds from Jamaica and San Andrés to grow the breadfruit, ackee, mangoes, oranges, and avocado pears that nourished their families. And everything grew: the fruits, the coconuts, the cocoa, the families, the schools, the churches, the villages.

For nearly a century the Afro-Caribbean settlers lived in relative isolation on the coast they chose as their home. Then, as time went on, trading boats sailed the coast, steam engines puffed through the bush carrying bananas, foreign companies came looking for oil and lumber and even sand. And so the coast that was known only to the Afro-Caribbean pioneers for a century has been gradually "discovered" by buyers and sellers and preachers and teachers and community organizers and government agencies and land speculators and tourists, all of whom bring with them progress and problems: change.

The oldest native of the Talamanca Coast alive today is Mr. Selles Johnson, who was born at Cahuita Point in 1894. Mr. Johnson, in addition to being a first-rate sea captain, mechanic, cocoa farmer, cricket player, horse racer, fisherman, and quadrille dancer, is also a most entertaining storyteller. I enjoyed listening to Mr. Johnson recall his boyhood along the Talamanca Coast many times before it occurred to me that Mr. Johnson's own grandchildren who live in Limón, San

José, and as far away as the United States, may not have heard these stories. And the children growing up in Cahuita, kicking their footballs and throwing their gigs between the hoofs of Mr. Johnson's horse as he plods out to inspect the coconut walk that his grandfather planted more than a hundred years ago ... how many of these children know anything of the struggle and the laughter that went into building the community that is their home? And how many of the tourists who take advantage of the new road to come and relax under the coconut palms that line the beaches of Cahuita and Puerto Vargas and Puerto Viejo ... how many of them could imagine the horse racing and ranch building and crocodile hunting and oil making and quadrille dancing and canoe carving that took place for years under those same palms?

A great breadfruit tree was felled in Puerto Viejo last year to make way for the new road that will follow the coast to the Panama border. A man the people remember as "Old Dan" planted that tree more than eighty years ago, the people say, and it was the mother tree of all the breadfruit from Puerto Viejo down to Monkey Point. The people want the new road and the progress it will bring them. They also loved that old breadfruit tree. It stood strong for many years and now its *hijos* thrive and produce though it is gone.

We can no more return to the days of the past in Talamanca than we can resurrect Old Dan's breadfruit tree. But we can learn from them, draw strength from them, feel pride in them, and use them, perhaps, as a standard by which we can judge what is progress and what is not.

This, I think, is in part what motivates the Limón educators who are promoting the Ministry of Public Education's *Plan Educativo de Limón*. The Plan, coordinated during its development by Professor Eulalia Bernard Little, proposes many changes in the approach toward education in Limón Province, based on the concept that education must take into account and reflect the culture in which it functions, and actively uphold the values of that culture. A specific recommendation of the Plan encourages students and teachers in Limón to investigate the values and strengths of the Limón culture which are rooted in the experience of the Afro-Caribbean settlers.

When the members of the Education Committee of the Cahuita English School studied the ideas in the Plan, they agreed among themselves to sponsor the task of collecting oral histories of the people of Cahuita. Their hope was to make a book for the children in the Cahuita English School, a book that would ensure that the experience of Mr. Johnson and his contemporaries would survive through generations, just as Old Dan's breadfruit survives through its *hijos*.

In cooperation with the Education Committee, as teacher in the Cahuita English School, I began collecting the material for this book. With all except a few of the contributors I tape recorded the interviews. The quotations in this book are taken directly from my transcriptions of the tapes. There may be errors of interpretation on my part. There are certainly misspellings of personal names and locally-used words that are to be found in no dictionary. There are many dates given that cannot be verified. Actually, I have not tried to verify many of the facts. This is folk-history, which tries to be true to the folks and is less concerned than a historian would be with the facts.

The title of the book, "What Happen," is a stock phrase in Limón English, a greeting among friends, pronounced "wh'appen." "Wh'appen, man?" "What's happening?" "¿Qué pasa?" It is also used, as Spanish-speakers use "es que," to introduce an explanation: "What happen, the bus leave me." "What happen, rain wet me up and I take a draft." In the title and throughout the book I have used standard English spelling for words and phrases that are typically Limonese in their pronunciation and usage. Other examples are "patty," pronounced "PAH-tee" in Limón, "hawksbill," pronounced "OX-bill," "them," pronounced "dem." What happen, I am not a linguist, so I have not attempted phonetic spelling. Local English words (gig, wis, etc.) and plant and animal names (yuca, rawa, wari, etc.) appear with explanations in the Glossary.

The people who contributed to this book their memories, their experiences, and their thoughts about the future, have a strong sense of the value of history. They hope that this book will encourage others in Limón and throughout Costa Rica to explore the roots of their communities, the sources of their traditions. Even in Cahuita this is only a beginning. Cahuitans will look at this book and say, "Cho, man. How Miss Paula write this long book and she never go speak to John Bull? She never speak to Miss Gatha. She never speak to Lloyd McDougall and him living here all these long years!"

There are so many old folks with stories to tell. And young folks whose pride and selfhood can be nourished by them. And visitors whose appreciation can be shown in respect and sensitivity. Together, the old and the young, the heirs and the newcomers will determine the future of the Talamanca Coast. If we share an understanding of its history perhaps we will all be careful to protect its natural resources and to appreciate the rights and the dignity of its people.

Paula Palmer
Cahuita, Costa Rica
May 1977

# Collaborators

The contents of this book are selected from tape-recorded interviews with people of the Talamanca Coast[1]. Collaborators participated voluntarily, for the expressed purpose of publishing a history of their communities. Interviews were conducted between 1976 and 1989 in the communities listed below. All interviews were in English, with the exception of those marked with an asterisk (*), which were in Spanish. Since the time of our interviews, thirty-nine of these collaborators have died. Their names are marked with a (†).

## Cahuita

Mr. Clive Brossard
† Mr. David Buchanan
† Mr. Alphaeus Buchanan
† Mr. John Burke
† Mr. Irad Clarke
† Miss Ida Corbin
† Mr. Joseph Cunningham
Miss Pearl Cunningham
Mr. Delroy Fennell
Mr. Fred Ferguson
Mr. Walter "Gavitt" Ferguson
Mr. Ervin Grant
Miss Emilia Grant
† Mr. Aniel "Arnold" Hanbelamt
† Mr. Elton "Slim" Hawkins
† Mr. George Humphries

† Mr. Selles Johnson
† Mr. David Kayasso
† Miss Maud Kelly
† Mr. Martin Luther
† Mr. Frankie McLeod
Mr. Noel McLeod
† Mr. Sylvester Plummer
Mr. Claudio Reid
† Mr. Hernan Skinner
† Mr. Albert Slack
† Mr. Joseph Spencer
Miss Mavis Tyndal Iglesias
† Mr. Jonathan Tyndal
* Sr. Mario Vindas
† Mr. Ivan Watson
† Mr. Leslie "Sorrows" Williams

---

[1] The complete and original tapes and transcripts of these interviews are available at the Costa Rican National Archives in San José.

## Puerto Viejo (Old Harbour)

† * Mr. Clinton Bennett

†    Mr. Selven Bryant

†    Miss Adina Bryant

†    Mr. Cyril Gray

     Mr. Albert Guthrie

     Mr. Felix Hudson

†    Mr. Rufus Hawkins

†    Miss Daisy Lewis

†    Mr. Augustus Mason

†    Mr. William "Paul" Rodman

     Miss Christina "Dolly" Smart

## Hone Creek

† Miss Velita Parker

Miss Julieta Wright

## Punta Uva (Grape Point)

     Mr. George Hansel

† Miss Eudora "Sis" Matthews

Miss Olga Matthews de Myrie

† Mr. Vibert Myrie

## Manzanillo

† Mr. Thomas Bethel

† Mr. Willard "Crackerjack" Gaslin

† Mr. Hermenegildo "Minin" Hudson

† Miss Aurellita Hudson

† Mr. Enrique Hudson

† Mr. Samuel Hansell

## Puerto Limón

† Mr. Standford Barton

Mr. Alfred King

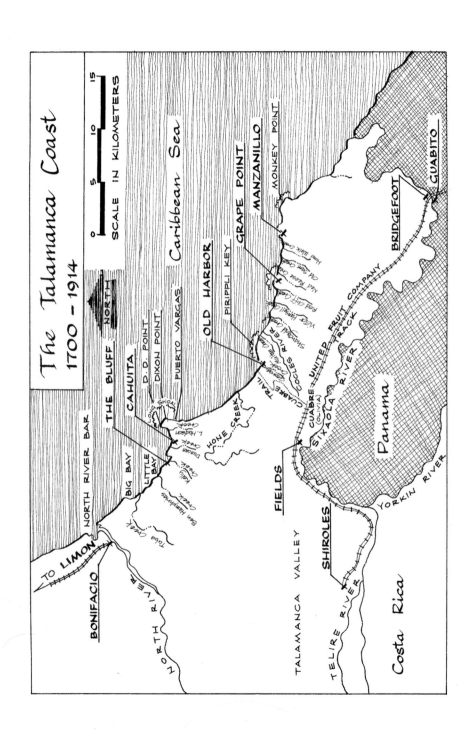

# The First Generation
## Immigrants (1700-1914)

"It was bush, but it was livelier than now. Oh, yes!"
Mrs. Ida Corbin

# 1. Legends of Indians and Pirates

The first English-speaking Afro-Caribbean family to make its home on the Talamanca Coast[1] was the family of William Smith. "Old Smith," as he is remembered by the few people alive today who knew him, rowed and sailed north from his home in Bocas del Toro, Panama (then part of Colombia), with fellow fishermen, following the northward migration of green and hawksbill turtles. The fishermen left their families in Bocas each year during the turtle season, May through September, to trace the path of the turtles to their nesting destination at Turtle Bogue (Tortuguero, Costa Rica). The fishermen made temporary camps for themselves along the Talamanca Coast near the shallow reef areas where the turtles gathered to feed. They planted provisions (cassava, plantain, yam, coconuts) that they would harvest each season when they returned to the camps.

In 1828, William Smith decided to make one of his fishing camps his permanent home. He brought his family to a calm bay protected by a broad coral reef on the north side of Cahuita Point. There he built a "ranch"[2] and planted the lime trees that mark his spot until today. Old Smith is the founder of the early settlement of Cahuita, and Selles Johnson, born in the house by the lime trees in 1894, calls him grandfather.

The history of the settlement of the Talamanca Coast begins, then, in 1828. But there are stories, handed down through the generations of Afro-Caribbean settlers, which tell of events along the coast before their arrival. The legends are of Indians and pirates.

---

[1] Geographically, the word "Talamanca" designates the Talamanca mountains (*Cordillera de Talamanca*), which extend from Costa Rica's Central Valley southeast into Panama, and the Talamanca Valley, the drainage basin of the Sixaola River and its tributaries. In 1970 the *Cantón de Talamanca* was established as a political subdivision of Limón Province. Coastal people use the word to describe the mountains, the valley, and the indigenous people who inhabit them. In this book, "Talamanca Coast" refers to the shores of the Caribbean within the Cantón of Talamanca, between Tuba Creek and the Sixaola River.

[2] rustic, thatch-roofed dwelling.

"Old-Time" Indians

Mr. David Alejandro Kayasso recounts a story that was told to him by his uncle, a Miskito Indian from the Nicaragua coast. Mr. Kayasso rowed a little canoe to Cahuita Point in 1903, landing with an uncle and a cousin in the bay in front of Old Smith's house on April 19. Mr. Kayasso was a young man of twenty years then, and he says he never intended to stay on the Talamanca Coast, but "there was about ten young ladies here, and I fall in love, so I stay." He was ninety-six years old and still in Cahuita when he began writing memoirs under the title, *The History of Cahuita Since 1880, A.D.* He died in July, 1976, five months after writing this story:

> "The history of the Cahuita Town was told to me by my uncle who used to come to catch turtle in his days. In his days there was no one to be seen on this place, but there was plenty of turtle, and as no one to trouble them on land or sea they were very tame. So every year they used to stay down here from March to September, then they go back home to Nicaragua.
>
> But one time as they were about to land, they saw some people coming up to them with bow and arrow, so they turn back aboard to see who the people were. So they anchor and put men out to watch. About midnight the watchmen cry out, 'Something is coming into the sea! Come quickly!' So they arose, and lo, there were two men coming to the boat. So they fit up their peg[1] quick, struck the two men. The mens ashore ran into the bush to hide. Then the men call aboard to send a tin of gun powder ashore, and when it came they sprinkle a little around the fire and went aboard their boat to wait and see what would take place.
>
> After not seeing no one, the men ashore start to come out. One go to the fire and touch a piece of the woods that had some of the powder, and seeing the sparks from it they start to see what it was. Then they take up the can and they cast a little into the fire out of their hands. Then one took the whole can and throw it into the fire and when it explode they all ran into the woods.
>
> The men in the boat started at them, and there the fight started. The Miskito from the boat, being more equipped, had more over those others. They keep arunning and killing them. So they chase them away to the place that is called 'Talamalka' up to this day, which mean 'the place of the blood' in the Miskito

---

[1] turtle-striking harpoon.

language. And the King give order to plant his flag there and came to the beach. And he call the long point of land Cawita after those trees with the yellow flowers."

The caway tree, from which Cahuita takes its name.

Mr. Kayasso explained that in the Miskito language, *cawi* was the name given to the tree that the Spanish know as *sangrilla* or *sangregao*, which flourishes in swampy lowlands. Many of these trees still spread their broad boughs over Cahuita Point, and in June they blossom with beautiful yellow flowers. Mr. Aniel "Arnold" Hanbelamt, of Cahuita, says the Indians of Talamanca used the great buttresses or "wings" of the caway (the local English pronunciation) to make musical instruments, especially tomtoms, because the caway drums give a high pitch that the Indians prefer. Mr. Milton Barnett, of Hone Creek, told Mr. Hanbelamt that the caway buttresses are also excellent material for making violins and bass fiddles. The caway has a sap that is as red and thick as human blood, says Mr. Augustus Mason, of Old Harbour, and some people have been known to get a fever when the tree is in blossom.

Most coastal old-timers agree that the name "Cahuita" originated with the Miskito name for the tree. Some say that the Spanish changed it to the diminutive "Cahuita", but Mr. Kayasso said that *ta* means "point" in the Miskito language, so the original name was Cawita, meaning "point where the caway trees grow."

Mr. Augustus Mason bases his knowledge of the "old-time Indians" on stories that his adoptive father, Mr. Joseph Hunter, told him when he was a boy growing up in Old Harbour. Mr. Hunter was well-named, Mr. Mason says, for he loved to hunt in the hills of Talamanca, following Indian trails through the woodland.

"Eight days he would go out with six or seven more men, hunting, and every day they bring to the ranch what animals they kill, and one stay at the ranch to wash the clothes and to cook. And banana they had, wild banana that was plant by the old-time Indians that never die against the Hone Creek River, and pejiballe tree, from the first set of Indians. Carbón was the Indian town. And afterward the Miskito Indian came in and run them, and they cut across from Carbón to Talamanca region. They take different creeks from Carbón to the Sixaola River at a place name of Bratsi, take the river up to Telire, keep traveling and go in Amubre and keep going up different branch of river. But I believe the Miskito couldn't conquer them. They kill a lot of them, but they turn back.

My adopted father told me he used to hunt way back a hundred years ago on that hill Pirripli and find skulls of Indians that was killed by the Indians them from the Miskito coast that run these Indians them into the hills and kill some of them. And he see plenty of those skulls and still have the hair. The hair on the head. The skulls never rotten and the hair never rotten. They strike them with the bow and arrow."

Pirates and Treasure

Selles Johnson says that when his grandfather, Old Smith, was coming and going along the coast during the turtle seasons in the early 1800s, he found two shipwrecks in the bay on the north side of Cahuita Point. Mr. Johnson is sure that those two ships were pirate ships, one Spanish and one French, because of the inscriptions in Spanish and French on bottles and other relics that he found diving around the wrecks when he was a boy.

Bob Bernthal

Mr. Selles Johnson

"Pirates was all around here those old days. They was wrecking the people, robbing the people, in Bocas, Portobelo, and all along the coast. You see they go over and rob the Indians and tell them to show them gold, where the gold mines is, and the Indians know, and then they rob them and kill them.

So them pirate boats was on the sea and the English gunboats was somewhere out in the ocean, square rigger, I know that. I see them come to Bocas, square rigger. They depend on breeze. So the pirate boats goes in at Puerto Vargas or at Old Harbour where calm sea, and the Englishmen can't attack them because they in Costa Rican water.

They can't attack them except they catch them on the high sea which is outside three miles from the land.

So those two ships that wreck at Cahuita Point, I tell you what I believes did happen. Them was hiding in Puerto Vargas and leave from there and come around the reef, and they must have stopped because at those days the British ship did have coal. You could see the smoke steaming in the air. So the pirate see it out in the sea and they comes in here to hide.

When I was a boy there was a chain come from one of them wrecked ships, come up on the beach and bored to a tree, a big tree. They take and bore a hole right through the tree, you know. And that chain go right through and fasten with a turn buckle on the other side. So they must be try to pull the ship off the reef, but she couldn't come across so they leave her there.

According to bottles and other things we found there, it was in the 1717. They had some bottles we found in the water. Those bottles was made in 1717. It marks it. But we don't know if the wreck was that said year, because maybe the bottles was older than that.

When I was about fourteen years old we had a piece of corn plant down the beach and my grandfather and my brother was going out to check it, and we saw a Spainaman sit on the beach just where I have my ranch there now. Him looking out to sea and we come right up to him and we boys ride past and the old man stop to talk to him. We leave him there talking. He had a big white beard and talking Spanish. And the old man, my grandfather, say to we, 'You hear what that man said?' We said, 'No, we don't hear.' He said that the ship got wrecked out there and it have iron chests, and it's true. We see one. But the Spainaman said no money in this chest. All the jewels and all the money in gold is not in that chest in the sea. It's ashore. They bury it. Now that show the Spainaman is from that boat and all that is in that iron chest is documents.

That's what the old man tell we when him come, and we leave that Spainaman there. Now where him come from we don't know, and how him get here we don't know. And a few days after that, we had a pasture right in the back there, and we went in there one morning to get a horse, and I see a hell of a hole. That Spainaman dig out what was there, what was his, and he gone. But we don't see him go."

Divers can still see wreckage of the two ships at Cahuita Point, although the water is deeper there than it was when Mr. Johnson was a boy. Mr. Johnson says there are still two iron cannons in the water, but the two brass cannons were taken up, one by Maduro and Sons, a Limón trading company, and one by a man named Bob Martin, who worked for the United Fruit Company. Mr. Johnson says a boat from the United States came once and took up silver cups, silver spoons, a French sword, and links of the chain that tied the ship to the tree that washed away years ago. He says every once in a while he still finds links of that chain in his coconut walk along the beach inside the bay.

People in Old Harbour remember a chain that was hitched on Pirripli Key years ago, a reminder of pirate days in that port, which takes its name from the fact that it served as a harbor for the old pirate boats. Mr. Augustus Mason, who came to Old Harbour as a boy in 1910, says the key just offshore south of Old Harbour was attached to the land until about 1830.

"Every seven to ten years when you have a eruption in the sea you can see the anchor chain of the ships of the pirates wash out on the sand by Pirripli Key. That was the hiding place for the treasures of the pirates. All these coast is with treasures, you know. They bury the treasure in different spots on the land. There is one right beside the tree there, by the school where a breadfruit tree is, and we always see the man that watching it in full suit of white but no head on. And several people come from outside to dig that treasure, but they could never get it. They always faint away, get sick and have to go.

Different people that can see spirits, if there is, I don't know, but different people can always see him stand up there looking. Because when they in piracy, when they land on the coast they ask who will stay and watch this till we return. And you say yes. They take your head off or shot you, and you have to stay. And at Pirripli Key there is one there. He have the full uniform: white and with braid to the sleeve and marks like the sailors' and white cap with black braid. He is watching there. And right along this coast, right round to Cahuita to where the place where Selles' grandfather was living, even to the place where he had a beautiful flowers garden, a treasure is there. And further up the creek that they call Cahuita Creek, there is something there, a spirit, in the form of a bull.

The different spots that there are treasures, my adopted father show me and tell me: Pirripli Key, and this side of Pirripli Key coming around there where the new *carretera* [road] pass through, there is one there by a big mango tree. And this

Bob Bernthal

Mr. Augustus Mason

breadfruit tree by the school, and in our *potrero* [pasture]. When we was boys we see the lights and the sign all the time in different years. Light surround where the treasure is. And I see the chain. The chain mark the chest that is buried there from the sea in. Whenever the sea wash every seven to ten years, that is a big eruption of rough sea, you may see the chain. But we see light and when we go after it, when we reach there we don't see it, we see it over there further. And the boats also. The old pirate boats come here sometime at nights, come in all the way from Limón, and when she come she will come right here and you will hear the anchor chain running out, 'rrrrrrrrrrrrrrr.' My wife see it also.

People came from France and take out a big iron chest the size of this refrigerator right up there by the plane base. And when it came to the surface, my adopted father told me that, the whole earth open and she went right down back till now. And once there was a Frenchman came through the trail from

Panama to take the launch to Limón, and he slept by my adopted father two nights until the boat arrive, and one morning after coffee, he left us and he went north. And when he return he said, 'Mr. Hunter, you are a rich man, but it will be of no use to you nor to me because we cannot get it. But between two pear [avocado] trees that you have, there is a treasure there and it is in gold. But I am a scientist and I cannot get it.' And it is true because we see the sign of the lights watching all the time from we was boys, right there.

And about a hundred meters from that spot that he told us, that was where my father told me they take out the iron chest. And they was there weeks working there. And got it up on the surface with a lot of equipment to draw it up, and it went right down. He say the earth open and a big noise, and it went down and everything close up until now. Yes, there is a lot of wealth on this coast."

The Talamanca Coast may be rich in pirates' gold, but the risks Mr. Mason describes of unearthing it may discourage most treasure hunters. There is only one man, in addition to Mr. Johnson's "Spainaman," who is reputed to have been successful in his search. This man was a North American named Klines, who located south of the mouth of Hone Creek in the late 1800s. "Klines came here for treasure," Mr. Mason says. "You know the pirates have their families and they give them the map and the chart. And so Klines came and locate here and start to plant vegetables, coconut, cocoa, but it was only for a show. And after they went away and never return. They found what they want: treasures that bury on the coast."

Deirdre Hyde

# 2. First Settlements

If any one thing can be said to be responsible for the settlement of the Talamanca Coast, it is the tiny marine animal, the coral. Coral colonies grew up over the ages in the warm, shallow waters around projections of land in the Caribbean Sea. As the animals died, their skeletons formed rocky reefs, a protective environment for a wealth of marine life. Tourists who come to the National Monument at Cahuita Point in the Twentieth Century are drawn there by the same natural phenomenon that drew the earliest coastal settlers, for the coral reefs that are so lovely to look at were also feeding grounds for the great fleets of turtles, green and hawksbill, that the Eighteenth and Nineteenth Century fishermen came looking for.

The turtles were plentiful in those early days. Today, after centuries of fishing and consumption of turtle eggs, the population of green and hawksbill turtles has diminished so seriously that the Costa Rican government prohibits egg collecting and restricts turtle fishing. The coral reef at Cahuita Point is also protected by the National Parks Service. Perhaps the reef should be seen not only as a natural monument, but as an historical monument as well, for the plant and animal life in its waters nourished and sustained human life on its shores.

Turtle Fishermen

The fishermen came in small rowboats and sailboats from Bocas del Toro and the Nicaragua coast, beginning in the late Eighteenth Century. They came each year as early as March, and stayed as late as September, spearing turtles on the sea and planting provisions on the land. For shelter they made small ranches out of the rawa palm, roofed with pin-thatch.

A few houses built partly or entirely of rawa can still be seen along the coast today. The only reason one doesn't find it in use very much in modern times is that one has to walk far into the woodland to find the trees. All the rawa palms within easy hauling distance went into ranch building decades ago. As Mr. Kayasso said, when he arrived at Cahuita Point in 1903 the village was "bare rawa."

Bob Bernthal

A panel of rawa bark.

Mr. Vibert Myrie, of Grape Point, describes the rawa tree as a palm that looks like pejiballe but without spines on the trunks. It's a tall palm with thorny roots branching out above ground level. To fashion building material from the rawa, Mr. Myrie says, the fishermen-turned-carpenters severed the trunk with an axe about eight feet above the roots, avoiding the lower section because there the wood is brittle. The ranch builders then cut the trunk the length they wanted the building material to be. With an axe they made blade-length cuts about three inches apart in a circle around the trunk. Eight or nine inches below the first circle of cuts they made another set, spacing them between the cuts of the first row. Having made these cuts from one end of the trunk to the other, the craftsmen then beat the bark with the axe head until the inner fibers softened. These were pulled loose from the bark, leaving split bark panels that were rolled together and carried home. Flattened and laid side by side, the rawa panels form a hard, strong surface, with just enough space left by the axe cuts to give some ventilation. Rawa ranches, unpainted, unprotected in the bush, can resist weathering, rotting, and insect molestation for more than forty years.

A cocoa dryer (barbeque) shelters bundles of rawa and mill-cut boards.

Mr. Oliver Matthews' rawa house at Little Bay.

The migrant turtle fishermen built most of their rawa ranches on sturdy wood posts, setting the floor a couple feet above ground level, as coast residents do to this day. They built a frame of rough cut boards, laid out the rawa strips and braced them against the frame with a board laid over the rawa, perpendicular to the strips, nailed into the frame. They brought enough nails with them to make the foundation and the flooring, but Mr. Mason, of Old Harbour, says they used a "wis" (vine) called kankibo for the rest of the construction. "They use the kankibo," Mr. Mason says, "for tying anything that they would like to last a long time. It don't rot. They use that to build house, to put on the thatch. You could use that kankibo in the place of nail for even twenty years."

Pin-thatch roofs were fashioned from the boughs of a common swamp palm, the silico. Mr. Johnson explains, "You cut the leaf a few days, about three days after the new moon. Any other time the insects trouble it, but you cut three days after the new moon and no insect going to trouble it at all. You cut it and then you strip it off the bone. And then you double it, and the same piece of bone from the main stem, you strip that and that pin it. The leaf it double over and then you pin it. One leaf, one leaf, like that. Then if you put it on right away, it shrink and becomes open, so you allow it to dry a few days and then you put it on. You can nail it on the rafter, but before they use the kankibo wis."

According to Mr. Johnson, the earliest rawa ranch-builders along the Talamanca Coast were his grandfather, William Smith, who settled on the bay north of Cahuita Point; Louis Hudson from Nicaragua, who settled just north of Old Smith; William Shepherd of Bocas, who built a ranch at Puerto Vargas; a man named Dixon, also from Bocas, who stayed on the southern tip of Cahuita Point; Ezekiel Hudson, a Nicaraguan, and Celvinas Caldwell, a San Andrés man, both at Monkey Point; Horatio MacNish, a man said to have been half Indian, half Irish, on the north coast of Old Harbour; and Peter Hansell, from Bocas, at Manzanillo. These were the original "bachelor" fishermen, all of whom eventually brought their families to share their lives on the Talamanca Coast, or made families with Indian women that they met on trading trips into the hills of Talamanca.

"All the work was turtle," Mr. Johnson says. "They get the hawksbill shell and bring it to my grandfather and he buy from them and carry it to Bocas, because he had the biggest boat. There was two company from Bocas that buy the shell. They sell to Germany and all about to make the comb and buttons out of the shell." Of the hawksbill Mr. Kayasso says,

Bob Bernthal

Felix James Hudson of Old Harbour shows his turtle-striking form with an apoo harpoon crafted by Clinton Taylor.

"There was plenty, and they were tame because they was foolish. They didn't see much people troubling them that time. You could stand right here and look and see the hawksbill floating out there plenty. They was so foolish and you could strike them easy.

My people from Nicaragua come here and strike them every year, March right until September. They go home, boats loaded. Turtle meat from the green turtle, turtle oil, and hawksbill shell. In Limón that time it was twenty colón[1] for the shell. I want to tell you, twenty colón was a lot of money that time."

[1]The exchange rate of the Costa Rican colón and the American dollar was four to one in the first half of the Twentieth Century.

A metal peg used to strike sea turtles.

To strike the hawksbill, the fishermen made spears of a palm similar to rawa, called apoo. The apoo palm is a taller, stouter tree, lacking the root spines of the rawa. The wood is so hard it is almost impossible to drive a nail through it. It is also heavier than the rawa, less easy to carry out from the woodland. But to make a turtle spear, Samuel Hansell of Manzanillo says, the fishermen only had to take a narrow strip about ten feet long, plane it to a round shaft, and attach to it a sharp, barbed metal "peg" or point. A cord was fastened to the peg and at the other end fastened to the shaft of the apoo "grip." The fishermen would hurl the spear from a standing position in their canoes, striking the turtle through the shell. The peg would be lodged in the turtle, and the fishermen would pull their canoes to the turtle by reeling in the cord. The turtles would be hoisted into the canoes and taken ashore alive, where they could survive without food or water for about fifteen days. The fishermen usually killed them by cutting their heads off with machetes.

In addition to turtling, a few of the early settlers made trips into the hills of Talamanca to trade with the Indians. Old Smith and Celvinas Caldwell, particularly, made regular trips to the interior, bringing out Indian rubber and sarsaparilla[1] for sale in Bocas.

---

[1]Sarsaparilla is a plant root used for flavoring, as in "root beer."

Farming on the Beach

Through the latter half of the Nineteenth Century, increasing numbers of English-speaking Afro-Caribbean families established themselves along the coast, grouping themselves into regions which they named after natural landmarks (Big Bay, Little Bay), and after themselves (Kelly Creek, Dixon Point), and using some names that existed prior to their arrival (Cahuita, Old Harbour). By the turn of the century many of the new immigrants called themselves farmers rather than fishermen, and cultivation of the coastal lands was taken up in earnest. As the farming families arrived, Mr. Mason says, they built their ranches by the creeks. The creeks came to be known by the family name, and they generally marked the boundaries of each family's claimed property. Creek names on the map reveal the names of the earliest settlers. In the Cahuita region they are Ben Humphries, Kelly, Duncan, and Louis Hudson. From Old Harbour moving south to Manzanillo, they are George, Multan, Sharegold, Victor, Ned Reese, and Old Sam. The Cocles, larger than the other rivers in this area, carries a name that survives, Mr. Mason says, from the pirate days.

Hone Creek, the large river on the great bay between Cahuita Point and Old Harbour, and the town of Hone Creek take their names from a palm tree. Mr. Mason explains:

> "Both side of that river was cultivate by the Lord with a palm name of 'hone'[1] that bears big bunches of a small fruit that the Indians use to make oil, rubbing it on a big stone like a mortar and pestle. They rub that fruit on it and throw hot water on it and the oil comes out. They skim off the oil and use it for cooking. That fruit is name hone. It's a palm tree but very short, with big roots. By the both side of that river grew those palms, so they call it Hone Creek. And the Jamaicans come in and some call it Home Creek, but the proper name is Hone Creek. You see a few roots still by the river, but not so much since the people start to cultivate and the river breaking wider and wider."

Town names south of Old Harbour obviously originated from natural phenomena. Mr. Hermenegildo Hudson, known as "Minin," says that Christopher Columbus himself named Monkey Point for the population of howler monkeys that still inhabits the swampy area, and

---

[1]Scientific name: *Elaeis olrifera.*

Hudson family of Manzanillo (left to right: Hermeneguildo, Aurellita, Enrique, Patricia) rest on the fallen trunk of the great old manchineel tree for which their hometown is named.

Manzanillo for a great old manzanillo (manchineel) tree that towered over the coast there. Of the manzanillo tree Mr. Mason says, "It's a poisonous tree, very poisonous. The milk of it, if it drop on you it burn you, blister you. And the animals don't know, but if an animal sleep under it, it affect them. You can take the leaves from that tree, rub it, and put it in a river and it kill all the fishes." "Minin" says that the original manzanillo tree, for which his village was named, died in the 1940s and fell finally into the sea in 1957.

Grape Point was given its name by José Hansell, an early immigrant from Bocas who planted the coconut walk there. When he arrived, says his daughter, Eudora "Sis" Matthews, the point was bordered all around with sea grape trees and coco plums. The sea has encroached so much upon the land in the century between the naming of Grape Point and today, that not a single grape tree is to be found along those shores, except on the bluff called Red Cliff, where the Hansells first lived. All the rest have been covered by the sea.

A minor "population explosion" occurred along the Talamanca Coast in 1903, the year of Panama's war of independence against Colombia. Afro-Caribbean families in Colón and Bocas del Toro who had little interest in politics and less in combat, fled Panama in small boats and rowed north, says Enrique Hudson of Manzanillo, whose relatives were already settled at Monkey Point before the fighting broke out.

Another source of immigration to the coast was the completion in 1890 of the railroad linking San José to the Caribbean Sea at Puerto Limón. Mr. Mason explains:

> "When Minor Keith was building the railroad to San José, he brought down people from the interior to work but they couldn't stand the climate. You had a lot of malaria then, and they die out or go back. So Keith go and contract Jamaicans, Barbadians, and the St. Kitts to finish the railroad. And after that was over the Jamaicans see that they didn't have so much privilege in Jamaica to cultivate. The lands was more for the government and the rich people, so they remain here. And the Hindus, the East Indians came too. And lots of them came to this side of Cieneguita bridge and take the sea coast and cultivate it in coconuts.
>
> As the Jamaicans came down the beach this side, some of them was looking to go to Bocas to find work. But the people would tell them, 'Stay and make farm.' And they would feed them even a two or three month to give them a help, just so as to have company, you know."

By 1915 the Talamanca Coast was dotted with population centers of as many as thirty families each at the Bluff (present-day Cahuita), old Cahuita (at Cahuita Point), Old Harbour, Grape Point, Manzanillo and Monkey Point. Most of these communities offered schools, churches, shops, organized sports, and cooperative forms of transportation and trade. The year 1915 serves as a cut-off date in this history because that year the President of Costa Rica himself established a new town of Cahuita at what was formerly called the Bluff. The remaining chapters of this first section of the history of the Talamanca Coast describe the way of life in the coastal communities until 1915.

Dennis Glick

# 3. Home Life and Cultivation

The Coconut Economy

The first cultivated product of the Talamanca Coast, and one that is still important in the economy today, was the coconut. Mr. Augustus Mason gives this account of the beginnings of coconut cultivation:

"The people that don't know or don't want to know, they say it was the sea that cultivate these coconuts, but there were no coconuts here in the olden days. These coconuts was plant from Panama and Nicaragua. When the people run from the war in Panama in 1903, they came this side, from Sixaola bar coming. They had was to come up in the calmer water, Monkey Point, Manzanillo, and right up the coast. And they land there in boats. After they land here they arrange among themselves that I am going to work from this creek to that creek, and you work from that creek to the other creek, as a limit against the beach. And then they build their ranches just out of leaf.

At that time the people never like to go in the hill. They were afraid from snake bite and get mud on their feet. And they cultivate the beach right along. And they plant pine [pineapple] melons, cane, yuca [cassava], just what to eat. And they go back to Bocas at night and take from the people there the plants of coconuts and sail back by night and land and plant along the coast. And they go to Nicaragua to sell the hawksbill shell and buy provisions, and there they steal coconut plant and come along back the coast and plant. All this coast is cultivate by Selles Johnson's grandfather, from Kelly Creek to Puerto Vargas. At that time there was another family name of Dixon, and they cultivate from Puerto Vargas coming down, father, brother, son and so on. The Jamaicans that come in after cultivate the north side of Hone Creek, but that was long after those Old Smith and Dixon. And from Hone Creek right down to Cocles cultivate by Horatio MacNish, he was a half Indian and half Irish. And then the others start from Monkey Point right down to Cocles. It was Reese, Michure, Lemmi Smith, William Downer, Jeremiah Brown, divide creek to creek. They were planting bare coconut and provisions.

Then the Jamaicans that was accustomed to work inland start to plant cocoa, but the real coasters, Panamanian and Nicaraguan, they keep along the coast."

The farmers carried some of their coconuts to Limón in small launches, selling them at three colons for one hundred nuts. Mr. Kayasso tells a story of linguistic confusion that he remembers about the first time he tried to sell coconuts to a Spanish buyer in Limón. Mr. Kayasso spoke the Miskito language and English, but he never learned Spanish. To understand his story you have to know that the Spanish word *coco* means coconut in English, but is pronounced the same way as the English word "cocoa" which in Spanish means *cacao*.

"I went to Limón lots of times and I know nothing about Spanish. Well, I don't know nothing about Spanish yet. I don't like the language and I don't learn it. And I had five hundred coconuts on board the boat and a Spaniard came down on the dock and him ask me if we have *coco*. I tell him no. But the coconut all there in the boat, and him see it and say again, do we have *coco*? I tell him no. He shake his head, stand there and shake his head. You see my mistake? It's *coco* I carry to sell him and I tell him I don't have none. When he say *coco* I think he means chocolate, and I don't carry no chocolate."

Mr. Selles Johnson talks about the techniques and problems of coconut cultivation:

"The coconut is specially for the coast. When it plant right by the beach it get a better result, grow very quickly. We have a caterpillar that did trouble the coconut sometimes, but it go away. That caterpillar grow from a butterfly, a white butterfly that live on the beach. You see those butterfly on the beach, sometimes hundreds, thousands of them, they make a big ring, and when they want to lay their eggs they go on the coconut tree and they lay their eggs on the limb of the tree with a big nest, white nest, and that stay there till it hatch. And then millions of caterpillar come out.

As long as the time is dry those caterpillar don't leave a leaf on the coconut. As they hatch they commence to go up and down the coconut tree.

They destroy this one, eat off every leaf, come down and go to the next one. But if you can know that they going in your coconut walk, you can go and get a piece of blue soap and go up there and put on the leaf. Then all of them go to eat that and them die. That's the old-time blue soap that made with fat and washing soda. That's what I discover once. The tree those caterpillar go on, they eat the leaf and every coconut drop off, so you lose that crop. But it will come back. The tree don't die. But if you hear rain coming, plenty rain, the caterpillar can't stand the rain, they drop quickly and they dead, it kill them.

Once they eat the leaves on a piece of the beach here, clean clean. Only the stump left. And after a while the rain come and damage them. And there is a bird that always eat them, but I don't see those birds these days. Yellow-tail, they call them. He come out and eat them. And get rid of them that way. But as soon as you have a dry year, you will see that caterpillar come and eat off the coconut leaf.

The marketing of whole coconuts was the business of coastal men. But much of the coconut crop left the Talamanca shores as cooking oil, and its production was largely the work of women. The oil-making process required a lot of muscle work for those women who didn't have a mill, and only a few could afford one. To make a "tin" of oil (twenty-five bottles) the women husked and grated the meat of about two hundred coconuts (sale value: six colones). They washed the grated meat with water to wring the natural oil out of the flesh, threw away the pulp ("trash") and boiled the milky liquid over open fires, burning the shells as fuel, until all the water had evaporated and pure coconut oil remained.

Mrs. Ida Corbin, of Cahuita, tells how she and her sister, Miss Maud, helped their mother make coconut oil:

> "To start, we grater the coconut, put it in something clean, a good pan, a good bowl. And we take the flour bag, we cut it small, and we put the coconut into the bag and wash it out in water in that clean pan what we have, and we wash that coconut trash a two time or three time, for some of the coconut give you plenty milk. So we have it properly done. And when we finish with the trash now we give it to the fowls or the pigs if we have.
>
> And then now the oil, we set it and leave it for the next day. We let it stay in the hot sun, and the sun cut the oil. And the next day we take a scoop, we have a calabash or such a like, and we take off that heavy part, the custard we call it, and put it in a pot. And we take the oil underneath and put it in the next pot. And we fry it out. We strain the oil through the clean flour sack. We used to use the sea fan, but you can't get that now. It come from the sea. So we use the clean flour sack. You have to keep stirring not to make it burn. Give it slow fire. Oh, as you fry it it smell nice! And then we strain it into the kerosene tin, and then when you look it's clean oil, pretty oil, and you just dip it and fill the bottles. We boil the custard then and get the oil from the custard, and we throw away the balance, nothing good in it. If you have chickens, you have pigs, well, you feed it to them.
>
> That was our living here in those days, coconut oil. People used to say, 'Miss Walker's coconut oil, we don't want nothing but that.' We used to drink it sometimes, but we have to run to the toilet!"

Still handy with a machete, Mrs. Ida Corbin demonstrates the first step in making coconut oil: husking the coconuts.

Miss Christina ("Dolly") Smart grates the husked coconuts.

She rinses the oily milk out of the grated coconut meat and strains it.

Paula Palmer

Miss Dolly skims off the "custard."

Arnold Hambelamt

Miss Maud Kelly stirs the coconut milk over an open fire in her backyard cooking shed, boiling off the water until pure oil remains in the Dutch pot.

Paula Palmer

Coconut graters, made from zinc roofing sheets, have their place in every coastal dwelling. Three graters hang from the side of this house.

45

A tin of coconut oil sold in Limón for twelve colones, giving the women six colones in profit for days of labor. But six colones went a long way in those days. Ten cents a pound for almost anything you wanted to buy: salt, sugar, rice, beans, flour. So the coconut oil business was more profitable then than it may appear today when in Cahuita you will pay Miss Maud or Mrs. Grant ten colones for a bottle of the same oil, prepared in exactly the same way.

Another home-manufactured product of the coast was yuca (cassava) starch. Mr. Mason tells us about it:

> "There was no sale for the amount of yuca that everybody did have. So when the yuca come in to perfection, they dig those yuca and make starch. You grater it like the coconut and wash it like you wash the coconut, and when you skim the starch off the top you put it on the barbecue,[1] rawa barbecue, you put a leaf over the flooring and put the starch on that. And when it is dry you bag it up in fifty-pound sacks and send it to Limón with sailing boats. And you will get only ten colón for one hundred pounds. They use it to starch clothes.
>
> There was a man in Limón named Isadora Ash, a Jew that buy all the starch and all the coconut oil that the coast can produce, from Cahuita to Manzanillo, and he dispatch it to the interior on the train."

Getting the produce of the coast to the buyers in Limón required ingenuity and cooperation in those early days. Mr. Mason describes how the "men of the sea" and the "men of the land" worked together to market the coast's products:

> "The Jamaicans is the ones that love to cultivate. The day will light him going to farm and the night catch him coming from farm. While the others that go out to sea, they go from three in the morning, come back in at nine o'clock, bathe, and they sleep in their same boat until three o'clock in the evening they go out again to see what they catch, and come in at night again. Those ones don't like the land, don't go in the land.
>
> The Jamaicans was the hardest working people that you could ever come across. They live from nothing but they make something. And they start to go inside the land and plant their

---

[1]Barbecues are platforms built about a meter above ground which slide under zinc roofs. They are used to sun-dry yuca, coconuts (copra), and cocoa.

own provisions and cocoa, and they build their own boats that run with sail. They build those out of any kind of wood and use calico cloth for sail.

There was no launch. So they come together and you will say, 'I going to build a boat,' and they all go together and build the boat, but not in partnership. And when that boat is finished, whatever product have to go to Limón, we will acquaint each other, five or six of us, that we going to make a trip such and such a date. And you will get so many bunch of plantains, and so many pounds of yam, and so many bags of yuca starch, and you will bring it out and load the boat.

The water was very calm here that time. There was a little point of land running out into the sea from in front the school there, so inside was very calm. And they carry the load on their heads and load the boat. And then five or six farmers become sailor, and between you you pay one confident seaman and call him the captain. And his trip from here to Limón and back, if it even take him two days or a week, his pay is twenty colones. And when you go there and sell the product then all of you come together and pay the captain, and he take the twenty colones and buy his provision and come back and feel happy. No freight pay to the boat because all the farmers are in it together.

They have to choose for captain somebody that know about the sea. The Jamaicans them didn't know nothing about the sea at that time. Them is the sailors, and they pull with oars. The captain was a man, a Honduranian name of Santiago Arzú, he was a famous captain here. And another one down at the point named Bartimos Ellis, all those is confident seamen, and at Manzanillo, name of Deen. They don't cultivate, they don't build boat, but they can handle it at sea. So you select from one of them. And that captain can live from that merchandise for the twenty colones for up to months."

With sea transportation as difficult as it was, and unpredictable because of weather, the coast settlers grew as many of their own provisions as they could. Selven Bryant, of Old Harbour, remembers harvesting callaloo and chocatow, broad leaf plants that grew wild in the bush and made tasty vegetables when boiled or cooked with dry codfish. Farmers planted cabbage, melons, cucumbers, tomatoes, scallions, okra, red beans, and gungu beans, and a vegetable they knew as "quash," a soft, watery vegetable with a skin like a melon that they ate both cooked and raw.

"We never left for hungry," Mr. Mason says. "We make sugar from sugar cane and give everybody a portion who don't have cane. We was living very easy that way. Rice and beans we don't have to buy because we cultivate that. We cut the wild palm [*palmito*] in the bush and use it for vegetable as cabbage, turnip or anything. All the cultivators coming and going to farm you will see them carrying *palmito* that may last a week, cutting it joint by joint. And we cook it in the coconut milk with meat and yellow yam. It was nice!".". Mr. Mason goes on to explain how fruit trees came to be planted on the Atlantic coast: "At that time this country was short of fruits, so the San Andrés boats come here twice a year with fruits, all class of fruits. And they bring dog, cat, chickens, everything that can be sold, because things was very poor in San Andrés and they want to sell everything. All the fruits you see in Costa Rica on the Atlantic came from San Andrés and Jamaica. Imagine mangoes used to come from Jamaica in barrels. But all the plants you find here is from Jamaica and San Andrés."

## Home Crafts

While the fruit trees were growing, the coastal people were making do without most goods that would have to be purchased. Money was scarce, but the woodland abounded in plants that the people converted into useful objects.

To make sandals, Mr. Johnson says, "you get a piece of board and mark it out for the size of your foot. And you get a piece of mahoe bark from the mahoe[1] that grows along the beach. You take the bark and peel it, dry it, and it come like rope. And then you plait it and fix it across the board and fasten it like sandals through a hole you bore in the sole. We call it sandals." Mr. Mason says the people used the same mahoe bark to weave cribs for babies.

The Jamaicans used the cotton-like fluff of the balsa seed to make pillows and mattresses, Mr. Mason says. The balsa, known locally as "bark log" and "down-tree," was also one of the favored materials for making musical instruments. Mr. Mason tells how the Jamaicans fashioned their instruments for the earliest music band in Old Harbour:

> "To make the drum they get the bark log, the down-tree, *balsa* the Spanish call it. They cut according to the length they want and they dig that right out or burn it with fire and make it as a barrel but without bottom or top. Then they go to hunt and kill the wari [peccary] or the mountain cow [tapir] and they dry

---

[1] Scientific name: *Hibiscus tiliaceus*

that skin. And from the same skin they cut slips of skins after it is dry to make the lacing around. And they make the hooks out of wood and lace it to the top and the bottom to make drum.

And they will get the wild bamboo in the bush to make a flute with different holes. We call it fife. And in case a horse die, someone who are interested in music will take the skeleton of the head and dry it. And they hold it with the two rows of teeth, they just knock them together. And you get a grater with an iron spoon, and you grate that. And you get a comb, wrap a piece of paper around it and blow. And that was the way we make our bands down here and we dance and enjoy ourselves."

Mr. Mason also described an instrument that Old Dan made and played. No one can remember the name of the instrument, if it had a name, but Mr. Mason said it made sounds like a bass fiddle and a saxophone at the same time. It was a five- or six-foot piece of bamboo, hollow, with a hole cut into the side at the center. The bowl of a calabash gourd fit into the hole so that the sides of the calabash projected outward from the hole like a funnel. Six strings made from the fibers of the wild pine (wild pineapple)[1] were attached to both ends of the bamboo, supported on bridges so that the strings stretched tightly just over the rim of the calabash. Old Dan made the bass fiddle sound by plucking the strings or bowing them with a bow also made from the wild pine fibers. At the same time he would blow through the bamboo and the sound would come out through the calabash, mocking the sound of the saxophone.

Mr. Mason also remembers making salt from sea water:

"There was an old-time Jamaican that came from Jamaica even before my adopted father. At that time salt was so cheap, at ten cents a pound, and yet many couldn't buy a pound. There was this old man name of Frasier. He call everybody 'daddy' so we all used to call him 'Daddy Frasier.' He had one eye. And he say, 'Daddy, we can do without buy salt. I can make salt.' And he take fifty percent sea water and fifty percent of fresh water, and the amount of hours to boil it down to salt we don't know. And he wrap it in leaves. But it is not white. And he tie it with the wis that we call mahoe bark, tie it in leaves and put it on top of the fireside. That time everybody use wood to cook. And you may have it there for even five years and it become as hard as a stone. And whenever

---

[1] Scientific name: *Aechmea magdelanae* (Spanish common name is *pita*).

you need, you just chip off a piece to the amount that you need. And that was what the most of us lived from when there was no salt to buy, as in the 1914 war. If you boil the sea water alone it is bitter, so you have to use fifty percent of the fresh water."

## Making Charcoal

To aid the burning of their wood fires, the coastal people made charcoal. The process is an old one, but just as efficient today as it was in 1900. Mr. Clive Brossard and Mr. Elton "Slim" Hawkins make charcoal to sell to their Cahuita neighbors today according to instructions handed down to them through generations of Jamaicans. Their tools are axe, machete, and shovel, their materials consist of wild lilies, dirt, and various sizes of pitch pine and *madera negra* logs.

The first step in the process of making a charcoal kiln is gathering materials. Mr. Clive and Mr. Slim pick up old railroad ties washed up on the beach, which they splinter into narrow kindling strips, calling them "pitch pine." They cut green trunks and branches of *madera negra* into three different lengths, about one foot, two feet, and three feet, respectively. Sizeable trunks of *madera negra* they axe into chunks a foot and half long by a foot in diameter. And from the bush they bring out sacks of chopped lily plants. Then they are ready to construct the kiln.

They start by making the "baby," placing about twenty strips of pitch pine kindling over two support logs, one-foot by four inches. Under the kindling they place the "lighter," extending out from under the "baby" eight feet toward the sea side of the kiln, the direction the breeze comes from. Around the support logs and the pitch pine, they erect twelve-inch "burn wood" sticks from a previous kiln in a circle. They pack the center hole with "chop chop," two-inch by one-inch pieces of green *madera negra* sticks. That's the "baby."

Now they are ready to build the kiln by stacking green sticks of increasing length and width vertically around and on top of the "baby," filling in holes with "chop chop." Several layers of one-foot sticks, then the two-foot sticks, finally three-foot sticks, called the "dressing," form the outer layer of the kiln.

Mr. Slim says the key to successful charcoal making is packing the kiln tight, especially the center part directly above the "baby." This is where the "crown logs," the thick, short trunks of *madera negra*, are placed. Their function as slow-burning green logs is to hold down the fire so that it burns slowly, spreading its heat to the sides of the kiln rather than breaking through the top in flames.

Pitch pine, crown logs, "chop chop," and dressing sticks encircle the site where Mr. Slim Hawkins will build his charcoal kiln.

Mr. Hawkins stacks green sticks of increasing size around the "baby," filling in holes with "chop chop" to make a tight kiln.

The completed charcoal kiln, packed with lilies and dirt, burns for several days.

Mr. Clive explains the function of the crown wood:

> "The crown wood is not to be too long. The crown wood,
> the shorter the better, because while the sticks inside burning,
> the crown wood drops down on to the baby to hold the fire
> down. But when you cut it too long it hitch on the side, don't
> fall through, and leave a big space of air on top of the baby,
> and then the fire get enough play to start burn the bush on
> top. So when you have the crown wood shorter, as it burning
> it falling onto the baby, and that's what you want, to hold
> down the fire."

If the kiln is not packed properly, with plenty of "chop chop" and
heavy crown wood on top, the fire, starting from the lighter under the
"baby," breaks through the crown and explodes the kiln before the
green wood can be reduced to charcoal. Perfect hard coal is the product
of a slow-burning kiln, requiring as many as five or six days of steady
smoldering.

With the crown wood properly packed with "chop chop" on the
top, and two tiers of "dressing" forming the outer layer, the kiln is ready
for its bush coat. It now stands about five feet tall, six feet in diameter
at the base.

Mr. Clive and Mr. Slim build a frame around the kiln with four-
foot logs on the ground, called "heels," supporting tiers of railroad ties
called the "lace." They stack lily stems vertically between the dressing
sticks and the lace, piling the lilies a foot deep on the crown of the kiln.
"You can use banana leaf," Mr. Clive says, "but the lily is the best. It
consume plenty water, make it like steam when it burning." Then they
pack dirt eight inches deep and five inches thick on the bottom tier of
lace, place the next tier of lace on the packed dirt, and build up toward
the crown. They cover the bush layer with a solid layer of earth, and
the kiln is ready to light.

Mr. Slim instructs:

> "Then you haul out this stick, the lighter, from under the
> baby. You get a piece of bag and wrap it around that stick.
> And you get a piece of string and tie it. Then you pour some
> kerosene oil on it and you light it. After it start to burn you
> shove it through the hole and right under the baby there. The
> breeze come through that hole in the bottom where the
> lighter come in, and between the heels at the base, and that
> start the burning."

Once the kiln is lit it requires some tending. "The longer it burn, the coal come bigger and harder," Mr. Clive explains. "If it burn too quick it come fine like dust. If you find that it burning too rapid you got to take the same dirt and pack it, block up the crown so you have it under control with just the right breeze coming in at the bottom."

After five or six days of even burning, Mr. Clive is ready to "draw" the coal. "When you are going to draw it you take a shovel, take off the earth and the burn bush, that the dangerous part. It carry terrible heat. That time you have to be careful that rain don't wet you because you catch a pneumonia. If you go and draw it and rain wetting you same time it not going to do no harm. But if you in that heat first and a shower of rain come and catch you, it bad. It can kill you."

Mr. Clive and Mr. Slim sell a sack of coal in Cahuita for twenty-five colones. A medium-sized kiln nets them twenty-five sacks if they keep the kiln burning slowly and evenly. In the early days along the coast a sack of coal was a good trade item for beef or coconut oil. Often neighbors built kilns together for their mutual benefit.

Home Brews

The do-it-yourself spirit that motivated the coast settlers to plant their own provisions, to make their own shoes, musical instruments, salt, and coal, also enabled them to put spice in their lives with homemade liquor. Red rum, Mr. Mason remembers, sold in Limón at two colones a bottle, but not many coast folks could afford to buy even a pint for Christmas. That didn't worry anyone on the coast, though, because they were accustomed to making their own strong drinks: guarapo, cane liquor, and ginger beer. Mr. Johnson tells how the people made guarapo and cane liquor:

"For the guarapo they just mill the corn and put it on the fire and boil it. Then they put it in a calabash and bury it in the ground nine or ten days and it become extra sour. And they drink it and it drunk them.

And they use the cane liquor too. They have a mill and they grind the cane, take that juice and scald it and bury it and it becomes sour, and they take it out and it drunk them bad. They don't buy no liquor from the outside, they use that for their Christmas. Each house try to have it, guarapo and cane liquor."

To understand about ginger beer, first one has to know about "chewstick."[1] According to Selven Bryant, "chewstick is a wis about an inch thick, with very soft leaves. We use that wis for cleaning our teeth. We cut it to the length of a toothbrush, wash it off, scrape off the outside and beat it with a stone. And as you wash your teeth it froth just like toothpaste. It have a little bitterish taste."

Here is Mr. Mason's recipe for ginger beer:

"It make from chewstick, ginger and cane juice. First you got to beat and boil the ginger, beat and boil the chewstick with the ginger. Same time you scald the cane juice and throw off the scum that comes on top. You put the cane juice, ginger, and chewstick all together in a wood crock with a wood cover, and band the cover down with kankibo wis. Then you let that crock sit in the sun to let it ferment. When the cover start to lift it coming to perfection. It sour and strong."

For milder refreshment, the coast settlers had a wide range of fruits, blossoms and grasses that they used to make soft drinks and teas.

A favorite drink for the Jamaicans was, and is, sorrel, a popular drink in their mother country. To make it they peeled the red petals from the sorrel flower, a relative of the hibiscus, and boiled them with ginger. The bright red drink could be kept bottled for months. It was often saved for holidays.

Coffee was cheap, for it was produced along the railroad in the Central Valley, but the coastal people generally scorned it in favor of "bush" teas: fever grass (lemon grass), sorosi, cowfoot, burr bush, Spanish needle, and others.

So even without cash in their pockets, the coast settlers managed quite well, having learned to make use of the abundant products of Nature. Among themselves they practiced a custom of bartering and sharing so that money was of little use or importance. Fishermen exchanged their day's catch for a few pounds of yuca or plantains from the farmers. Hunters exchanged dried meat for charcoal, coconut oil, or garden vegetables.

Mr. Johnson's grandfather raised cows in pastures at the Bluff and in others scattered through the hills of Talamanca. But Old Smith's beef was never for sale, always for exchange. "In the

---

[1] Scientific name: *Gouantia lupuloides*.

Christmas time," Mr. Johnson remembers, "we kill two cow sometimes, because we had plenty cow. Every week we kill cow, and we never sell meat. Same as turtle. We catch turtle and make crawl and put them in, and we kill a conch and blow the shell. You cut the point off the conch, and you blow—'ooooooooohhh'—and call, and everybody know that meant there was meat down there. That's the signal of meat. And then the people come and they bring in their plantain and yuca and banana, whatever they has, and everybody get a slice of the meat."

"We was living good," Mr. Kayasso says of the early days in his adopted home. "Everything we have. We want nothing. You may say now the living that time look hard, and it was hard, but we never know better. Times was lively, man."

Deirdre Hyde

# 4. Hunting and Fishing

The plants that grow wild in the Atlantic lowlands provided the early settlers with raw materials for housing, clothing, utensils, food, and drink, as we have seen. The other half of Nature, the animal kingdom, was for the most part benevolent too, providing food, sport, and adventure.

Mr. Mason's adopted father, Joseph Hunter, liked to hunt. "He always hunt," Mr. Mason says.

> "When I was a boy I had was to go with him in the bush day and night. He go and stay in the bush for one week or eight days, hunt, and we dry the meat. When we reach inside I have to stay at the ranch. I don't go in the bush. And we only carry for the first day a bottle of kerosene oil, matches, and salt. The first day we cut rubber off the tree and tear it off and make it into a lamp with a wick, and that's what we use for lamp: the rubber milk. And the salt is what we eat with the meat, and bananas and pejiballes that grow along the Hone Creek river right up to Carbón from the days of the ancient Indians."

Mr. Hunter, together with eight other Jamaican immigrants, made a clearing and built a thatch shelter ("ranch") on the summit of a hill, which served as the camp for their hunting expeditions. Each day the hunters went out from the ranch in pairs, following machete-cut trails they had hacked through the woodland in the four compass directions. They returned to the ranch each evening with the day's kill, eating meals prepared by the one adult who remained at the ranch. The hunters stayed on the mountain a maximum of eight days or until they had sacked enough meat so that each of them would walk back to Old Harbour carrying a full load. Their targets were "wari" (white-lipped peccary), "sina" (collared peccary), "mountain cow" (tapir), "gibnut" (paca), and deer. Mr. Mason elaborates:

> "They was hunting by trade, to make a living. They always go out, nine of them. Eight go out with dogs, two in each trail that just a man can pass, chop out with machete, and the ninth one remain at the ranch. And whoever kill whatever class of animal, they bring it back along the same trail to the ranch, and that man in the ranch dry all the meat without salt. Just by wood fire. Smoke it. And that is the one that do the cooking, the drying of the meat, and the drying of the clothes when you get wet, over the wood fire. The ranch built by all those men on the summit of the hill. And I have

to stay by that man at the ranch because I was too young to go hunting with them. And I have to help to dry the clothes and dry the meat. In eight days time they return back home. Every man with the dry meat in big bags on their back, and they come home.

The wari is wild pig, and the sina, that is the same breed of wari. We call it sina [SIGH-na], and the Spaniard call it *saino*. It's a little raw, high smelling. The wari meat is most like pork or mutton, while the sina has a wild smell, and the wild smell is from the gall in the back. As you kill it you cut out that gall and throw it away and the smell gone. The sina and the wari looks alike, but the sina have longer hairs than the wari.

They are wild pigs, brown and dark brown, with long teeth coming out and very dangerous, especially the white-face one. That one seek to kill you. If in case you meet a drove of a hundred or two hundred coming travelling according to the feeding trees that they meet, you cannot shot the first set in front. You have to wait until the first hundred or so go by and then you start to shoot in the center of the drove. Or else, if you start to fire at the first set they will kill you. And you have to tie down the dogs or they will kill them, eat them so you don't find a bone left.

The wari, the large and fat ones, weigh as much as sixty pounds. You kill whatever amount you can carry out. Each man can carry three of them to the ranch. At the place you kill them you cut the head off and skin them, take the insides out and carry to the ranch with leaves on your back. After you dry the meat one man can carry six of them home 'cause it dry.

Then the gibnuts, what they call *tepezcuintle*, you can get them at nights with headlight. They come out to feed at nights. They live in the holes in the day and come out at night in the feeding tree, and then you can shot them. And you have dogs for the gibnut, apart from the wari dogs, different dogs that dig them out the hole and you kill them in the day.

And the mountain cow, the Spaniard call them *dantos*, it's a animal very short and thick like a big hog, round. It have the appearance of an elephant, but a very short thick animal. It will weigh all four hundred pounds and more. Very hard to kill. You have to make special bullets with iron that when you shot them you get them by the arm, under the arm, or right in the chest or the head. But firing on the body it hardly affect them, the skin is so thick. They make the special bullet from old iron and old file. There are bullets to sell that you can buy anywhere out of lead. But for killing mountain cow you have to have special bullet, and you make it round, more or less. You can't make it long. And the mountain cow always looking, when you shot at them, for the river. She will go in the river and you don't see her while the river is deep, you know. And she will come out when she reach a half mile and go on the land and travel on. So the hunters will know that she go down into the river, but they may not know if she go up the river or down. It depend on the amount of you, so a portion of you will go down and a portion will go up to see if they can find her. And when they have young ones they are very cross.

And the deer, the deer always be on the riverside. Not so much in the forest. And we used to kill the monkeys too, the red monkey. That are nice meat.

Smoking the meat the way that man at the ranch do it, it can keep for three months. After you reach home you will hang it over your fireside. At that time nobody know about stove or nothing, bare wood fire. And they have like a frame built out of wild cane over the fire. And you take a piece of meat, the wari, mountain cow, or the deer, and you cut it. You cut it in long lengths, thin, for drying. That mean that the sun and the smoke penetrate through every inch of it so that it cannot spoil."

Mr. Johnson says the wari is very scarce in Talamanca these days. He remembers seeing a huge drove of them passing from the hills along the beach, heading north toward Nicaragua at the time the United Fruit Company was blasting to make a tunnel for its railroad from Sixaola into the Talamanca mountains. Mr. Johnson was out fishing in the bay by Cahuita Point when he saw the drove of wari break out onto the beach. That night he came home not with fish for supper, but fresh wari meat:

"The United Fruit Company started to make a tunnel and they use plenty bombs. Dynamite. Blast up the whole of the rocks to make that tunnel. And the animals got scared and come out the bush and take to the beach. Because I was coming from sea one day, and when I look I see a whole group of them, a pile of them was there. And I come on with my boat and I stay in the boat and with the harpoon I strike one. Him rear up and I hit him again. Kill him. And the whole group come and pass right by. People kill as much as they want right up to Cieneguita. They went on to Moín and right up toward Nicaragua. You find them now at Colorado Bar plenty."

Another animal that was more plentiful along the coast in the old days than it is now, is the "sea cow" (manatee). Mr. Johnson says the sea cow truly resembles the land cow. It's a large animal, weighing as much as six hundred pounds, that lives in rivers, passing along the coast from one major river to the next, feeding on the grasses at the river edge. Mr. Johnson has seen young ones following their mothers just as young cows do:

"My grandfather strike them out here at Cahuita. A certain time of year they pass from the Sixaola River to North River, you see, and we know and waiting on them out there. But most time you find them on the river bank. They feed on the grass along the river side with head out, you see. And you see them so. But they hear very quick, so you goes up very easy into your boat. And you harpoon him and him run. You got to put a piece of wood on the end of the line and let him run because him coming back. And him go way around and come back the same place you give him the peg. And you let him tow you a little, tire him with the peg in him. And then to kill him now, you got to hit him on the nose. You hit him on the nose and he die. And you have to sink the boat to get him in. You can't lift him yourself. You tow him to a shallow place and you roll the boat, big boat, you know. You lean it down and make it fill with water and roll him in. And then you take a calabash and throw out the water and you go home.

And it make bacon! Why, it's one of the sweetest meats known. I love that one. They take the meat and they cut it in big flakes, big flakes, and they salt it and hang it up on string in the sun and dry it, and it come bacon. You want to take a piece you just fry it. Bacon! I love it. It's been many years now since I eat that."

Another of Mr. Johnson's favorite meals, the tarpon, came from the sea. Mr. Johnson had plenty of practice spearing tarpon when he was a boy at Cahuita Point. He tells this story of tarpon fishing at Mr. Kayasso's expense:

"The English-speaking people, we call them tarpon, but the Spaniards call them *sábalo*. That's one of the cleanest fish in the sea because all it eats is the little fry fish that we call 'sprat.' That's what he feeds on. He got big scales and heavy flesh. I love that fish. That's the only fish that I love. I always strike them. Go out in my boat, harpoon in hand, and I stand up and see them coming, in clear water you see them all the time. Some of them is a hundred and fifty pounds, the big one them. I use the harpoon out of apoo and strike with that and put a bob on the line. And when you strike you see that bob going on the water and you chase it down. You quick with the paddle and get at it and haul him in and hit him again. Oh, it's easy. I alone do it. I alone. I had the practice. Sometimes as you hit them they don't move. I haul it in as a joke.

I see Kayasso was out there one day. He was there looking for the same fish, you know. It's a eatable fish, people like it. And Kayasso out there. Every minute I see him do so, and him miss and don't get it. Every minute him throw at the fish and he miss it. I was on the shore, me and my lady there. I had a little piece of old canoe, shove it out there, and I look and I see one coming. Big one. Throw, and I hit him, one time. I don't miss them, because I had practice. My grandfather had me go out there every day, every other day, when we want fish."

Mr. Kayasso may not have been the greatest tarpon fisherman, but he tells of shooting crocodiles on the beach at Cahuita that is now National Park land. Eighteen-foot crocodiles used to inhabit Kelly Creek on the south side of the Bluff, Mr. Kayasso said, and neither horse nor cow nor dog nor human being was safe passing through that creek. "As it see you it chase you," Mr. Kayasso remembers, "and to get away from it you have to run back and forth like a zig-zag, not straight, because the crocodile can't make the curve like a man. And so you escape him. Him run on him tail and two hind legs."

The crocodile, being such a menace to the livestock, was hardly a popular animal on the coast. Mr. Kayasso and a few other young men eventually rid the rivers of them by attracting them out on the beach at night with lanterns. "We climb a grape tree, put on the light and up they come from the river, straight to the light, and we shoot them." The self-appointed crocodile exterminators got a little help from an American company that came one year to hunt the beasts for their hides. But for Mr. Kayasso, crocodile hunting was never for profit, only for safety.

Smaller game that promised the coast settlers tasty dinners were inhabitants of river beds, tide pools, and tree tops. River shrimps cooked with rice was a favorite dish. Whelks and conches made savory stews. A variety of wild birds provided the ingredients for poor man's "pigeon pies." Mr. Samuel Hansell remembers the birds he hunted as a boy in the woods of Manzanillo: the billbird (toucan), parrot, macaw, tapno-chick, wild turkey, and curassow.

The vast variety of fishes, small game, and wild and domestic meats available to the coast people, in combination with the foods they cultivated on their land, kept them well fed, to say the least. Preparing a meal rarely entailed a trip to the shop. It was merely a matter of "running down" the ingredients in the bush, in the sea, or on the farm. The thrifty housewife put everything together in one pot, simmered it in coconut milk, and called it "rundown" for everything she was able to "run down" that day. If it included fish, yam, plantain, scallions, palmito, and Panamanian pepper, it could hardly be better.

# 5. Trade in the Talamanca Interior

The Talamanca settlers prided themselves in being as self-sufficient as possible out of necessity. But they were always looking for avenues of trade to sell their farm and fishing products, to acquire rare goods, and to make cash profits. Within the Talamanca region there were two groups of people that welcomed trade with the coastal farmers: the North Americans of the United Fruit Company and the Indians of the Talamanca highlands.

United Fruit Company Trade

The United Fruit Company's banana plantations on the Panama side of the Sixaola River were so successful in the early 1900s that the Company decided to expand into Costa Rica. It built the bridge across the Sixaola River from Guabito (Panama) to Bridgefoot (Costa Rica) in 1908, and began construction of a railroad into the Talamanca mountains, planting bananas on either side of the tracks. H.M. Fields, an American, was the contractor for the banana company who later gave his name to a settlement established by the Company in Talamanca, near the present-day cantón capital, Bribri.

Mr. Johnson well remembers the coming of the United Fruit Company to Costa Rica because his father owned property on the Costa Rican side of the Sixaola River. "They got from me a big piece of land," Mr. Johnson says, "because my father dead and I was a little boy and I was here [Cahuita] and when I go see, they take it over and cut it down and plant bananas. And all they give me was two hundred dollars Balboa [Panama currency]. They had a *comandante* which rule there, and since the land didn't title, he give them access to go as they like. They came right up to Cuabre."

Cuabre[1] was the original name for the settlement which the United Fruit Company later renamed Olivia. It was at the base of a trail that the Indians chopped through the hills to the sea at Old Harbour. For years Old Smith and Joseph Hunter had followed the Cuabre road from Old Harbour into the Talamanca mountains on trading expeditions with the

---

[1] *UkábLe*, in the Bribri language. For a history of this trail, see Barrantes and others 1990.

Indians. But when the United Fruit Company railroad from Bridgefoot (now Sixaola) to Cuabre was under construction, the Cuabre road became an important trade route. The Company landed boats in Old Harbour and hired young men from the coast and Indians from the hills to carry loads of supplies over the Cuabre road to the Company camps. Mr. Mason sometimes made the trip twice a day, a two-hour walk one-way for a strong young man. From Old Harbour the trail climbed a steep mountain which came to be known as Rest and Be Thankful Hill.

Mr. Selven Bryant recounts the arduous hikes "over road" on the Cuabre trail:

> As you climb up Rest and Be Thankful Hill, you see all kind of old grip [suitcases] and shoes and old things throw away there. The people get tired. What you don't really need, you can't carry, you dump it there just to fight your way out to reach Olivia.
>
> Used to have man that trade over road with horse and mule, drawing freight. You had a man here named Knight. Him carry a foot machine [pedal sewing machine] right over the hill, and those days those machine was pure iron! Him back it right over the hill. The people call him "Local." All him do is draw freight from Old Harbour to Olivia, from Olivia to Old Harbour. That was his living. I think he was a Barbadian. When him reach Old Harbour, him blow; you hear him in all of Old Harbour. You know the "Local" is coming.
>
> The government compel the people to clean the Cuabre road twice a year. Olivia people work that side and meet the Old Harbour set; anywhere they meet up, the work finish.
>
> And we keep the road through the coconut walk clean right from here to Cahuita. You never see coconut leaf or husk in that road. Everybody keep it clean, clean, and people travel up and down, night and day."

The products of the coast found new marketing outlets as the United Fruit Company expanded into Talamanca. Farmers sent their sons up the Cuabre road to sell coconuts, oil, and provisions.

Women whose husbands had small cocoa farms ground fresh chocolate with a mortar and pestle to sell to the company workers who preferred it over the packaged chocolate that came in through the commissaries from the United States. And Joseph Hunter discovered a lucrative business in animal trading. Mr. Mason recalls:

> "My adopted father used to buy cows and horses. Mules was very scarce. He trade on them, go to Alajuela, Puntarenas and buy maybe ten or twenty heads. They may cost about sixty

colones each. And when you bring them here the Company pay you thirty-five dollars a head, and it was four colones to one dollar, so it was a big trade.

My father bring the animals to Limón by train, and then walk them up the beach, cross rivers until he get to North River bar. And that bar have sharks in it and alligators. So he take two or three of the worst class horses or cows and put them in the river. And the shark and alligators will eat them. And meanwhile they are eating those, you see the water in blood, then you drive in the good ones to get across. And we tie together balsa logs like a raft that we use to float on."

From North River, now known as the Río Estrella, Mr. Hunter drove the animals up the beach to Old Harbour and from there across Rest and Be Thankful Hill to Cuabre, where he sold them to the banana company.

Indian Trade

Trade with the Indians in the Talamanca highlands flourished during these years. It offered a few Afro-Caribbean traders an opportunity to observe Indian customs first hand and make a living at the same time. Mr. Mason describes the trading this way:

"My father used to trade in the olden days with the Indians, buying cows and pigs, but not with cash. Exchanging articles. If you go to the Indian and ask them how much you want for that pig or that cow, they don't know. They don't know money. But they will tell you, you show them this thing and the next thing, and they say they will take this and give you that pig. And no pig they give you less than one hundred pounds. You may buy something in Limón, especially anything in red, and combs and perfumes that smell sweet with a red color, or a dress ready made or only cloth. You carry a kerchief while it has red spot on it, or a perfume that is red and sweet. A plain white one, they don't want that. And they say they will take this and give you that. And this article may cost you five colón in Limón and you can get a pig for the value of ten colón. And they won't accept the change from you unless it is in the coffee tree money. The first silver in Costa Rica was with the coat of arm of a coffee tree, silver. Fifty cents and a colón. And they will accept that and nothing else. And anything else they won't receive, and they bury that. They don't spend from it, they bury it. And they would rather have it in exchange for some article. They don't have no use for money.

And they carry the article you exchange, say a ten pound of salt, further in and trade with the other Indians and take animals from them the same way and come and change with you again this side. They travel all the way from Talamanca. But they never want money. They want sugar, they like the refined sugar, or salt or blankets and anything that look pretty."

## Customs of the "Old-Time" Indians

Mr. Mason goes on to give this picture of daily life among the Bribri Indians of Talamanca, as he knew them in his boyhood:

"The only thing that you found the Indians with is pejiballe. It's a wild plant, you know. Anywhere that you walk and see an old pejiballe tree and if it even woodland, you can be sure that was a settlement of Indians. Because when I used to go in the woods with my adopted father we found only cultivation of pejiballes and bananas. Where they got the plant from we don't know. The square bananas, the Spaniards call it *guineo*. It is very short and thick. That's the plant the Indians have. It never die, especially by the riverside.

And the pejiballe, they boil it to eat and they make *fresco*. Because I travel with them sometimes, coming through the trail, and when they reach to a creek they will dig a hole and cut a leaf named the *bijagua* leaf, and they will dig that hole and line it with the leaf. And at the home they grater the pejiballe and mash it with a mortar that made out of wood and put it with leaves in the *chácara*[1] and a woman carry that. And when they get to the river they will throw it in that hole and take a calabash with water from the creek and throw in it. And they have a thing called *molinillo* with sprang, and they rub it between their hands, use it in the pejiballe like an egg-beater, and beat it up till it dissolve fine. And when it ready now, without sugar, everyone go right around and they kneel on hands and knees and drink from that hole. And refresh themselves, no sugar nor salt.

And they take chocolate, beat it in the mortar, and they pound it again and boil it. And they will roast two or three ripe plantains, well ripe, so when you taking off the skin it look like something that will fall away. And then they bite a piece of that plantain and drink the bitter chocolate behind it, and they is quite satisfied, refreshed. With no sugar.

---

[1] A shoulder bag woven out of natural fibers by the Indians.

They have a wild cocoa that they use for the chocolate. It smell funny. But they dry it and take off the skin. Then it lose that smell. But it is white. The pod is yellow, but the seed is white.

At that time the products of Talamanca was rubber, sarsaparilla—that is a kind of roots—and pigs and cows."

Mr. George Humphries, of Cahuita, remembers making a trip up Tuba Creek to an Indian settlement. He said the Indians built their ranches in separate clearings, at least three hundred meters between each family. The ranches were made of thatch with no flooring, and the family members slept on cow skins. The yards were planted in the indigenous plantain Mr. Mason described, a flat, short fruit. Mr. Humphries saw lots of pigs, chickens and ducks in the yards and smoked wari meat hanging from rafters. And he says the Indians kept a fire smoldering day and night.

Mrs. Ida Corbin grew up along the shores of Big Bay, north of Cahuita, near Indian settlements. She remembers the fires that the Indians kept going "all year long, day and night without matches," and she liked to watch the women cook. "Everything they roast. They wrap the meat up in leaves and they dig a hole and put ashes from the fire in there and then the meat wrap up in the leaves and then more ashes on top." Miss Ida's mother, Mrs. Walker, baked cakes to sell, and on baking days Miss Ida remembers the Indian children coming into the yard to taste the sweets. The big basket with a cover that Mrs. Walker carried her cakes in was made by the Indians. Miss Ida remembers:

"Momma make coconut oil. She make Johnny cake, she make bread, she make sweet bun, pudding, and all that. Oh, my mother, she always bake, you know. Mommy bake in the pots and the kerosene tin. Oh, nice baking. We have to go carry the basket and the tray. The Indians them make the basket with two handles. Nice. Sometimes they paint them nice, you know. Big baskets with a cover. Mommy tell them she want that one, big one, so, with a cover. And now when you see she pack the buns them in that, she fix the paper inside, was pink paper she get in Limón. And she take the buns and fix them right around, line the basket pretty, pretty."

Miss Ida and her sister, Miss Maud, spent many days in their childhood playing with the Indian children, singing and bathing, fishing and catching crabs. "Oh, yes," Miss Ida recalls, "we always fishing. But sometimes they burst the line, and sometimes we can't draw them in, big fish! You have to let it go. Oh, fish! Crab! We catch crab all the time with the Indian children them. Yes, we boil crab and put on lime. My mother beat we. But we don't mind. Hide it all about."

The skill of the "old-time" Indians in using natural materials to make utensils, tools, and clothing, won the admiration of the Afro-Caribbean traders. Before they were able to trade for cloth, the Indians made their clothing out of the bark of a tree they called *tuno* (in Spanish, *mastate*). Mr. Mason describes the process as he observed it:

> "The small *tuno* trees are round, and they cut it and they carry it on their shoulder to the riverside. They lay it in the river and using the hard wood we call *níspero*, they split it or burn it out to the size they want. They cut it with machete when they get, but if not with stone. And they cut it. They keep beating the bark and wash it with the river water and beat and beat and beat until it give way. And then afterwards they spread it on a hard log, the insides of it, and keep beating. And every juice and every skin come off and leave it thin thin, but soft. And they dry it in the sun, and they make hammocks, clothes, bags, everything from that."

Mr. Kayasso says the Indians used the bark of the same *tuno* tree to make mosquito nets, the sheets of bark seamed together with fresh rubber milk. As for blankets made of *tuno*, he says, "You don't want a better blanket. That is a first class blanket."

Mr. Mason admired the sewing and weaving work of the Indians. He says, "From the wild pine, that's a wild pineapple plant, they make the thread and the needle, and they sew with it. They beat the wild pine and dry it and the thread come out white and pretty and very fine. They used to make rope from it. And they have a wis in the bush that cut and give the different colors, and they paint the thread and make these shoulder bags what they call *chácara*. And all these different colors that you find on it, they make it from a wis or different bush, and it look natural as if it come from the United States."

The Indians usually made their settlements on river banks, and they were skilled fishermen. Mr. Johnson remembers, "They catch all the fish they want. They use the bow and arrow to strike the fish. They make the arrow with the apoo and the bow from the same apoo or the wild cane. They make the string from the trumpet tree. They strip the trumpet tree and take the inside bark and they weave it into string. Gum up the string with rubber milk all around so it hold together, tight. Make hammocks out of that same string. We always buy those hammocks in Talamanca. But the rope is strong. Tie pigs with it. Do plenty things with it. And the arrow strong and sharp out of the apoo. They kill tiger [jaguar] with it. They kill wild pigs with it."

Mr. Johnson tells how he saw the Indians make their strong drink, *chicha*, and celebrate their fiestas:

"They take a bunch of pejiballe, a lot of it, and they boil it and peel it and take out the seed. They put it into a big thing they have, the jar. You know they make their own big jar out of clay. They put the pejiballe in there and then they throw a little water in it and they bury it down in the earth. And they make it stay there till it sour. About a week. And they take it out.

Then they take the ripe plantain and they boil that and they put it in leaf and tie it and they put that under the earth till it get sour. Then they take that, they do gets nasty, you know, they take that, and they chew it. They chew the plantain and throw it in with the pejiballe that already sour, into a big calabash. And then they mash it up all together and they go back and throw a little water in it and bury it again. Have to tie the jar mouth tight.

Then they open it now. It's strong, I tell you. Very strong. They take it out and put a little water with it into a calabash, and they dip them hand in that and mash it up. Then they give you to drink. And you got to drink it. If you don't drink it you can't live among them. They would feel bad and you couldn't get nothing out of them.

And they got drunk. You see them staggering all about. They have that when they having their fiesta time. They drink and they dance. They dance with a stick. I stop and look at them. I dance with them too. I dance with them. And then they sing and they have a skin drum, from the baboon[1] skin and bamboo. And they 'tunka, tunka,' and their song was 'waya, waya, dipay, subum, subum, hang!' And they sing that and they jump the more high. They jump up in the air. They don't hold one another, you know. The women and the men, but everybody dance single, no holding one another.

Some of them drunk too much. They goes into the river. They always have the house near a big river, you know. And they go and dive in there. Because they didn't wear much clothes. They take a big piece of cloth and tie 'round them waist, stick it together at the hip.

If the women is bathing, suppose you coming on, they see you coming on there and they having a bath in the river and they are naked. Don't figure that they are going to hide their puss. They're going to hide their breasts. I ask them, I say, 'But why you hide the breast? You should hide the other special part.' They said, 'No, no, no, no. We born with that, so you can see that as you like, but we didn't born with this.' That's why they hide the breasts."

---

[1] Local word for the howler monkey.

Antonio Saldaña, last king of the Bribris.

Mr. Johnson remembers that the "higher grade" Indians, the members of the King's family, wore gold jewelry. This is what he says about the Indian royalty:

> "King Antonio, he was the last Indian King of Talamanca. His older father I don't know. And his mother I don't know, but his father was King before him. King Antonio I did know personally because anytime any problem with the government up there in Talamanca, he took twelve Indians along with him and he came by Indian road, he walked right in and stay at my grandfather's place, sometimes two or three days. And he walk the beach to Limón, and he walk until him get to San José. And you can sure he talk to the people in government and make them change over. But he was friendly with my grandfather. He died, I think it was 1910. From there, after he died, they don't get any more King.
>
> He had one daughter the name of Victoria. She didn't have no children. So the tribe go down. He had a brother that had some sons, but at the time the Fathers, the Roman Catholics, they were in Talamanca, and they have school there. And they studied one of the boys. That boy is in England now. He came here about five years ago. And was to come back. He carry a group of them to San José to ask the government if they would allow him to be King of his granduncle's place. And they said yes. But him don't return. Him must be think it strange to come back to the woods and him live in a big city. He went back to England."

The Indian customs were strange to the people of the coast, but their products and trails were valuable in trade, and Indian women became mothers of many half Afro-Caribbean children.[1] Mr. Selven Bryant describes the destiny of many Jamaican men in the early years of the Twentieth Century:

> "They joined up with Indian women and made farms up in Talamanca. Some of the Jamaicans learned the Indian language, and their children grew up speaking English, Bribri and Spanish, same way. Luke Miller, a man name of Pití, some others name of Frenchi, Hamilton, Nelson, Paddyfoot, Clark, George Crum—all of them were Jamaica man who came over with the Company and they stayed on in Talamanca."

---

[1] For more information about the indigenous groups of Talamanca, consult the Bibliography, especially Bozzoli 1979 and Palmer, Sánchez and Mayorga 1991 and 1992.

Dennis Glick

Mr. Joseph "Boyse" Spenser shows children in Cahuita how he makes a net for fishing.

# 6. Sea Trade and Transportation

Until 1967, when the road connecting Fields (Bribri), Old Harbour (Puerto Viejo), Hone Creek, Cahuita, and Penshurst was completed, the people of the coast depended on the sea for transportation and trade outside the Talamanca region. Newcomers to the coast today, who never see launches docking in Cahuita, may find it difficult to imagine the way of life locked in the memories of the old-time residents whose transportation choices were simple: walk, or wait for a calm sea. A trip down the coast to Grape Point or Manzanillo can give the modern visitor a glimpse of the past, for while the people of these villages wait for the road to be built from Old Harbour south to Sixaola, they still have only the two transportation options. Motor boats, of course, have replaced the old sailing vessels, and the sea trip from Manzanillo is only a half-hour hop to Old Harbour where the road awaits passengers. But in the early years a twelve-hour sea trip to Bocas or a two-day journey to Graytown under sail were routine to the coast people.

The coastal waters were a bit calmer in those days, and the shorelines extended out as much as two hundred meters beyond today's beaches. The Caribbean has been growing in this last century, tossing its waves farther and farther inland, until now it hides from view the beaches and docks and even some dwelling sites of the early settlers.

"You had a pretty beach a-way out there," Mr. Johnson says, stretching his arm out over the bay that covers the beach of his boyhood days at old Cahuita. "It was a different sea from now. That was a big beach out there. That time the reef was nearer to us and houses all about where you see the sea come in right now. Sea come in little by little and wash those places away."

Early Sailboats

The first boats along the coast were those that brought the original turtle fishermen from Nicaragua and Panama. These small boats, and the ones that the early farmers made to carry their coconuts and oil to Limón, were all dugout canoes, no more than twenty feet long and four feet wide. Three months of work with an axe, an adze, and a turning adze produced a boat that could carry four hundred coconuts and a couple men.

Mr. Kayasso describes the effort of making a dugout canoe as "terrible work." This is how he recalls the process:

> "I didn't believe that man was so powerful. You had some trees here—big! You want to know how big? You go over that side, I stay on this side and we can't see one another. They call them sandbox.[1] Some of the trees were so large that you chop till you can't no more. One, two men, chopping, chopping, chopping with axe, you know. Sometimes it take all day, two men chopping. And after the tree fell, you cut it to the size you want. And dig, dig, dig it out with axe and then, you know the adze? That's what you use to dig out the inside. But you have to be careful with these tools, I tell you. When you work with these thing, if you make a mistake you chop this leg. Then you have another tool with shorter handle, they call that the turning adze. We use that now to finish the boat, to make those curves. From the day you fell that tree you going to be working on that boat all two, three months."

Mr. Willard Gaslin, called "Crackerjack" by his neighbors in Manzanillo, is reputed to be one of the best dugout builders on the Talamanca Coast today. He learned the trade as a boy, and has crafted all the small boats used for fishing and transportation in Manzanillo in recent years. The sandbox tree, he says, is still the best. His work is made easier by power saws used to fell the trees and to dig out the rough shape of the boat. But the finishing process is essentially the same as it has always been, still requiring about three months of labor. A painted boat, Crackerjack says, will last many years.

It was Old Smith who brought the first real sailing boats to the area. He bought the *Alquina* and the *Whisper* in San Andrés in the early years of the Twentieth Century and sailed them to his port at old Cahuita. The *Alquina* was a two-and-a-half-ton vessel with sprit sails, about fifty feet long, as Mr. Johnson remembers her. Old Smith sailed her up and down the coast carrying coconuts and hawksbill shells to Limón and Bocas del Toro.

The trip from Cahuita to Limón, Mr. Johnson recalls, "was two hours and a half, when you got plenty breeze. When you don't got breeze, take you all day. But we get there quick with the breeze. You had

---

[1] Scientific name: *Hura crepitans* (Spanish common name is *javillo*).

Bob Bernthal

Manzanillo boatmen shove off their dugout canoe from the shores of Old Harbour, carrying plastic-wrapped supplies and passengers down the coast.

to depend on the breeze, you know. And to go to Graytown, if you get a good breeze, a day and a half. And that's about eighty miles. If you catch a real good breeze, you cut it down to a day, but if you don't got breeze, well, it take you two or three days. But we don't care. We carry water and food."

The *Whisper* was a larger craft, Mr. Johnson says, five tons and eighty feet long, of the "shoal and batten" type. She made longer voyages than the *Alquina*, sailing to San Andrés and Jamaica with hold and deck full of turtles, returning with coconuts, avocado pears, cocoa plants, sheep, dogs, goats, linen, furniture, books, and anything else Old Smith could purchase that would make life on the Talamanca Coast more comfortable or profitable. It was the *Whisper* that brought the first pine boards and corrugated zinc roofing from Bocas to build Old Smith's "real house" by the lime trees at Cahuita.

For years Old Smith traded as he pleased among the countries and islands of the Caribbean. In the meantime the Costa Rican government was establishing laws involving import duties and defining contraband, and one day a government boat intercepted the *Whisper* just sailing in with a full load from Bocas. Old Smith spent four months in jail for dealing in contraband. The *Whisper* was confiscated.

But by this time there were a few other ships sailing the coast. Mr. Mason talks about the first launch that offered somewhat regular

75

(weekly) passenger and cargo service, beginning in 1909: "The first launch was made by a man name of Ernest Williams, a Jamaican. That launch name was *Perseverance* because it take about five years building it, and he was poor. He had to get the Limón Trading Company to import the motor for him. He built the boat because he was a shipwright himself. He charge one colón and fifty cents for passenger and one colón for a quintal of cocoa, and ten cents a bunch for plantain that sell in Limón for forty cents a bunch."

Maduro and Sons, an American-owned trading company based in Limón, launched its ship, the *Vanguardia*, in 1912, hiring the eighteen-year-old Selles Johnson as engineer. Thus began Mr. Johnson's forty-year career on the sea.

The *Vanguardia*, Mr. Johnson says, was an eighteen-ton boat with sprit sails backed up by a small gasoline motor. It was built in the United States and brought to Costa Rica primarily for local use in Maduro and Sons' turtle export business. During the turtle season, June through October, the *Vanguardia* carried turtles exclusively, but in the off-season it shuttled passengers and produce up and down the coast from its home port, Limón.

Mr. Johnson describes turtling on the *Vanguardia*:

"They always draw turtle from Turtle Bogue [Tortuguero]. They monopolize the whole beach here and the beach at Turtle Bogue, too. They get the turtle and ship it out on the big ships to the United States. Green turtle. They sell the whole turtle. They build some boxes and cement the boxes that no water come out. And they put one turtle in each box, alive. The small one they call 'chicken turtle' and the big one 'turtle,' but they is both green turtle. The shell of the hawksbill, they ship that sometimes to Germany. They make comb and all thing there.

At Turtle Bogue they put watchman on the beach and they walk with lantern. They turn over the turtle when they come to lay eggs, turn over on them back, and the next morning they put a rope on the hand and let them go. Then we outside, we have the small canoe, because you can't land on the beach there, the surf too big. So the turtle fight their way through the surf and come out. When they come out the men in the small boat see them and catch that stick and haul them in and carry them to the *Vanguardia*. And we hoist them up. When the hold is full then we put them on the deck 'round. The *Vanguardia* carry eighty turtle. Take them to Limón where they put them on the big ships that go to the States. And we in the *Vanguardia*, we go back up to Turtle Bogue and get the next load."

Sailing Lore

Mr. Johnson says the *Vanguardia* and many of the trading boats that came after it to do business along the coast, carried engines so small that the machines were employed only when the breeze failed to fill the sails. Eventually, as engines got bigger and better, the reverse system was used: the engines powered the boats unless they broke down on the sea, then the sails were raised to get the boat back to port. So even into recent years, sailors on the Caribbean coast had to be skilled in "manning the sails" and reading the sky for signs of wind and weather. Mr. Johnson explains the old sailors' verse:

> Rainbow in the morning,
> Sailors take warning;
> Rainbow in the evening,
> Sailors's delight.

"The reason why that is, the rainbow that makes in the morning, the weather going to be bad. The poor sailors, they are suffering all day, and in the evening if they see a rainbow, it may mean a rest, you see, the 'sailors' delight.' They are glad to know that the weather is going to change for the balance of night.

But the next one we call the 'windgall.' That is a shorter one, like a rainbow but shorter with a different color. That one from any point of the globe give you trouble. You see one of those, you can be certain you're going to have a heavy wind that day and may come to a hurricane or a cyclone or something is out there. But it will be a terrible wind any time you see one of those. Where you is, you on sea, you better try to come to a safe place.

Even with birds, if you see the booby birds come and one come and light on your boat you know you are going to have a heavy storm that day."

There are other thrills for the seaman, not from the whims of Nature but from the realm of the supernatural. Mr. Johnson tells of seeing the sea horse and the Flying Dutchman:

"I saw the sea horse out at Monkey Point coming from Bocas one broad day. I into my boat, and I see a big reeling of water. Come close, coming up to me now. But my boat was fast, you know. And I look and I see a big reeling of water, big reeling water, and I see a big animal stick out his head and gone. I said, 'That thing favor horse head.' And when I got near up to it I see it come right up again and it braying as a horse, same as a horse bray, 'heeeiiiigh,' and gone again. That's why I certain there is really sea horse. It have the head, the mane and everything. The head have a red color, same ears as a horse. And we had an old sailor on board, a Nassau man, and he said, 'That's a sea horse, boys.'

And one night I come in from Gandoca [south of Monkey Point] at night. I coming and I come right up Long Shoal, and coming up Long Shoal I see a boat, light up, coming towards me. Hear the motor working on that boat. Small open motor boat, and I see the people in it, walking up and down, and that boat trying to force me on the reef. My boat was a big boat. And that boat come across my boat and turning, and it went right across the shoal. And if I did follow him I would get ashoal there and my boat would turn over, but I turn to the side, and I came up here. That's a bad boat. He went across that shoal, straight across, and he was gone, and I didn't study him. We call that on the sea the Dutchman, the Flying Dutchman.

There's some people, you see, that die on boats, and they have boats there on the sea after, same way. There are people that say they're the Devil. But I don't say they're the Devil. The Devil don't have no time to worry about it. Him have something else to do.

But I believe it dead people run those Dutchman boats. But we don't worry with them, me and my crew. That's not the first Flying Dutchman we see. All the time we see them. I go here to Colón. Here to Colombia. Once I see big Flying Dutchman ship coming down on me. And if you say it not the Dutchman, then I say, Why it disappeared?"

Despite the sailors' skill, chance plays a large part in the life of the sea, and for this reason superstitions about sailing abound. Near the end of his days, Old Smith rebuilt a boat, painted her nicely and christened her the *Cahuita*. With a new motor imported from the U.S., the *Cahuita* carried cargo and passengers up and down the coast, but only for a short time. Old Smith wouldn't let just anyone captain his pretty boat. In fact, says Mr. Mason, he would allow her to sail with only one man as captain: Simeon Hudson, of Manzanillo. When Captain Hudson took a job on another vessel, Old Smith brought the *Cahuita* to rest in the bay in front of his home, and there she sat and rotted. Coastal farmers, bewildered, complained that they needed transport for their produce. But Old Smith shook his long white beard, Mr. Mason says, and kept his silence. When he had made up his mind, for whatever his private reasons, he was not a man to be persuaded.

Travel to Puerto Limón

There were some coastal residents whose superstitions or fears about the sea kept them away from boats entirely. They became terrific walkers. It was not uncommon for men, women, and children to walk the beach between Old Harbour and Cahuita (seventeen kilometers) to ex-change visits or do business. A horse was a great help, but few families owned horses in the early days. With a launch scheduled to sail north from Cahuita only once a week, and landings sometimes impossible because of high seas or bad weather, folks without produce to carry often opted to walk to Limón. Mr. George Humphries remembers a Cahuita man, Amos Dixon, "would get up and walk to Limón in the morning, turn 'round, walk back the same evening. He was a very good walker." At eighty-six kilometers round-trip, that's an understatement.

When a launch did stop in Cahuita, heading north to Limón, its charge was to take the produce first, the passengers only if they could be accommodated after the freight. "When I was a boy," Mr. Humphries says, "down there the place they call the Hole, down at the Bluff, those days the boats dock up there to take the cargo. Sometimes the boat come overload from Puerto Viejo with foodstuffs. They can't take it all. Cahuita people lose all their yuca, yam, plantain, it all spoil out there at the Hole." At such times, of course, there was no question of taking on passengers, unless someone was seriously ill.

So the people rejoiced the day in 1910 that train service started between Limón and Bonifacio on the North River (now called the Río Estrella). Twice a week the trains ran between the United Fruit Company banana plantations in the Estrella Valley and the docks in Limón. For the people of the coast, the locomotive shortened their walk to Limón by thirty-four kilometers, and for the Colombian Bonifacio family it created a booming business of river transportation from the river mouth up seven kilometers to the train tracks.

The Bonifacios lived at North River bar. For years they had ferried coast walkers across the river mouth—famed for its sharks, alligators, and strong currents—in a small canoe. When the train service started, the Bonifacios extended their shuttle upriver, charging passengers fifty cents for a one-way trip. Train fare from Bonifacio, the end of the line at that time, to Limón, was one colón. It wasn't long before the Bonifacios had set up a shop and a little settlement where the tracks met the river. The location bears the family name until today.

Mr. Cyril Gray, a long-time resident of Old Harbour, was one of those Jamaicans who distrusted the sea. He describes the alternate route from Old Harbour to Limón:

> "I don't like sea. I used to sea sick. So in the old boat days, I preferred to ride horse. We used to leave here in the morning, early, ride right from here to North River bar to take the canoe, go up to the station to take the train. Who didn't have horse had to walk or sleep in Cahuita first night and get up next morning and go again. But we did this way: Say you coming from Limón today. You come down the river and I ride out to the river bar and give you my horse, and you come home. Tomorrow anybody coming out from Old Harbour, you give him my horse, and he ride it to the river and meet me and I come back. And that's how we get through."

Mr. Gray, at eighty-nine years of age, now travels happily from his home in Old Harbour to San José by bus in less time than it took him then to make the trip to Limón by horse, canoe, and train.

Deirdre Hyde

Game of skitlolly.

# 7. Community Life and Organization

By the year 1914, residents of the coast identified themselves as belonging to specific regions, each one with a center for community activities: the Bluff, Cahuita, Old Harbour, Grape Point, Manzanillo, and Monkey Point. Of these communities, Cahuita offered the most sophisticated social organization, with two churches, a school, a judge, a shop, and a cricket club.

## Old Cahuita

Between Duncan Creek and Louis Hudson Creek, on the north side of Cahuita Point, some twenty-five families lived in houses ranging from rough rawa and pin-thatch ranches to the board and zinc houses of the Smith family by the lime trees. The beach between the two creeks extended two hundred meters into the present-day bay, and the water was calm. Mr. Johnson tells of houses built over the water in the Cahuita of his boyhood:

> "There was some Jamaicans come in that time. They make house out over the sea. They plant big posts and build house and make like a sidewalk going around the house. Like a dock nearly, and they hitch their boats there and go on boat to the land. Over there, over the sea, you don't get no mosquitos and the sandfly in the night. But on the shore now, the mosquitos come down in the night, but if you have a good breeze blowing there's no sandfly.
>
> So the people build their house right out over the sea. My grandfather did have two house out there, but he use them as storage for the coconut. But we use the stuff to keep away mosquitos by our house. We burn the ducks ants' nest, the big black thing you always see on the coconut root. We call that duck ants.[1] We burn it with sulfur and that keep away the mosquitos. The smoke of it. They smell it and they

---

[1] A local word for termites.

don't come. You put the duck ants and the sulfur into a old pot and light it, and it burn. We always use that to keep away the mosquitos."

Old Smith built two large houses near his lime trees, one for himself and his wife and their overnight guests that included Indian kings, missionaries and travelers, and one for his children, who numbered fifty-two, according to Mr. Johnson. They were all half-brothers and sisters, brought under the same roof by the old man who sired them with the cooperation of his many Indian "wives." Old Smith took pride in his impressive paternity and insisted on rearing and educating his children after their Indian mothers cared for them through early childhood. By the time Selles Johnson was born, an upstairs had been added to the children's house, which was occupied by the younger of Old Smith's children and the older of his grandchildren. The boys slept upstairs, the girls below, as many as thirty altogether at any given time.

A Swedish biologist, Carl Bovallius, who walked from the Talamanca interior to Cahuita in 1882, recorded these observations and impressions of the community he found at Cahuita Point:

> It was difficult to walk, although the path was not too rough, because sometimes we had to wade through the sea or burn our feet on the fine sand; sometimes we had to climb over an inferno of sharp rocks and pass through spiny, scratchy undergrowth; sometimes we had to cut open a path for ourselves with machetes …
>
> Finally, we arrived at our destination; our eyes were delighted to see a number of pretty buildings surrounded by enchanting flower gardens, right on the sea shore. We walked by a score of huge, live sea turtles (*Chelonia imbricata*), that were lying belly-up on the sand …
>
> Cahuita is a large colony of blacks, with about fifteen houses spread out along the beach. The residents make their living by extracting rubber and by fishing. The green turtle is their most prized catch. They sell the rubber and the hawksbill shell in Puerto Limón. They are valient and able sailors …[1]

The Panamanian, Nicaraguan, and Jamaican settlers in Cahuita were English-speaking Protestants, inheriting their language and

---

[1] Bovallius 1977 (translated from the Spanish).

religion from the British colonies of the Caribbean. The first church established on the coast was the Baptist congregation at Cahuita. Its founder was a North American missionary, Parson Soby. Mr. Johnson tells of Parson Soby's work in Cahuita:

> "He was an American, tall, big man. He had a big beard, too. He could sing, oh, he was a great songster! He came here on my grandfather's sailing boat when there wasn't no church. That was before I born, 1890. And he stay by my grandfather and he himself went and square lumber and built the Baptist Church there. Built it himself. And then he always go and come. And after we get another minister name of Henderson. He go and come same way, stay a fifteen days, give service and Sunday School, and go on back to Limón, for years."

It was Parson Soby who made the arrangements for the first school teacher to come to Cahuita in about 1905. Selles Johnson was a student in that first class at the Baptist Church, along with about sixteen of his brothers, sisters, and cousins from Old Smith's house, the Dixon children, and the newer families of Cahuita and the Bluff.

"That first teacher name was Grant, I think," says Mr. Johnson, straining to remember. "He was a Jamaican. And after that, another one, next one, about two years after. That's the way we get English School. English School it was. We didn't have no Spanish School. And we got the next teacher, name of Johnson. Him from Jamaica too. And after that we got the next one, a colored man from Limón, named Hilton. Teacher Hilton. That was a great teacher, and he teach English and Spanish. He came here 1914, I think it was, and that was the first Spanish we ever learn."

The Church of England, St. Mark's, was built in about 1900 just on the Cahuita side of Duncan Creek. By this time Jamaicans were building ranches and planting coastal farms at the Bluff and to the north along Little Bay and Big Bay. Families walked down to Cahuita for church services and church-sponsored picnics, concerts, and religious holidays. Mrs. Ida Corbin lived with her mother, Mrs. Walker, at the same spot on Big Bay where she now lives with her husband. She remembers walking the beach to go to church in Cahuita. "Sometimes all in the night, rain, the creek come down heavy, you reach the creek and you can't cross."

The largest creek between Big Bay and Cahuita was Duncan Creek. At that time it flowed to the sea in two branches, an island in the center. Mr. Johnson says the people finally "bridged the creek so the people can come and go. We built a standing bridge, plant posts, and the bridge go from the land to the island and from that island to the other side, two bridges out of wood. We square wood and build it. Ride horse right over it when the creek did high."

The swelling of Duncan Creek (now called Río Perezoso) keeps visitors to the Cahuita National Monument from crossing to view the coral reefs around the Point during rainy seasons. But since the decline of the community at the old Cahuita, there has never been another bridge spanning the river.

The first Cahuita cemetery was the Smith family burying ground near the houses by the lime trees. One of Mr. Johnson's uncles, Peter Smith, was the first person buried there. To this day Mr. Johnson tends the flowers above the grave of his mother, now surrounded by coconut palms Mr. Johnson planted there years after old Cahuita was abandoned.


Bush Medicine

The people of the coast were a remarkably healthy lot. Old-timers scarcely remember a sick baby, a stillborn child. The hardiness of the population can be attributed to the mild climate, pure water, strict sanitary habits, ample and nutritious diet, and the genetic resistance of the African descendants to the tropical killer, malaria. The United Fruit Company hospital in Limón rarely received a patient from the Talamanca Coast, and this was not entirely due to the difficulty of transportation. The people of the coast lived healthy lives because they knew how to accommodate themselves to their natural environment, and when someone did become ill or suffered an accident, they knew how to cure the illness with natural medicines: bush.

Mr. Johnson isn't sure where the medical knowledge of the old people came from. From the Indians? From Africa? He doesn't know. He thinks they were born with the knowledge.

"Listen to me. Everybody that born, born with a certain thing. From when I was born, my delight was to be a mechanic. Nobody did learn me. But that was my delight. I born with it, you see. Now some people born to know the bush, be midwife, snake doctor, and so on. They can't say where they learn it. They born with it, and that's their delight. My grandmother could cure fever without any doctor. She knew to do it with bare bush, but I don't know them things. The Indians, they can cure fever, but the bush they cure the fever with, you wouldn't be able to use it. That's the bush we call stinging nettle, some people call it scratch bush. They beat themselves with it and it blister them and they get rid of the fever. But you couldn't use it 'cause it scratch bad, you know. The old people, the old parents, they did know plenty medicine, but they die out."

Since the people were generally healthy, the main events that called for medical attention were childbirth, snake bite, and accident.

Childbirth was traditionally in the hands of women, midwives, who learned the essentials of the skill from their mothers or just through experience. Of Jeanette Johnson, a famous midwife at Grape Point, Mr. Johnson says, "She never study. She couldn't even read. But she know. The old people teach her, and she know. Bare bush she use." At old Cahuita, Doloras Dixon was in charge of midwifery, and her daughter Eunice became a great midwife later in Old Harbour. Samuel Hansell's grandmother, Antonette Hansell, delivered babies in the Manzanillo region, and, as if to prove that she knew her trade, she bore twenty-five children herself. In Monkey Point, Personette Hudson was the midwife.

All through a woman's pregnancy the midwife made visits to check progress, mixing and prescribing bush teas and salves as necessary. For the last month of pregnancy the midwife usually moved into the house of the expectant mother, helping her with household chores and making preparations for the birth and the newborn. Mothers, sisters, and women friends assisted the midwife in the delivery, after which the midwife stayed nine more days tending to the infant while the mother was confined to bed. "Very seldom did you hear a woman dead from having baby in those times," says Mrs. Adine Bryant of Old Harbour. "Very seldom you hear a baby dead. And look how many baby die now in Limón hospital."

Whatever knowledge the midwives possessed, they earned great respect among their neighbors. To say of a woman, "She is a midwife," carried the same quality of admiration that goes with the statement, "He is a doctor," today.

To say of someone, "He is a snake doctor," carried a sense not only of respect but of awe, for the snake was the most feared enemy of the coastal farmers, and the methods of the snake doctors were mysterious indeed. Mr. Johnson gives this summary of the snakes that were feared in the area:

"You had the same snake those times as you have today. You had the *terciopelo* [fer de lance]. You had the tommygoff, you had the sleeping goff, you had the coral snake. Then you had the whip snake, the banana tommy, and the green whip snake and the boa. Well, the boa is all right. The boa is a good friend of mine. He don't make much trouble. The biggest boa, we call him the 'wola,' but as he the biggest now, he eat all the bad snake. And you have the next one, named the guinea-hen snake. He don't do no harm. And then you have the two-headed snake. That was here, but I don't see them now. I never heard anybody get bit by them. But I know in Cahuita you have the sea snake. The same one is bad to bite us. It sleeps in the coral. I used to strike them with my harpoon."

Deirdre Hyde

Mr. Johnson says Old Smith, William Shepherd, and one of his uncles used to cure snakebite in Cahuita, but the most famous snake doctor in the early years was Celvinas Caldwell, of Monkey Point. Celvinas was a San Andrés man who is said to have learned his snake doctoring from an African. "Minin" Hudson, of Manzanillo, says he visited Celvinas' house and saw his great collection of bush—herbs, bark, vines—and snakes crawling all over the house and yard. Minin says Celvinas "never lost a case."

Mr. Johnson describes how Celvinas worked his cures—and Mr. Mason backs it up in every detail.

> "Celvinas was the best snake doctor 'round here. Him cure everybody here. Him always have a dirty handkerchief, and if you call him and him don't want to come, he send that handkerchief for you and say, 'Stay there till I come. Tie it where the snake bite you.' And when him come later, he only put his hand on your head and you vomit all the poison and him say, 'You make that fellow bite you, don't it?' And you say, yes. And him say, 'You want to see which one?' And he call them, and the snakes come from all about in the bush. And when they come he point and say, 'It that one did bite you.' And you kill it. Him don't kill it. Him don't kill snake. It would go against him. But he gives you authority to kill it."

Midwives and snake doctors were community resources, people who practiced their skills with a sense of responsibility to their neighbors. But within each family there were mothers or grandmothers or aunts who dressed the daily wounds of children and farmers and boat builders. These wounds could be nasty, for the daily companion of the menfolk, young and old alike, was the machete. For a machete to be useful, it must be sharp.

Mr. Selven Bryant, of Old Harbour, describes the common method of treating machete wounds:

> "First time we used to get some bad machete cuts and nobody never go to doctor. You get a young green cocoa pod, and you just peel off the skin and you take your knife and scrape it. It kind of gummy. You put it on the cut and take a piece of cloth and tie it, and anytime you take that off, the cut well. Big cut. One time machete cut these three finger, all three right to the bone. Go to no doctor. Just get the cocoa and scrape it on there, tie it up. Machete chop off this finger, too, when I was a boy, and I wave it till this end piece practically come off, and my mother take it and just clamp it on back and get cocoa and bandage it up. Go to no doctor."

The Judge

One way of ascertaining whether a community is "on the map" is to ask if it has a representative of the government, a police authority, a judge. As early as 1900 Cahuita and Old Harbour were "on the map." A government agent in Limón appointed a local resident to be the authority, should any civil disturbance or dispute arise, and to register newborn children and record deaths. In Cahuita, predictably, the first "judge" was William Smith. In Old Harbour, equally predictably, the first "judge" was Joseph Hunter.

Neither of the original judges, nor their successors, spent much time on the job, Mr. Johnson says, because "in those days everybody that live here was good. Good people. No thieving or nothing. I never remember any trouble like that."

"At that time," Mr. Mason says, recalling his adopted father's tenure as judge in Old Harbour, "you didn't need much education to be a judge. You keep up the books however you can. And all the inspector was interested in is to get the money that you may collect. Everything was ten colon and seventy-five cents for whatever crime. No one have anything different, no matter what it is they do. It was plenty money at that time. And now and again some inspector come out from Limón to check up the books and take the money if there is any."

Old Harbour

By the year 1914, Old Harbour boasted two shops, a Catholic Church, and an English School as signs of its social organization, in addition to its judge's desk. The American treasure hunter, Klines, built the first shop, Mr. Mason says, right where an old barge rests today, submerged in sea water. David Sharegold, a Jamaican, took over Klines' shop and competed for business with Francisco Ramírez, a Colombian. Both shops bought coconuts and oil from area farmers, paying the producers fifty percent in cash, fifty percent in provisions from the shop.

Selven Bryant gives this account of the establishment of the Old Harbour Catholic Church:

> "The Catholic people from Limón come in and build a
> church. But the majority of the colored people wasn't Catholic.
> So they just have the few Spanish, some Indians, and a few
> colored people. You have a bishop from Limón who used to

come here, Father Blessing they call him. Then after that you had one named Albert. All of them was German. They come from Germany to the church in Limón and from Limón they transfer all about. But what used to keep them back a lot was that they don't know English. So they had was to study English and Spanish so as to get along with the people."

The first English School teacher in Old Harbour was Teacher Duffies, a San Andrés man whose original assignment was in Monkey Point. Ezekiel Hudson brought Teacher Duffies over to give lessons to his own children at home. After a few years Teacher Duffies moved to Manzanillo, where the community offered him a house and a better income, since there were more families there to support the school. Eventually Teacher Duffies settled in Old Harbour.

Merrymaking

The early settlers of the Talamanca Coast were a lively bunch. At Christmas and Easter they gathered first in their churches for worship and then in their homes and on the beaches for merrymaking. Every family produced liquors: *guarapo*, cane liquor, and ginger beer. Women baked special cakes, and whole pigs were roasted in backyard pits. Music was supplied by "bush bands" using, for the most part, home-made instruments like the ones Mr. Mason described in Chapter 3. Every community had its own music-makers.

Miss "Sis" remembers bright full-moon nights at Grape Point when the people were itching to dance but no musicians could be found. "There was a man named Ruel, could whistle good. He start to whistle and the people dance out under the almond tree till morning with just him whistling." Miss "Sis" says the people celebrated Christmas sixteen days until New Year's, and the first eight days of the New Year they called "Old Christmas" and kept partying.

Of the Christmas celebrations at Cahuita's St. Mark's Church, Mrs. Ida Corbin says, "The church always have recitation, invite us to come and recite. We recite, we sing. The big people they sing too. Everybody sing. But the practice was to recite. 'Joy to the world, the Lord is come.' 'And Mary wrapped the Babe in swaddling clothes and laid Him in a manger.' Like that. You have to recite. If Mommie don't give me a nice dress to go, big bow in my hair, two here, and a pretty dress ... and then now she make a little cake extra."

Miss Eudora "Sis" Matthews (center), with her daughters Gudelia and Olga, at Grape Point.

Children kept themselves busy year-round with homemade games. The favorite of the boys was a merry-go-round which they constructed on the sandy beaches. The old-timers in Manzanillo still laugh over their first experience with the merry-go-round. The local inventor of the game (it appeared all along the coast in slightly different forms) was a boy named Charles Nelson, whom everybody called "Charlie Pretty."

Charlie Pretty cut a trumpet tree into a section about fifteen feet long, eight inches in diameter. He bored a hole about four inches deep through one side of it at the center. In the sand on the beach he fixed a solid vertical post, ten feet tall, its top end penetrating the hole in the trumpet tree. So the merry-go-round had the appearance of a giant letter T, with the trumpet tree balanced on the post and the post rooted in the sand. Over the two ends of the trumpet tree Charlie looped ropes, forming swings, and invited his friends to sit in them.

With one boy in each swing, he looped another rope over the trumpet tree and pulled on it, racing around in a circle under the flailing feet of his riders. The merry-go-round was a great success until one of the riders got dizzy with all the circling and fell off. The trumpet tree tilted, off balance, and the surviving rider crashed to the ground just as the lower end of the trumpet tree smashed into Charlie Pretty's jaw, knocking him to the sand. He got up, swooned in a circle as if he was still running the merry-go-round, fell again. Got up again, swooned in a circle again, fell again. He was sick for a month, says Samuel Hansell, laughing, but the merry-go-round was firmly established from that day as the favorite sport for the boys of Manzanillo.

The girls had their own game, skitlolly. To play, they would stand behind a line about fifteen paces from a set of ten wooden "pins" and roll a heavy wooden ball into the pins, knocking down as many as they could. The wooden pins were cola bottle-shaped, set into a round board about three feet in diameter. Each pin had its own value in the game, up to ten points for the "king-pin" which stood in the center. Each girl scored points for her team according to the value of the pins she knocked down with one throw.

"If you knock down the king pin, it's a rejoicement!" says Mrs. Ida Corbin, clapping her hands as she remembers the game. "And sometimes you so lucky you take one ball and you clean the board. And if there's a prize, then you get it. Oh, skitlolly!"

In later years, during the 1920s, skitlolly became a league sport for girls throughout Limón Province. Teams wore uniforms, "a lovely shorts, little short pants, nice, and the cap. We pretty, you know," Miss Ida recalls. Teams competed in Estrada, Matina, Siquirres, marching onto the ballfields, Lady Captain in the lead, followed by the Color Guard carrying banners.

"We play in Limón," says Miss Ida, "we go on the ballground and they march us from there to the park. That place where the park is now was beach at them time. We march down there and we sing the hymn and the music play, and we go back and we march. That march called the 'Grand Chain.' Oh, that was what the Spaniards like to see. Money! Some of them just take it and tie it in your hair. Oh, yes, I had a good time."

While the children amused themselves with merry-go-round and skitlolly, adult men of the coast were taking one game very seriously: cricket. From the first matches played between teams from Cahuita and the Bluff in 1909, until the beginning of World War II, cricket was the major sport of the Atlantic Zone. The Afro-Caribbean sportsmen inherited their love for the game from British colonists in the West Indies. Trading companies in Limón imported the gear (bats, wickets, balls, uniforms, and leg pads) from England, and in all the communities of Limón Province men chopped out ballgrounds and formed teams. In 1914 the farmers in Old Harbour were organizing their first team and laying out a ballground where the health dispensary has since been built. But the earliest cricket matches on the Talamanca Coast were played in old Cahuita, at a ballground just south of Duncan Creek. The competing teams were from Cahuita, David Kayasso, captain, and from the Bluff, David Skinner, captain. Mr. Johnson remembers the games:

> "I play on the Cahuita team. Mr. Kayasso give it the name 'Walpa,' some Indian name. I don't know what the meaning of it, but later on Kayasso give the same name to a racing horse he did have. They play with their own clothes. I was the only one did have a uniform. I was a boy, and my aunt buy me a uniform, buy the cloth, and they sew it. No one else. We got the gears in Limón.
>
> The captain of the team up to the Bluff here was old Skinner. It was Skinner, Theodore Buchanan, Pablo Maroto (that's Miss Katherine's brother), Mr. Cox, I don't remember the rest. But it was a stronger team than our own at Cahuita, I tell you straight.
>
> We was Kayasso, me, Sylvester Plummer's brother, a fellow from San Andrés, that is Cahuita team."

Manzanillo eventually put together a first-class cricket team to test its talent against Old Harbour, Cahuita, and the Bluff, and the competition soon expanded from the coast to include communities with teams throughout the province (see Chapter 12).

How to sum up life on the Talamanca Coast through the year 1914? "It was bush," Miss Ida says, "but it was livelier than now. Oh, yes!" Many of the daily activities of the coast people continued unchanged as the years passed. In 1977, as in 1937 and 1907, women make coconut oil, men cultivate coconuts and cocoa, children recite verses for Holy Day programs in the Protestant churches. But events which originated outside the Talamanca region after 1914 made themselves felt in the lives of the settlers, and things changed. Some of the changes were brought about by foreign companies that entered the area. Some were results of policies of the Costa Rican government. Some came hand-in-hand with a growing population. Some were a simple matter of the passing of time and ever-developing technology.

Part II of this history of the Talamanca Coast records these changes as the people of the coast experienced them, from 1915 through 1948. It begins with an accidental visit by the President of Costa Rica and ends with a revolution that instigated even more rapid change in Talamanca in the years following.

Ruben Hansel and Enrique Hudson demonstrate the cricketing they enjoyed in their youth in Manzanillo.

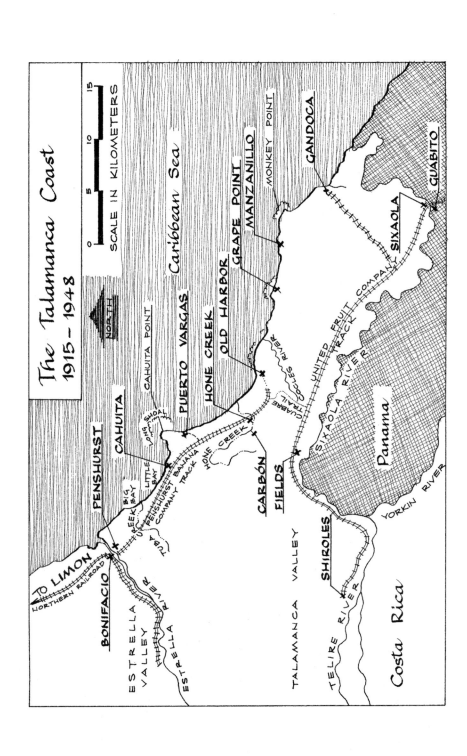

The Talamanca Coast
1915–1948

SCALE IN KILOMETERS
0    5    10    15

NORTH

Caribbean Sea

PENSHURST

CAHUITA

CAHUITA POINT

LONG SHOAL

LITTLE BAY

BIG BAY

CREEK

TUBA RIVER

PENSHURST BANANA COMPANY TRACK

PUERTO VARGAS

HONE CREEK

HONE CREEK

OLD HARBOR

GRAPE POINT

MANZANILLO

MONKEY POINT

GANDOCA

CARBÓN FIELDS

JUABRE RIVER

COCLES RIVER

UNITED FRUIT COMPANY TRACK

SIXAOLA

GUABITO

SIXAOLA RIVER

Panama

YORKIN RIVER

SHIROLES

TALAMANCA VALLEY

TELIRE RIVER

Costa Rica

BONIFACIO

TO LIMON

NORTHERN RAILROAD

ESTRELLA VALLEY

ESTRELLA RIVER

ESTRELLA RIVER

# The Second Generation
## Community Builders (1915-1948)

"You could call it no more than a hand-to-mouth living."
Mr. Fred Ferguson

"Yet the people pressed onward and they kept trying."
Mr. Leslie "Sorrows" Williams

# 8. The Founding of Cahuita

Only three people can tell the story of the founding of the present-day Cahuita as first-hand witnesses of the event: Mr. David Kayasso, a Nicaraguan immigrant who was thirty-one years old at the time; Mr. Selles Johnson, a native of the old Cahuita, twenty years old; and Mr. George Humphries, a boy of eleven then, who was brought to Big Bay as a baby from San Andrés island. The three accounts reveal a few discrepancies, but the basic facts are clear, for these are stories that have been told over and over to new generations of Cahuitans.

Mr. Kayasso writes in his *History of Cahuita Since 1880 A.D.*:

"I believe it was in the 1915 we saw a big launch passing by going south, until evening late she was going up again, but into a very hard wind. Then about eight o'clock in the night we saw lights coming through the bushy road, for there was no street then. Then we learn that the launch we saw passing was the government boat and she was blown ashore on the beach, so these are the men from aboard. And the President of the country was also aboard. They were all wet to the skin, so all who were able to help with something to change the wet clothes did so, and oh, it was a great thanks to all. Then the fire was made up right away, and coffee was made. Some house to give them to lie down and rest until morning. Drank coffee and try to make their way on the beach to Limón. Oh, it was a hard time for some. But all was safe at home that night to tell the loss of such a fine boat on her first trip. But thank God, there was no loss of life.

But after a few weeks the President return to give thanks with some of his men. As they come they ask for the place where they were the night they had such a fine time. They were carried to the house. And as the President asked, 'Who do own this place?' they told him Mr. William Smith. 'Where is he?' He ask if he was present. Answer came back, yes. He was called and ask if he will sell the place and for how much. He reply, yes, for five hundred colones. The President agree and the bargain was fix right away, cash paid, men put to work right away to square up by manzana and run the street. Each block was divided into four squares leaving a street on each side. So each person who was there got a piece of each square after it was cut in six pieces. It was not sold. It was given to them as their own with title also.

So that was the starting of Cahuita. And now the name Cahuita is known over the world. That was a good President. His name was Alfredo Flores. Now out of all who were there that morning to see the start, is only two alive, that is Selles Johnson and the writer, David Kayasso, seeing and enjoying the improving of Cahuita."

Mr. Johnson tells the story from the point of view of his grandfather, who lost a pasture while everyone else gained a town, and from his own point of view as a sea captain who got caught in the same storm that sent the President's boat to ruin:

"In those times some Jamaicans and Colombians all from San Andrés and Panama, they start to come and live here, begin to make ranches and things, and my grandfather get against them and went to Limón to get them off this place because this place was his own. He cut it down, plant coconut and fruit trees and have cows. And they start to fight him with law. Squatters, you see.

And in 1915, a President get cast away in a boat going to Limón. I was on the sea same time, in that same storm, but I smarter than them. I run away from it. I take shelter up by Cahuita —the old Cahuita—in the bay there, and I riding that storm the whole night with the anchor down and the motor running. Every time the sea hit us we put on the motor, kick her ahead, give her ease and she ride over, she ride over till daylight. Daylight I move her from there.

But the President boat, she name the *Cristina*, she get cast away, and the President come in at Tuba Creek and walk the beach. And when he came here the people them attack him and show him the necessary, that they lives down there and they can't make no farm where they can cultivate because the front of the land is with coconuts and the back of the land is swamp. And they want to make farm.

Well, he called my grandfather and asked him how much he would sell the place for, this place they call the Bluff, because it was my grandfather's pasture. And he was like a damn fool. He go and say five hundred colon. Just because he believe the President wanted to force him. Well, the President said, 'Well, I'll give you five hundred.' And the old man said, 'No, that's not what it worth. For twenty-five years I using this place.' And the President said, 'Well, my word carry. I can't change it. I give you the five hundred colones and you let the people live there.'

And a few months after he sent an engineer and cut it up, block it out, you see. And he made them understand that anyone that find a fruit tree on their lot, they must pay the old man for it. Say there is a mango or a coconut tree, any tree, orange, pear, they have to pay the old man for it. Five colones for a coconut tree.

The lots was thirty-two meters by fifty meters. Six of them to the *cuadrante*. Plummer take a lot. Skinner, he take one. Theodore Buchanan, Willie Dixon. They come in and take lots. And they call that main street 'Avenida Alfredo González Flores' after that President. They put up a sign, board sign, with the name on a gate just by where you see the bank is now, and for years it always there till sometime round the Forties. 'Avenida Alfredo González Flores,' it said.

They send a special train from Limón when he cast away here. Send messenger and call a special train to Penshurst. He rode Mr. Masters' horse through farm down to Penshurst and take the train back to Limón. They didn't send no boat because he was afraid of the boat. He wouldn't go back into a boat again. He sleep that night in Mr. Isaac's house, that a Chinaman had a house right by where you see Mr. Lam. That's where he sleep."

George Humphries, as a boy of eleven, was more interested in the shipwreck than in either presidents or land ownership. This is what he remembers of the event:

"It was a big motorboat, have in two motors, named the *Cristina*. That time the United Fruit Company just start working up banana plantations in Sixaola, but the rail never put through neither. So the President went up the Sixaola River to rectify something with the Company, went up in the bar there. Well, they turn back in the evening and when they get up by North River bar there, they catch a very terrible weather. Hard weather. Breeze. The sea get rough. From that day I never see sea get rough like that in Cahuita. That was a terrible storm. So the engineer get sea sick, couldn't tend to the engine, and the engine got shut down. And the breeze blow them on the beach, but they was lucky now. None of them die. Some of them come without clothes. There was a man living up the beach name Edward Masters. He give them some clothes. And I think they had to walk it to Penshurst. Train running that time, and they get to Limón.

Well, up to now that boat is down in the sand up Tuba Creek. Boat way up on the beach. That was a good boat, come from the United States. Have in good convenience. Up to now I think in Wagner yard have that bath tub what they have in the boat to bathe with. Right now I believe that tub in Wagner yard, a hell of a big thick tub. Boat was a metal boat. They tried was to work on her, see if they could get her off, but the weather come down, the sea full her up, and they didn't see her no more. It went right down in the sand. They get out the two eighty-horse-power gasoline motor. They get them up. But they lose that boat. It can't rotten neither, because it's metal."

So it was a trick of the sea that led to the establishment of the town Cahuita at the point called the Bluff. Previous to President Flores' accidental visit, the name "Cahuita" had applied specifically to the long point north of the Bluff, to the settlement spread out between Duncan Creek and Louis Hudson Creek, and to the region as a whole, from Cahuita Point north as far as Tuba Creek. During the ten years following President Flores' visit and the surveying of streets and lots at the Bluff, Old Smith and his wife died at old Cahuita, and one by one the other families there moved onto lots at the Bluff, building for the first time board houses roofed with zinc. They attached the old name "Cahuita" to their new town, and so it has always been known officially, but folks who live along Big Bay and Little Bay still say they're walking up to the Bluff, meaning the town Cahuita.

Richard Kelly built the first house in the new town of Cahuita, just to the north of Kelly Creek. Behind Mr. Kelly, Sylvester Plummer's father built the second house, which still stands today. Sarah Dixon put up the next two houses, one next to Mrs. Lam's current lot, one next to Mr. Henry's present house. David Skinner was the fifth house owner in the new town.

The carpenter who constructed all these early houses was Mr. Cox. Pine boards from the United States and corrugated zinc roofing were imported from Bocas, brought to Cahuita on Old Smith's sailing boat and the Vanguardia. The pine was cheap material; it wasn't until World War II interrupted trade that the people of Cahuita started using Costa Rica's own lumber resources, primarily laurel, for construction.

By the early 1920s, St. Mark's and the Baptist churches had abandoned their sites at old Cahuita, constructing new and larger buildings at the Bluff, and the Seventh Day Adventists established a new congregation there also. Two Chinese, two Lebanese, and a Spanish man were operating businesses in the new town. A farmers' cooperative maintained two grocery stores and a cooperative cocoa farm. Miss Priscilla Wier taught six grades of English School, and the Universal Negro Improvement Association claimed active membership of almost every Afro-Caribbean family in the area, putting on concerts at which a pedal organ was played and Shakespeare recited. Cricket matches drew crowds of spectators to the new ballground at Little Bay every Sunday. Cahuita was booming.

Where did all these people come from? How did they get here? And why did they stay?

# 9. Getting Here

If you ask someone of the coast, "Why did you make your home here?" they're likely to give you a patient smile and say, "But that's a long story, man." Here are some of those stories, beginning with the people who arrived in the earliest days, continuing more or less chronologically according to when the storyteller came to rest in the Talamanca Coastal settlement he now calls his home. The stories span the first five decades of the Twentieth Century and involve travel through the lands and waters of half the Western Hemisphere. They are all offered in response to the question, "How did you (or your parents) come here, and what was the place like when you arrived?"

Mr. George Humphries was born on the Colombian island, San Andrés, in 1903, and came with his parents to Big Bay in 1905. He remembers:

> "My father did own a boat named the *Valkyrie*, a sailing boat. He was a captain, had his own boat. He was sailing around to Nicaragua, Belice, all around. He travel from San Andrés with his boat. He had a good-size shrimp boat. In those days he was running cargo from all different countries.
>
> Once he was making a trip to Limón carrying some cargo and he lost the boat up this place called North River bar. The boat get ashoal there and they lose it. Some people was living at North River bar in those days named Bonifacio, carrying on some business, have a little store. Them sell dry goods.
>
> We come on that boat. My mother and four of us children came from Colombia on that same boat. We land right here on this beach; the sea was calm. And we stop by a family that live up the beach inside the bush there, was family to we. I was to call that man uncle, name of Ben Humphries. They were living in a little ranch there. We stop there for a few days, and afterward my father build a little ranch just where Frankie house is there now. They thatch all the house in those days with palm leaf, and make the ranch with rawa from the bush.
>
> My father start to make farm. He was a hard working guy. Sometimes my mother fret, say he stay on the farm so late she don't know if snake bite him or what. Plant foodstuffs first and then the cocoa afterward. Plantain, coconut, yam, cassava, all those things they plant. Then they plant the cocoa after. So they have lots of food those days. Wasn't much cocoa in Cahuita in those days. Not even so much banana.

Sometimes people plant a little tomato. Tomato grow wild in those time. Chop a piece of maiden land there, and you don't know where the tomatoes come from. They bear all about, and I don't see them no more again. Not big tomatoes, more smaller but they eat good. Chocatow grow there wild too. When you cut maiden land that's the first thing you see coming up. It have a broad leaf. Eat very nice with codfish, too. And it good for your stomach. But for years I don't see that again."

Mr. Augustus Mason has already given a thorough description of the way of life he experienced in Old Harbour as a boy. Here he tells how he happened to be growing up there:

"I was born in Jamaica in 1904, but when I was six years of age my father die, and my mother gave me to the godparents. My godparents was half Jew and African descendants. My godfather was Alexander Cavalow, and he marry to Judith Shirley, and they was in business in store, and they got bankrupt and they run away from Jamaica, leaving everything, and come to this country. They brought me as their child.

We left Jamaica 1910, and land in Limón December 11, and then we land down here in Old Harbour December 23, 1911, on this beach in a boat name of *Santa Rosa* that was brought from the States. We land in that hole in front of the Chinaman shop. That channel name Joseph Channel because my stepfather, Joseph Hunter, always keep a sailing boat in there. He was a Jamaican from Spanish Town, and he leave there, run away from his parents 'cause he was very young, run all about Nicaragua as cook and sailor until he came here and marry to Horatio MacNish daughter."

Born in 1880, in St. James Parish, Jamaica, Mr. Cyril Gray tells this tale of coming to Costa Rica and making his farm in Hone Creek:

"We had a small banana farm in St. James Parish. My father died when I was just thirteen years old. I always assist the old lady with the farm, but I didn't like it. You know, farming is a hard thing when you young. Not everybody like it. Not like now. I becomes a lover of farm. I've tried many other business and I'm not successful. The only thing I'm successful is to till the soil.

I was a shoemaker from when I was about fourteen years old. I leave home when I was twenty-one years old. Just feel like leaving. I wanted to travel. I came from Panama to Guabito and from there over here. I could make my living as a shoemaker. I came here 1914, same year that war break out. I came here and I work for two colon and fifty cents a day when I start to make farm. I started my farm in Hone Creek. I came here with a little money from there, but that could not keep me. I had to do something. Cost of living was very small, not like now.

I made that farm. It was woodland. I bought a little piece but the river take it away, Hone Creek river. I still have a few trees, but river cut it off. There's somebody occupy it over the other side now, and it's bearing cocoa, fruit trees bearing. You see, the river cut from my side and throw it over on the other side.

I planted that farm with banana, plantain and cocoa, provisions too. When I came in those days you know how much was the price for cocoa? Five cents for a pound. But I just had a determination to plant, that one day it would worth something. When the cocoa start to bear I got ten cents a pound. I planted tomatoes, cabbage, turnip, potato. I planted tomatoes that weigh one pound—one tomato, one pound. The soil good for the vegetables. Cabbage with big heads and they're hard. Now I plant nothing at all. Can't get labor and I can't do the work anymore. I like to plant grains, you know. Beans, they bear good, and corn. I don't like rice. Rice scratch too much when you picking it."

Mr. David Buchanan, born in the house in Cahuita where he lives with his family today, tells how his father came to be one of the first residents of the new town Cahuita:

"My father was a Jamaican, Robert Samuel Buchanan Sterling. He went to Panama in the days of the contract to build the Panama Canal, but he could not get work, and he could not stay in the country because the police don't allow you to light on the street in the daytime. So he had to leave that country and come to Costa Rica. He went to Siquirres and was working up there on the railroad. At that time he said they were building the La Junta bridge. He worked there for quite a while and afterward he came to Estrella when they were putting the railway in to Estrella Valley.

He was among some of the first settlers of this side. Up here was still in woodland, while the people lived up at Cahuita Point, and then gradually the people started moving in.

You could only walk the beach in those days because there were no roads, only woodland. Can you imagine when they had a heavy weather, the rivers was high. People had to wait two or three days until it goes down so they can pass.

My father built this house right here out of board, but it was not completed, only two rooms, half finished. In those days it was hard to get materials down here because the only way you have transportation was with boat from Limón, and that boat would come once a week. And if you have no money to pay, you just can't buy anything."

The McLeods of Cahuita descend from Thomas McLeod, a Jamaican who had ten children. Wilfred "Frankie" McLeod, one of the ten, says his father came from Jamaica to work on a contract with Minor Keith, the railroad builder who founded the United Fruit Company in Costa Rica.

"My father told me say, that he was contracted with Minor Keith, a company that came out to plant cocoa in this division. But after they came down and start to work there was some disappointment came in and the boss didn't return. So the laborers, the land that they cleaned, they divided it up between the whole of them that was working. So my father remain with a part over by Tuba Creek.

We were living at Big Bay that time. I remember hardly any fruit was in Cahuita. Only six or seven orange trees bearing that I did know of. One pejiballe tree was there by Humphries' yard. This water apple, there was only three trees of it that I did know of. We had one lemon tree right where Sorrows is, another was in Mr. Mike's yard. That breed of lemon die out. Afterward they start to bring sweet lime. But we lose the lemon complete out of Cahuita. The lemon is a fruit more like the sweet lime but it has a pointed bottom most like a lime. Yellow when it's properly ripe. That lemon is die out from Cahuita. About ten star apple tree we had here. And there is another fruit that a Spanish woman in front of Tabash shop there had, called fig. I think it was the real fig they take and make prunes. But it die out.

We used to do a lot of little tricks as boys all over. Maybe we go by a yard where have fruit trees and steal off the fruit. But we do it by tricks. We go now, maybe six or eight of us together. Maybe one or two go in the yard to ask for water to keep the owner of the yard occupied. While one of us is on the tree picking the fruit and throw it over to the other boys a distance away, and we scamper off with those fruits and divide it. Because fruits was scarce."

Mr. Joseph Spencer, known locally by his "hill name" or nickname, "Boyse," came to Cahuita from Siquirres with his mother in 1919. Mary

Spencer, Boyse's mother, sought a home on the coast because of the healthy climate, but she couldn't persuade her husband to stay because he found the transportation frustratingly difficult. Mr. Spencer gives this account of his family history:

"My mother told me that I were born twelve o'clock Sunday morning, first day of March, 1908. We lived in Siquirres then. My father was working for the United Fruit Company, and my mother used to bake. She did a lot of things. She was a midwife also, what you call a nurse. That's her living in those times. She train for that in Jamaica. My father was a straw boss, that mean a man see the next person work. We call them straw boss, foreman. It was in the banana plantations.

My father leave Jamaica just like so many others, just people traveling. In those times you just up and down and nobody ask you any questions. You get permission to leave and to land, and that's all you need, not even passport they didn't use in that time.

My father came to Cahuita from when I was a boy, but he didn't like this place. Why he didn't like it, they didn't have no transportation. They used to use sailing boat, come up and down this place, boat with sail. Sometimes the boat leave here a day, sometime stay a week in the ocean, can't get to Limón when you have north weather. That's a breeze coming in from the north. And they can't go to the north because the breeze coming from that way, so they got to do a thing, a system that they call tack. They go this way, triangle this way, you know, zig-zag. And sometime the breeze is so strong they can't make no point, and they just up and down, for days. You see them out in the ocean there, don't know where they're going. That's why my father didn't like the place.

Well, my mother was sick up in Siquirres. She couldn't keep no health, and she liked to get a fresh air from the sea, the ocean, and then she come this way and like it out here, and we all come with her. That was 1919. Her sister was living here at that time. They were in Siquirres and then they come this side because they had some lands here they like to work up, work farming and so forth. Then they started planting cocoa beans and yam and yuca, pejiballe and all those things, and they take them to Limón to sell.

They didn't have to buy the land in those times. The government say that the people was to come and cultivate the place, and so everybody come and they take a piece of land and cultivate it, and after they was cultivating it for ten years time, then they could call for title. You have to go to a lawyer, a notary lawyer, and then that's where the problem come in. Because most of these lawyers they have 'tomorrow,' everything they say is 'tomorrow,' and then for days or months the people can't get the title. So most people never get title to their land.

So I start help to make farm that way from when I was small, and I still making farm to this day."

Mr. Joseph Livingston Cunningham arrived in Cahuita in 1937, where he married a native of old Cahuita, Pearl Dixon. Mr. Cunningham's story of getting here involves economics and politics of three different countries: Jamaica, Cuba, and Costa Rica. This is how he tells it:

"I was born in 1893, the 26 of September, in Jamaica, the parish of St. Elizabeth. I worked in the fields, 'cause the parents was very poor. I had but little education. I had was to go out in the field and work from I was twelve years old just to support the balance of the children in the home. I do all kind of work outside just merely to get a day's pay, you see. There was so many of us. It was fifteen of us in the home, and don't have anything to support us. So you find life was hard with me.

Well, a friend of mine went away to Cuba and he promised me that he would send for me to work in the sugar cane fields over there. And 1914 I left Jamaica in the month of March and reached Cuba and worked in the sugar cane field. The trip take us twenty-four hours at that time. That was a sailing boat, twenty-four hours from Kingston to Santiago de Cuba. But when the world war started I wanted to go back to Jamaica. I went back to take care of a sick brother that I have. He was mad. They had was to carry him in straight jacket and hold him this way. And then they carry him to the doctor. He don't dead. He was still alive. He's still alive today too. I have three brothers still alive in Jamaica right now.

Then, in going back to Cuba, there wasn't no steamship service. All the steamship gone to the war. They got only sailing boat. Those sailing boats was from Grand Cayman. Then them give wrong advertisement telling the condition of the boat, say that the boat work with gas and sail. Never had one inch of gas. Only bare sail.

My dear sister, we meet a rough sea there with that sailing boat. The sea come up and wash off everything off the deck. Seven women was on board and they started to sing, they started to pray. The sailors said to them, 'Women, it is too late now. You should pray before you come on the boat.' Think of that. And they still continue to cry and pray. But I keep everything silent here in my heart. I asking God to deliver us. And the sailor them started to curse now. Say that when you curse it's better than pray. And they started to curse. Oh, I never forgot that as long as I live. The captain said to them, 'Take down the life belt and give it to each passenger and show them how they is to pin on the life belt until further orders.' Well, that is what they do. But God in His tender mercy—well, after five hours of that, the sea go down. And we take four days to Santiago de Cuba.

Then in Cuba it was rather rough there to work, but you get good money when you work. The more you can work is the more money you can get. And I work. About sixty-five thousand Jamaicans was working in Cuba then. So I never regret going to Cuba.

But in 1917 they had a revolution over there. The Cuban government soldiers killed eleven Jamaicans in Cuba. Let me give you a story which is very difficult for you to believe.

You see, the rebels took charge of Havana. They monopolize the country and commanded all the citizens that was by the cane factories to smash up the place, all the commissary and all places. They commanded all the Jamaican young men that was there to go with them to destroy the place. And they smash up the cane factory.

Well now, the government come in back with a strong force, and the rebels cut short. And when the government soldiers go and see how the place was there, the people told them that the Jamaicans helped smash up the place. The government officer did name Carena. He was a German man, but he was naturalized as a Cuban, you see. He was one of the officer that carried the government soldiers that day. At that time the war was hot, you know, the 1914 war. Carena say him gonna kill every one of the Jamaican he see because he hate the whole of them. Germany fighting now against England so him taking revenge there against the Jamaicans because Jamaica belonging to England.

You know what that German did? He put eleven Jamaican in the field there for three days and make them work, cut cane and feed the horses, without them eat a morsel. And when them hungry he put them into a ring like that and put the machine gun into the middle and mow them down. That's what that German commander did. It was eleven of them killed right there. The balance never report at that time.

Well now, there was a woman was living at a place called Cuatro Caminos. They took her husband out of the house in the night and carry him down to the cane field there and kill him in the cane field, and come back now to go and advantage the woman. But the woman smarter than them. As them gone with the man she did go and take refuge in the cane fields. And when they went back they don't see the woman.

Well, after the revolution the woman was still there. She said the English government must know about this because you know what they do? There wasn't no communication in the country. They disconnect everything. They burn down the bridges, no train. And that woman walk to Havana, the capital of Cuba. It was four hundred and seventy-five miles. She said she wanted the English government to know what was going on. If she had told Santiago it would be more nearer, but she said she wanted the English Ambassador. The guy was only a consul in Santiago, and she make up her mind to bear the opposition by the way, you see, and she walked it, take her twenty-one days.

And she reached there, she met the Ambassador and let him know what was going on. Then the Ambassador sent out a cablegram to England same time and tell what was going on in Cuba. And in quick time the report come back to the Ambassador, say he must find out if they kill any more of the Jamaican them. And if they continue killing, the British would declare war on Cuba. And you know, they didn't kill no more. England say that the Cuban government will have to pay for every head. And the money was paid in 1921.

And all that time, I was there. I sit down nine months and never work as much as a five cent. But I live on what I did have in my pockets. I sit down and wait till they say Monday work is going to start. When Monday come, they say fifteen days, and that was the way I going until I spend nine month there. No work started.

Well now, the government of Cuba called our government in Jamaica to take out the people from there because no work for them. Jamaica government said, if you don't have no work there for them, you have to send them yourself because we send them there to help the situation in Cuba, so you must send them back. And I take the first trip out. The boat carry eight hundred passengers, five hundred Jamaicans and three hundred Haitians. They take the Jamaicans first and then go back to Haiti. And we land safely in Jamaica.

So then that was the ending of that revolution in Cuba. Smash up the country too, I tell you. That why I had to leave it. But if not, I wasn't going to leave Cuba at all because you could get plenty money there for work.

I stayed in Jamaica until 1926. In November my brother sent for me to come to Costa Rica. He did have a farm in Parismina. He say he have fifty hectares of banana, and I must come and help him along with it. And I did came, and when I went there I saw banana bear in such a way that a man could hardly lift up a bunch of bananas. Yes, I can tell you. When I take the banana up I have to do so to see if I can lift it up to my shoulder. The plantation was very beautiful.

And five months after that the [United Fruit] Company stopped buying bananas. There was some trouble between them and the government here. And furthermore, the Company say it doesn't pay because the banana takes disease. So the Company stop buy and the bananas stay there and perish.

Well, I do a little fool work outside. I go up to Turrialba to work on the railroad, on the bridge they got up there. Wages was very small, five colones and twenty-five cents a day. And then I came to Cahuita, 1937.

I came here a stranger. Only one man I did know. After I came here I work with a man in the cocoa industry. I work with him until I could able to make a farm of my own. Work very hard. I buy a little farm and then I work it till I get some more land, until now. You see, I get old, I can't manage it now."

The oldest person alive today on the Talamanca Coast is Mr. Thomas Bethel, of Manzanillo. At the age of one hundred and eight, by his own reckoning, Mr. Bethel chides his seventy- and eighty-year-old neighbors as "boys," and says, "What do they know about history?" Having traveled the Caribbean and the Pacific by sailing ship and North America by train, Mr. Bethel sings songs of the sailor and the working man in a strong raspy voice, and on special occasions he throws away his walking stick and breaks into a tap dance on the porch of Maxi's Manzanillo shop. Mr. Bethel's life story deserves a book of its own, but these are the highlights of his travels, which ended in 1942. At the age of seventy-three he decided to settle down in Manzanillo.

Thomas Bethel was born in the state of Florida in 1869. His mother took him to Nassau, Bahamas, as a child of two. When he passed his fourteenth birthday, he'd had enough of comfortable home life, and so began his wandering by hopping a sailing ship bound for Alabama. He hired on as a cook in Mobile's Bottle House Hotel, but it wasn't long before he was back on the sea as cabin boy and apprentice sailor. During the 1898 war between the United States and Spain, Bethel manned the sails of the schooner *Herald*.

When the call went out for laborers to build the Panama Canal, Bethel sailed south, arriving in Colón in 1905. His first assignment was to a railroad construction gang, heavy work which he soon gave up in favor of cooking. The Canal laborers ate well, Bethel says, but they

Bob Bernthal

Mr. Thomas Bethel, at age 108.

suffered terribly from malaria and work accidents. Train wrecks and machinery mishaps took the lives of Spanish, American, and West Indian workers alike, but Bethel developed a lasting respect for the "tough contract laborers" from Jamaica and Barbados who resisted malaria fever and bore the stress of the relentless physical labor. When Bethel signed on for construction work at one of the Canal locks, he says he watched two thousand laborers meet violent deaths, falling off scaffolds and being crushed by uncontrolled machinery and collapsing tunnels. It sickened him so much that he left the Canal Zone to seek his fortune on the Pacific coast.

He found only a little less violence in the French and American gold mines of southwestern Panama. Contract laborers from the Caribbean islands and as far away as Africa were put to work digging and dredging pits four hundred to five hundred feet into the earth, pulling up bucket loads of soil to be strained for gold. Cave-ins that crushed hundreds of laborers at a time were not uncommon, Bethel says, but the practice that most infuriated him was the pocket-searching at the end of each work shift. In 1908 he joined the crew of the U.S. steamer *Alianza*, headed to California.

Bethel crossed the North American continent by train, reaching the Atlantic just in time to catch a steamer to Bocas del Toro. From there he joined a United Fruit Company work crew building the bridge over the Sixaola River at the Panama-Costa Rica border. He remembers seeing two laborers fall to their deaths. The old man talks of the death toll of all these construction projects not as a sentimentalist but as a realist: to build a canal, to mine gold, to construct train tracks and bridges costs not just in dollars, but in human lives, he says, a terrible but inevitable cost.

Bethel occupied himself in Bocas until 1921 when he got on a boat that landed in Manzanillo. But he wasn't ready to settle down yet. For the next twenty-one years he worked for the United Fruit Company on the main train line in Siquirres and in the Estrella Valley. In 1942 he made a trip to Manzanillo, and this time he stayed there and began planting pineapples and subsistence crops, which he does to this day.

Mr. Bethel gives this response to people who ask him for advice on how to prolong their lives past a hundred years:

> "God didn't make man to die. He make man to live forever, if he wants to live. I can't tell you what to do to live. You must know. For myself, I eat any kind of meat, well, I don't eat snake. Still, if it come to a crisis that I have to eat snake, I eat it. But I never eat it yet. People fry too much. How I like meat is to boil

it in a good soup. Meat soup, turtle soup, fish soup, and fish with the eggs, that I like. Smoking pipe goes against me now. I always smoke cigar, smoke cigarette, pipe, all the time. I feel sometimes now that I want a pipe, but every time I smoke it I feel sick. So it's just chewing tobacco I take now. It comes from the United States.

I was a drunkard too. I don't drink rum now from I had ninety-one years. I was drinking rum for about eighty years. Now it's only Good Friday I take a few drinks, and whenever I go to dead house for Nine Night or Set Up, I'll take a few drinks. But I don't particular for it again. I love dance, stage dance, and I love the singing. If I could win some money, I'd marry to an old lady, and we could talk, talk in the night about all history, George Washington and the independence of the United States. If I had money my life could be plenty better. Have a woman to cook for me, clean me up every day. But for that you want money. Anyhow, I'm contented."

John Burke, deacon of the Cahuita Baptist Church, made his home in Cahuita in 1949 after years of traveling and working in Jamaica, Cuba, Nicaragua, and Panama. This is his story:

"My grandmother was born just a couple months after slavery was abolished in Jamaica. My daddy was a Methodist preacher, Robert Burke. He had twelve of us children, six boys and six girls. I was born in St. Andrew's Parish the ninth of July, 1901. I went to school in Jamaica. And after I left school, I think it was in 1919, I went to Cuba by boat. It's about ninety miles across from Jamaica to Cuba. I was nineteen years old. I went because the rest of the boys were going, friends of mine. We wanted to know something about the outside.

Those days was a big day in Cuba. You get plenty of money. All kind of work. You have men work in the railroads, you work in the farms cutting cane, you work in the factories and all different places. I worked chiefly in the sugar factory and in the railroad department. Well, I had me ten years in Cuba, popular days they were. The companies always prepared good places for us, houses properly laid out.

Well, I left Cuba because they were expecting a big revolution in 1928. I went to Puerto Cabezas in Nicaragua, and I worked as a pruning foreman on a banana plantation for the United Fruit Company. Then I decide to leave Puerto Cabezas, and I took the launch from there, the launch named *Lindo Es*. And we sailed on to Limón. We left about four o'clock in the evening, and about two o'clock we had a storm. And it was such that I laid down on the deck and just make up my mind to die. But it happened one of the sailors walk around and say, 'You better hold on properly there or else you get overboard.' So I hold on to one of the ropes and I say now if anything happen the boat got to go down with me. And we did get over to Puerto Limón.

In those days Limón were very ugly. You know, I'll never forget. When I get to Limón I get off the boat, I went to a hotel that looks like a hotel that I were accustomed to in Cuba. And when I went in to ask for a room to stay in, I saw a white-head woman came down. She looked at me and she said, 'No, we don't admit Negroes here.' I looked in the canteen and I saw two young men, colored men they were, working. And I said to them, 'If I were like you boys, I wouldn't work here.' And they gave me a three-quarters smile, that was all. And I left. I went to another hotel and I stayed there. It was the Park Hotel that refuse me. That was in 1929. I'll never forget that statement. The Park Hotel. It looks like the kind of hotel that were accustomed in Cuba. But the rest of hotel, they were ornery places. Limón was nowhere to compare to some of the cities in Cuba. But it isn't so now. I had a meeting at the Park Hotel Friday night. The pastors of the different churches, all colored men. I don't think there's any place in Costa Rica or in Limón where a colored individual couldn't go today.

Well, I took another launch from Limón they call the *Ana Chicuna* right on to Colón and from there to Puerto Valdía, near to Colombia. I worked there with an overseer, a German, as stockman to look after the horses and mules. I had a very good time there. One night we had a party with all the overseers. And they were drinking beer all night, and Mr. Blash and I got two bottles, a glass, and I show him how we drink beer: every minute we take a sip and we talk. And he said, 'Now I'm going to show you how Germans drink beer.' And he put it up and tu-tu the whole glass, and it finish.

In those days I was not known as Burke. While I was traveling around I was known as John Jellicoe because I like that name.

I didn't like Puerto Valdía so I return back to Costa Rica in about 1930. I went down to Siquirres and I walk around till I get a good job at Indiana Branch as foreman. I left there and came down this line to Bananito. I went on the lines. At that time abacá [Manila hemp] was taking up the [United Fruit] Company. I worked with the abacá for quite a few years as a foreman. And when I got paid off, that was in 1946, I went to Germania on the Old Lines and I went doing farming. I had a friend down here in Cahuita and they said if I could get down to Cahuita they'd give me a property to manage, a cocoa farm. So we came to Cahuita

1949. That last house in front of the police office is where we stayed until I start to make my own farm.

I was a farmer from boyhood. I had no profession decide for me, so where farm is concerned I got a full experience about it. And I like it. You become more independent. I go out and do my own work. Nobody come tell me, boy, you got to do so-and-so. I just don't like that. That's why I love farming. I see for myself that you become more independent that way."

Mr. Martin Luther was a well-known, active man in Cahuita until his sudden death in March 1977. Although he was born in Matina, Costa Rica, he spent his childhood in Jamaica and Cuba, and came back to his native land as a stowaway. Before settling in Cahuita in the late 1940s, Mr. Luther took his last journey outside the country to work in the Panama Canal Zone during the Second World War. His story is that of a restless young man, fighting to make a living in a unknown and some-times unjust world:

"My mother told me that I was born in Matina in 1914, October the nineteen. And she took me to Jamaica when I was around five years old. She went there because she were belonging to Jamaica. Maybe she were tired of staying here, and she take us to school and so on, there. She wanted us to learn English. She were interested in English more than Spanish.

In those days, my grandmother was alive, and she didn't like me much because I was accustomed to eating bread here, and they have a custom of eating breadfruit in the morning for breakfast. The breadfruit was much more cheaper than the bread in Jamaica. She didn't like me so much for that, because I always want bread.

My mother left me there with my grandmother, and she went to Cuba, and I stayed in Jamaica and went to school until I was in the third grade, and she came back over from Cuba and she come for take me to Cuba. She was there working. She used to wash and iron for the Spanish people. So she took me there and I went to school at the beginning. But I couldn't get along with the Spanish children so much. They speak only Spanish, they have colored Spanish and the white ones. But in those days when them know you can speak English and they know you are from Jamaica, they call you *Jamaiquinos*, just nickname, and we used to fight a lot. So I never go back to the Spanish school. My mother sent me to English school. They had a colored woman from Jamaica teach English, and I carry on until I complete fourth grade, and I never had the opportunity to go to no more school.

I start to help my mother, assisting my mother by selling the newspaper, and I used to make good money. Get up very early in the morning, I take a big lot of newspaper, go sell it in the street, come back and begin to sell some more. I went to Cuba in 1926 and I was there until 1932 when the country started to get very bad. The crop was much shorter. They used to make sugar about nine months of the year. Then they bring it down to three months of the year, and many Jamaicans, the government used to pay their fare back to their country. There were not enough work in Cuba in the years 1931 to 1932, and many went home without even five cents in their pocket.

Well, in that lot I went. I didn't have no Jamaican documents but in that lot I went. I get an opportunity to go, and I left my mother there and went back to Jamaica, and it was very hard for me to get a job, for I didn't grow there. I didn't have things so very good, and I was there until 1937. I got to know it. I got to know the place very well, even the capital of Kingston. And I like it, but it was very hard to get a pick of a job.

I was about twenty years old then, and one day I come down to the dock in Kingston. I see a ship loading, and I wanted was to get in the dock yard, and I couldn't get in because there was a watchman at the gate. So I went outside and pick up a stone and get a piece of paper and wrap the stone in the paper and hold it in my hand. I had my shirt out as if I had been working inside and I come out to buy something, some lunch to take in. So I got a chance to pass the watchman. And when I get there I take a chance and I went and I took away a grip [suitcase] from a passenger that was going in the ship, assist him to take it up, and then I hide myself away in the hatch.

It was a Dutch boat. It was I and the next guy, but he was born in Cuba. And I went down and hide behind there in the hatch. I was there that whole night, and the next morning the ship sailed. But I didn't know the ship was going to Colombia. Before we reached the port, they caught us on the ship and they feed us, and we reach there and we try to get away. We went on the dock, they catch us again and put us back on the ship. Then they send and call the Immigration Officer, and they land us there to transport us to the Canal Zone. That's the first time I would be to jail. Slept in the jail, but I wasn't locked up in the cell. Sometime they take me for a walk out to the market. I get an opportunity of knowing the market, but I didn't like there because they have many flies on the thing you buy to eat, and I scorn it.

And they transport us to the Canal Zone, took our picture and name and everything, and they put us on the next ship, sent us back to Jamaica. But when we reach Port Royal, before docking at Kingston, they sent and call us midship, question us why we stow away. Because we wasn't born in Jamaica, we say, and things very hard, we couldn't get a job, so we stow to go back to the country where we were born. They told us to go back on the ship and stay and they'd call us again. So the ship travel to Kingston, and a watchman came on the boat, a Jamaican watchman, and he asked, 'Boys, what are you doing on this ship?' We said, 'Nothing, sir. We just came on here to get something to eat.' So he told us go down now, and we embrace that opportunity to come off.

And while we was on the street the following day, we met some of the sailors and they says, 'You boys, if we catch you again you're going to be locked up in the jail forever, for the Captain was looking for you both to give you a job.' We didn't expect it was something so good, because the law there is any stowaways to get thirty days in jail. So we were running away from thirty days. We never expected to really get a job if we had stayed on.

But anyhow, we said that since we have lost that opportunity we are going to try a next boat, and we wait till eight days after we take a next ship, this one named *Simón Bolívar*, and it was much easier to get on board. That was a big tourist ship, and she sail out, and she came by to Costa Rica. But they catch me and say, 'Who and who on board?' I say I alone. I was on a shelf, and there was a floor mat they wanted. So the man come pulling it out, and I try to ease out, and I couldn't get out fast enough. A couple minutes later they catch my partner. Now they put me to wash pots, and they put him to paint. They treat us very good. Dutch boat. Eat a lot of cheese, nice cheese sandwich.

And after the boat arrive to Limón. And at the dock the man came and ask us if we have any papers, and I show him my birth certificate, that I was born here. So him give me some money, was very little, and I come off the dock. But it was very strange. I really didn't remember much because when I left here I was small. I only know what my mother told me, and so I came to Limón Town.

At that time they used to buy a lot of banana in the Pacific. The train used to take banana from the Pacific to Limón, and we get into one of those empty cars and we stay there one day. And in the night we go to a bar with some Spanish boys because we both of us know Spanish, and they treat us very good. We drink beer all night. We told them we were going to Puntarenas, and they told us the way that we could go and catch a ride on a train. But at that time I couldn't hop a train, and we have to hop it passing by, so we started to walk, and I walked all the way to Puntarenas.

I stay in Puntarenas looking a job. But at that time there was a President name León Cortés, that was in 1937, and he show a law that the colored people should not go on the Pacific side of the country. And we met with the boss there, was American man, and he was glad to see us. He told us that he was some boss in a machine shop in Limón some years ago, and asking us for several person if they was still alive, and we tell him yes, we know them. But was just a lie because I didn't grow here, you know. But he gave me fifty colones, telling us to go back. He try to help us but he not able to employ us because it's against the law. And I took the money and we went behind the curtain of a car that carried us to Siquirres.

But I wanted to know this famous Matina where I was born. So I walk to Matina. I inquire about a woman they always told me about, and she was my mother's good friend. And I have a talk with her and told her who I was and so on. A couple people remember me. And I stay there with them until I start to learn to work as railroad foreman. I used to do some pretty cheap work. Then I wasn't satisfied with the living, and I left and went away to Limón. It was 1941, and I sign on the contract there to go to the Canal Zone to work in the war. It was seventeen cents an hour they pay. You got a trade, tradesman get twenty-eight cents.

1941 we left here in March. But before that I had a next trip out. I didn't tell you about that one. I went to the Canal Zone about a year before. I stow on the boat and they catch me there, coming off the ship on the dock, put me back in jail, took my picture, and I say, 'Don't worry with that, you have it here already!' Well, anyhow, two days later they send me back to Costa Rica because I had all my papers in order. When I reach back here they put me in jail one day and let me loose. Then I signed the contract, and when we reach on board, all the sailors was my friend because we only had one year since I had stowed away on that same ship, the *S.S. Tolowa*. So all the sailors was my friends. Yeah, they treat me very good.

We went to Colón, and I fell in electric camp, went out to work. I had a very good boss, they call him Smokey, an American fellow. He liked to make a lot of scandal. Like to take a lot of liquor, and we like him too, because at that time we used to drink a lot. And we go working, and when I see a lot of people making money I just don't feel to work anymore. You know what I used to do? Start to get very fresh with the boss, because when you get fresh he give you days off and you go to the dock and then work with the United Fruit Company and the Standard Fruit Company. Used to make around five dollars a day. We could work in the night, we could work in the day. There was a lot of work. So sometimes I behave very rude with the boss. Well, he finally sent me to the camp to go home. They have a camp in Balboa where when we misbehave ourselves they take us from the labor camp and take us there till they send us home. That was around six of December in 1941.

But, really, it was a great experience for me, because I never knew I could go under the water. Working underneath the water, and the water is on top of my head, and the ship is on top of my head, because you have a tunnel from one lock to the other one on the canal, under the canal. The ship is on your head when it going through the locks. We there splicing cable, the cables that work the canal. Those were all in automatic machine at Gatún Locks. So that opportunity in those days was very great to me. Even to get into where the canal is, you have to have your photo badge and your identification card. The first thing the guard meet you with a gun and a bayonet, and you have to identify yourself.

After working there for that period of time I start to get lonely. They put me in a camp and from there we had fifteen days wait on a ship to come to Costa Rica. I spend about a month in Limón, then I decide to go back. I pass through Penshurst, pass Cahuita outside. I never know this place yet at that time. Walk it through the trail to Olivia, down to Almirante on the train, and take a launch from Almirante to Colón. I got myself a job in the naval supply department, and I worked there for about a year and learned to drive the hoister and from that I could drive a truck. And then I quit where I was and worked for the Army for about a year and then came back home.

But in the time I spend on the docks in Colón I always ask the sailors, 'Why is it the colored American only get to be a messboy on a ship?' Well, one gave me the answer. He told me that riot on the ship is the worst riot you have, and it will cause riot on the ship, and that's why. Because the colored don't want to take order from the white, and the white don't want to take order from the colored. I see ship and aircraft carrier with captain colored and whole crew colored, so I believe it was true what that sailor told me.

And the next thing, I'm telling the truth. I didn't like the system in the Canal Zone. We wasn't so well-treated. Sometime I go out with my boss, and we, the colored, weren't allowed to purchase in the commissary. The boss had to go in and purchase our lunch. They have discrimination. That's why, when the American folks come around Cahuita these recent years, I wasn't feeling so good at all at the beginning. You see, wherever you work in the Canal Zone, they have a water spout to drink ice water. You see one there silver, one there gold. The one marked gold, if we make a mistake and go drink water there, we may be locked up in jail. I didn't like that. The commissary, they really make one for you and one for them.

And at that time, there are many Panamanians and Costa Ricans that know some of the jobs more than even some of the Americans because the Americans did it by study, but the Costa Ricans and Panamanians had it by practice, such as fixing a car. But the American, the boss, maybe getting five dollars a hour. And you that know it only get thirty cents a hour. It was unlegal. And you got to do the work, and he gets the money. So many of us wasn't feeling so justified. We didn't like it. And we think all the Americans was like the people that we met there. So at first I didn't have good mind for the Americans that came around Cahuita. But according to how I see a few start to act I feel better.

Well, I left the Canal Zone and came over back in early 1943, and I was living in Limón working in the hospital. And then I met Miss Esther and that's how I come to Cahuita, because I take up with Miss Esther and she belong to Cahuita. So I start to make cocoa farm."

One last story of a traveler who became a Cahuita farmer is told by Mr. Ormington Demontford Corbin, born in Barbados in 1903. Since 1954 Mr. Corbin has adopted the home of his wife, Miss Ida, improving the farm on Big Bay that Miss Ida's mother began in the first decade of this century. In the peace and quiet of his yard he recalls his adventuresome boyhood and travels:

"I was born February 20, 1903, in Barbados, on a hill called Free Hill. And I grow there. After about ten years my mother left there and she go to a place called Elliot Village, and we build a house there. All that time my father was in the Canal Zone in the construction days. And I go to school up to the class of sixth standard. After I left school I was there cultivating the land while my father was away. And one day my cousin said to me, 'Let us go to Cuba.' I said, 'All right.'

At that time my father was in Cuba, and he wrote my mother and told her don't allow me to come to Cuba because the work is too hard, but she did not let me know. She kept the letter and she never said nothing to me. So when the cousin says, 'Let's go to Cuba,' I told her. Then she brought the letter and showed me. I said, 'Mother, it's too late. You should have told me before.' But when I go to the Immigration Office now, I so small, they wouldn't take me. And I said to my cousin, 'Let's stow on the ship.'

It wasn't a direct hiding. The captain know we was on the ship. Only Immigration don't know. We go on in the day. You see, the captain get an amount of money for each man that he carried to Cuba, so he don't mind. It's more money for him. He contract with the plantation owners in Cuba to take the men there to work. That captain carrying people to sell.

So then when the boat left Caroline Bay, we left under one sail, one sheet to the back. And we had eleven days sailing under that one sheet to get to Cuba. Eleven days I had to lay down in one place. I couldn't get up, I couldn't walk. The head was giddy. It's the first time I took such a far voyage. We had everything to eat and clothes to wear. When we did able to walk, we had nothing. And when the boat was three days out to sea I wish it could turn back, yeah. Never sailed so far before, and I was crying too. I leave my mother there crying, and when I get three days out to sea I start to crying myself, I tell you.

All right, when we got to Cuba, my father was in Cuba. When I got there, I asked and I asked, and I got to find out where he was. We go to there. He said to me, 'Don't I tell your mother not to let you come to Cuba?' I said, 'Yes, Dad, but she showed me the letter too late when I had already made up my mind.' He said, 'All right.' He was a foreman on the railroad, and I worked there with him all the time. In the year 1922 he went home. I go there in '21, he went home in '22. He wanted me to go but I wouldn't go, I said, 'No, no. Let I stay.'

So I stay till the fever took me. I went in the hospital, for weeks in the hospital. When I got out I couldn't cut cane. I go and work with the owner of a farm, cooking. And I cook there and cook there and cook there until in 1928 I left for Nicaragua. On the ship I dropped in Limón, and I go in jail for twenty-four hours. There were a gambler on the boat, and he gambled his money, no? And he suspect that me and my cousin had his money. And when he got there, he tell the government that we have stole his money. And when they got to find out it was a lie, he ran. He ran away.

Well, I was there, nothing to do, money finishing. I got to work with a man the name of David. He had a truck. There were only in that time three trucks in Limón and one bus. That was in the year 1928. And I go around with that man on his truck until I go to work on the track, the railroad. And when I left there I walked to Nicaragua. Walked to Nicaragua on the beach, three of us. We spend a little time in Nicaragua and walk back to Costa Rica. Take about two weeks walking. Then I went up to Nicaragua again and I took a canoe, a small boat, from Nicaragua to Monkey Point. And from Monkey Point I go to

Bocas, walking. I was working quite a while in Bocas. Got myself a horse, doing a little work, none of consequence. Money was too small, so I left there and go to the Canal Zone.

I first worked on the docks, and it happened that those people on the docks always try to take something and put it in the bag when they went home, you know. And they see I wouldn't take nothing. So one of them took a pear [avocado] and give it to me. He says, 'Here, you won't take anything. If we get catched, you get catched too.' And I called for my time the next day. They didn't want me to give them my time, but I tell them my mother's sick. I had to make some lie to give them.

And then I go and work with the Army, the American Army. And I worked there, worked there, worked there until I couldn't get work again. Because they had a system with the man who work over you, as a colored man. When you get your pay, he want you to give him a part of your money. And he keep that. And I tell him no. I says, 'I have a wife. I have a home, and I can't give you my money. You're getting more than me.' So any time the laying off come, I always the first because I wouldn't do what the others do to keep the work.

That time Miss Ida sick, and five years she sick. Well, after I couldn't get nothing I returned back to Almirante and I worked there, and the money small. Then Miss Ida got to understand that her stepfather was alone in Cahuita, and she said to me, 'Let's go,' and he sent and call her too. But we wasn't ready. But she said, 'Let's go,' and we leave and come over here with the intention to go back. But when we come, he says, 'Don't go back.' Well, we never go away again. We came right here to this house. This house was built around 1912, and now I'm fixing it up again."

Arnold Hanbelamt

"They comes and they goes, all the time," says Mr. Johnson of foreign companies in Talamanca. The Penshurst Banana Company left behind this steam engine when it abandoned the region in the 1940s.

# 10. The Influence of "Outsiders" and Foreign Companies

As temporary and sporadic as their activities have been, foreign companies have had an enormous influence on the development of the Talamanca Coast. We have already seen how the United Fruit Company stimulated local trade in the Old Harbour-Olivia-Sixaola region during the first decade of the Twentieth Century. Until Minor Keith's company built the railroad connecting San José and Limón, Costa Rica's Atlantic port was of little value as a market for the Talamanca turtle fishermen and early farmers. The United Fruit Company's expansion into the Estrella Valley, linking Limón and Bonifacio by train, provided the only land transportation route for the people of the coast from 1910 through 1976. Many of the families that came to populate the coast happened to be in Costa Rica only because the Company contracted their menfolk as railroad, dock, and plantation workers. The Company's impact on the Atlantic Zone is so great that it is impossible to imagine what course Limón's history might have followed without it.

The coastal land, however—from the mouth of the Estrella River southeast to Monkey Point—was never in the hands of the Company. Except for a few years in the 1930s when the Penshurst Banana Company took up a large inland concession for its plantations, the Talamanca Coast has always been a region of independent small farmers.

Other companies that came to the Talamanca Coast never stayed long. "They comes and they goes, all the time," Mr. Johnson says, as if he's been viewing an ongoing film over the last eight decades. The companies establish themselves with a flurry of activity that inevitably involves the local population, and suddenly they're gone, leaving behind a mixture of disappointments, resentments, and benefits.

The United Fruit Company, Sixaola Division

At the height of the banana boom in the early 1920s, the United Fruit Company occupied 28,202 hectares of Costa Rican land extending from the Panama border at Sixaola (then Bridgefoot) to the upper reaches of the Talamanca Valley. These plantations were known as the Sixaola Division, and they employed more than 5,000 workers. Although the Costa Rican government authorized the concession of these lands to the Company and charged export taxes on the bananas produced there, the Sixaola Division was managed from Company headquarters in Almirante, Panama. The products of the Sixaola Division (first bananas, later cocoa) were transported over 121 miles of railroad tracks to the United Fruit Company docks in Almirante. Workers were paid in U.S. dollars until the 1940s. Since neither roads nor rails connected Talamanca with Costa Rica's Atlantic port, Limón, most commerce and communication from Talamanca were directed toward Panama.

Between 1905 and 1917, the dollar value of bananas exported from Costa Rica exceeded that of coffee, the principal export crop of the central highlands. In 1920, the Sixaola Division alone produced more than three million bunches of bananas.

The people who grew up on the United Fruit Company plantations and those who gave many years of their working lives to the Company can give valuable insights into the social impacts of the giant multinational which was known in Costa Rica as "Mamita Yunai" (Mommy United).

William Rodman, known by his neighbors in Old Harbour as Mr. Paul, was born in 1926 on the Margarita plantation in the Sixaola Division. His godfather worked all his life for United Fruit; his father was an independent contractor in association with the Company; and his maternal grandfather leased a farm from United and produced bananas "independently," although the only buyer was the multinational.

Until the age of 15, young Paul Rodman knew no other lifestyle than that of the Company Town. At age 59, when he narrated his account of Company life, he was an independent cocoa farmer and president of the Administrative Board of Coopetalamanca R.L., a regional agricultural cooperative. His retrospective analysis of the impacts of Company policies on the lives of the Talamanca people is a story of corruption and cruelty, of human relations distorted by racial prejudice, of arduous work and collective struggle. Above all, Mr. Paul's story shows how the cultural values of the West Indian immigrants sustained them through their many years of subjugation to the unlimited powers of a multi-national corporation.

Mr. Paul relates how he came to be born on a farm in the Company's Sixaola Division:

"My father left Jamaica on contract to the Panama Canal. Yellow fever and malaria was killing off the workers that time, and the Jamaicans—the Negroes—was the group that could withstand most of the sicknesses. So he came to the Panama Canal on contract. You sign for two years, but if you pay your expenses for your passage, you were free, you were not bound to remain in the contract. You had to pay whatever expenses they had to bring you over, and if you could pay it back before the two years, then you could go seek other jobs.

So my father paid off his contract and came to this Division, following the banana business, because in Jamaica his family raise bananas. So he followed that Green Gold to Costa Rica. That was Green Gold days, they call it. A lot of money was made in those days.

It was English people that opened this Division. They worked their way north from Panama into Costa Rica. The United Fruit Company was formed by a lot of different people. There were a lot of English people that had investments in the United Fruit Company, and at first the super-intendents or the general overseers were English people. In the 1930s the Americans started coming in as administrators in the area.

A man named Fields, an English agronomist, opened the farms in Costa Rica from Olivia to Suretka. He got a concession from the government, and he bought out the rights from the people who had that land. He give the banana farms the name of the first owners: Olivia, Margarita, Volio, etc. Chase was named after an English superintendent, and Fields gave his own name to the place called Fields. Farther up, they used Indian names, like Suretka and Shiroles.

The Indians refused to sell their lands, so Fields just run them off. He offered them money, and if they refused he sent people to go and burn their houses and their crops. The Indians had to go hide in the mountains.[1]

---

[1]Some Bribri Indians suspect that administrators of the United Fruit Company arranged the assassination of their last king. Antonio Saldaña died of poisoning in 1910, the same year the Company started exporting bananas from the Talamanca Valley. King Antonio had firmly opposed the Company's expansion up the tributaries of the Sixaola River. A Bribri man who was a child when King Antonio was murdered commented: "Among the Indians there was a traitor. The Company paid him to kill the king so they could do whatever they wanted in Talamanca" (Simón Mayorga, quoted in *Nuestra Talamanca Ayer y Hoy*, p. 105, translated from the Spanish).

Both Indian and black residents of Talamanca protested to the Costa Rican government that the Company was taking their lands by force. "My father [son of a Jamaican man and a Bribri woman] formed a commission with several Indians and went to San José right to the President's house to defend their rights. Later the Company paid some of the Indians for the land they had taken from them. But my father also paid a price: the Company refused to buy the bananas he produced" (Alejandro Swaby, quoted in *Nuestra Talamanca Ayer y Hoy*, p. 86, translated from the Spanish).

"My father never worked for the United Fruit Company direct. He sub-contracted work as an independent. In his early days here he worked on building the railroad. My godfather opened this railroad from Sixaola right in to Shiroles. My father worked as a subcontracter to cut hills, clearing a path for the railroad. He hired his own workers.

Most of the workers were Spaniards[1]: Nicaraguans, Hondureñans, Costa Ricans. The Spaniards did most of the opening of the lands, preparing the lands for the planting of bananas. Later the Company contracted thousands of people, built big camps, and opened the farms. Then the Jamaicans that knew about cultivating the banana came in to do the planting. The Spaniards weren't interested in the farming part, except for a few Nicaraguans who did work in cultivation.

The Indians never worked for the Company. They were independent. They was, still is, and I think they always will be. They would work for subcontractors like me and my father, but not for the Company.

So my father worked opening the land for quite a while, until the banana start planting, and then he got contracts from the Company to plant banana and sell them. He worked in the Chase area. The Company owned all these lands, but they didn't work them. They leased the lands, a symbolic lease, I would say. They leased any amount of land for one dollar. It was just a formality, so that you know the land is belonging to the Company.

My mother's father was also an independent producer, leasing land from the Company. His farm was in a place called Rawa Town. He sent my mother and my uncle to Jamaica when my mother was around five years old. They grew up in Jamaica, and when my mother was 20 years old my grandfather sent for her back. She came over to Sixaola Division, and my father saw her, and then I came along!"

As a child growing up on the Company farm in Margarita, Mr. Paul observed the differences between the early English administrators and the Americans who replaced them:

"I liked the English administrators more than the Americans for the reason that they were less Negro-haters. The Americans seem to have a deep color problem. But the English didn't have that. They didn't care what color you were, they just treated you like a worker.

---

[1] "Spaniards" here refers to all Spanish-speaking people, regardless of nationality.

Paula Palmer

Mr. Paul Rodman

Most of the Americans in those days seems to come from areas where there was some deep conflict between the races. They really didn't like nobody. You could be Spaniard as well as Negro and they treat everybody bad. English overseers saw to it that each farm had certain vital commodities: water, meat once a week (very cheap, too), recreation for the people. And the living conditions were better. They know that if they keep a healthy working group they get more out of them.

The Americans came and they didn't worry: if there's water, there's water; if there's meat, there's meat, if there's none it's O.K. Sports, well they brought in baseball. The English were cricket and horseracing. Well, the Americans love horseracing too. There were races two or three times a year.

The English superintendent would come into the farm where the people was working, he would come into the camps and give instructions what to do, and you could see he wasn't snobbish.

The Americans didn't deal with the mass of the people directly. They dealt through the foreman or another intermediary; you just didn't see them. They wouldn't come and listen to no problems.

The English people did several good things. They saw to it that there was enough milk in the camps, and it was free. You just had to go get it. When the Americans came in they didn't worry with that no more. No time for that. They were smart enough to hire a few of the Spanish people in key positions and then those privileged few would help to oppress their own people. That's the beauty of the system they had.

It was when I travelled to Panama many years later that I realized that there is a difference in humans in general. At the beginning I just thought that all Americans were supreme. I didn't believe that any American could have any interest in me. But now I know there is a lot of good American people. And there is worse, too."

Of the educational options and opportunities available to young people in the Company camps, Mr. Paul remembers:

"There was no education program in the Company. They had one Spanish school in Sixaola (that was Bridgefoot then). But the only way you could get to that school was you go live down there or you go to school once a week when they have a passenger train. But most of the time there were no teachers there. That was the big problem. The teachers maybe stay two or three months and you never see them again. So I never go to Spanish school. I don't know what percentage of children went to that school, but it was very few.

But all of us colored children, we went to English schools run by private groups. Just a group of parents got together and hired teachers from Jamaica, somebody that was capable.

The United Fruit Company saw fit to educate some children within their system of business. They would take from each village two or three boys, 13 or 14 years of age, who just know to read and write. They would send one to the Merchandise Department and there they would teach him just to be clerk, to work in the Commissary. And they would send one to the accounting or time-keeping department, but those boys would only learn just what the Company need, no more. You weren't really an accountant, you just learn to keep their books according to their system. And others went to the mechanic shops, a few.

And the Company sent a very few boys abroad, but none of them ever came back. Most of those had parents who were more educated. I know one woman had a son and she wanted him to be a minister, and the Company sent him to England and he did become a Baptist minister, but he didn't come back. Sometimes the Company did something nice like that as a way of keeping somebody quiet. But the rest of us were just slaves in a diplomatic form.

I realized that there was no future for me with the Company. I could see it, I could feel it even as a boy. They would only teach you enough so you could serve them. And I say to myself, well, that isn't enough for me.

I was placed in the time-keeping office, and all I was given to do was to fill out the forms, to carry the time record, to prepare the pay sheet, and from me it would go into the main office. I was not even allowed to make the final calculations and additions, just prepare it. And then in the next section another group of puppets like myself finished the calculations. And finally it goes into the superintendent's office where there was somebody to sign it. If they were Negroes they were so proud they didn't believe they were Negroes anymore. They were not so well paid, but they were pampered employees, and they scorned the rest of us. There were only a few of them, but it was an ugly thing to see."

Mr. Paul describes working and health conditions on the Company plantations:

"The working conditions were ... well, they complain today of poor conditions in the banana companies, but this is a king's life compared to what I grew up with.

Snake was abundant in all the farms near the river or the lagoons and the woodland. People were killing big snakes every day, and plenty of them got bit.

There were a lot of machete cuts, and the men who worked with the mules were always getting hurt. They would bring in around 500 mules every two or three years from Nicaragua, but they were savage, wild beasts and they gave the men who handled them hell.

Malaria never used to trouble much the colored adults, but the children, yes. Us children would get malaria every now and again. And the Spaniards really suffered. They got weak and stayed in their bed for weeks and months, with no pay.

There was nothing like compensation when you get sick. If you can't work, you don't get no money, unless you were monthly-paid people like foreman, time keeper, railroad foreman (like my godfather), clerk. They were the only monthly paid, and they were very few. Everybody else on the farm were piecemeal job or contract. So if you can't work, you get no pay."

Relations between black and white workers and their families were very tense because of prejudices held by both racial groups against the other. Differences not only of color but also of language, religion, education, customs, and aspirations created an atmosphere charged with racism. In retrospect, Mr. Paul laments the racial divisiveness which, he points out, only benefited the Company by preventing the formation of cohesive workers' organizations.

Mr. Paul explains the cultural roots of the racial conflicts that characterized daily life in the United Fruit Company camps:

"The Jamaicans in my days had a faith that they were in Costa Rica only to make some money and go back. Most had that intention, but very few actually go back. Who made money decide it was worthwhile staying, and who didn't make money just couldn't go back.

Most of the Jamaicans didn't like to mix with the Spaniards, with the exception of a few that got their wives and husbands among Spaniards. But there was always friction. In those days the Jamaicans looked upon the Spaniards as inferior. It was just a racial way of thinking among everybody. It was passed from one group to another. Still, some of the Spaniards came to be like brothers to the colored. They gave up their customs and adopted the colored customs. They took up our way of cooking, they learned English; you could say they actually turned semi-Negro.

The Negroes would call the Spaniards nasty. The Spaniards would allow their children to go naked and they would stool about in the yard. And the Negroes would never allow that. We may be ragged and patched, but we were clothed, and clean, too. The Spanish didn't bother with those things.

In those days, I would say 99 percent of the Spanish couldn't read or write, while 80 percent of all Jamaicans could read, and they could write.

The Spaniards and Jamaicans in those days was real dynamite. Every payday there would be fights. It was just a hatred between the two groups. There were trouble makers on both sides.

Our parents, to keep the children from going into the Spanish quarters especially on payday when these people were drinking, they would frighten the children with terrible stories about the *paña*.[1] They said the *paña* would chop them up with machete. It is true that you would see Spaniards, drunk, who

---

[1] Derived from "Spaniard," a mildly derogatory term used by some English-speaking West Indians to refer to all Spanish-speaking people.

would chop up any damn thing they see, whether dog or cat or fowl or pig. I never remember them really hurting any children. But we were told that, and we were damn afraid of them, I'm telling you. We were brought up to be afraid of these people, and then, as we got bigger we would always be on our guard. Any time we see a *paña* pickney we start fighting him one time. It was something that was encouraged by the parents on both sides. So I'm not ashamed to speak it, because I'm speaking the truth.

The problem is, the man that made the most benefit from this was the United Fruit Company. Because if we had stopped bickering among ourselves we could have united against the Company, stopped picking his cocoa and chopping his bush until he paid us plenty more, made us better homes, water, electricity, better conditions. But instead of fighting together against the Company, we were fighting among ourselves. It's sad to say but we really didn't realize it at the time.

Mostly the Spaniards were simple people, they weren't fussy about living conditions. For them it would be the same thing to live on a wood floor or off the bare earth. They would have their place clean, but no furniture and no fuss, and they had the habit of spitting on the floor. And their cooking was different.

The colored people was proud in having their floors polished and shined, and if they couldn't buy furniture they get codfish boxes and line them with some kind of cloth. And the bed. They had to have a big iron bed. It was impossible to think that they didn't have a big iron bed, triple-sized, with about 500 pieces of brass all over it. And we children have to be cleaning them, polishing the damn thing twice a week. And curtains. And fine china, silverware. It was cheap and every year people would buy sets and sets. Those things were never seen out except for special occasion, but you had to take them and clean them every week.

The silverware was never kept in the cabinet. Those damn thing was kept in the trunk. They had some special big hell of a trunk. It take six of us little ones to move it, or two big strong man.

In the cabinet was where they had the chinaware. Whenever I broke one I was fretting for a month till mama found out, and then it was hell. Whenever the pastor was coming for dinner, then the chinaware come out. And if he's bringing some visitor from Jamaica, then the silverware come out.

And the linen that was put on the table, that was the finest thing you could ever see. I think I have some in my trunk here that my mama left me. She'd been travelling with that thing all her life. It was handmade linen, but it was starched and ironed. It was white, white as lily. And it was three pieces they use. The first one they put on the table, and another one on top of that, and another one on top of that one. It's lace, and each piece has a pattern, and when you see the three of them together you see the design of a duck or a roast turkey or a parrot.

The Jamaicans got these customs from the white people, because where they could learn about having these things? From the plantation owners in Jamaica. In those people's homes, the slaves and servants had to take care of those fine things.

But the Spaniards didn't know about those things. They were always on the move, and they never buy all those things, so they could just pick up and go. While the colored, it was always a problem to move because it was tons and tons of things. They were mostly preserving these things to take back to Jamaica, all wrapped in fine linen. Because they really had the intention of going back. And then when Marcus Garvey came on the scene, that strengthened the idea of returning back, but then they weren't thinking anymore of Jamaica, they were thinking of Africa as the homeland. It really created a dream in our people."

Marcus Garvey's Universal Negro Improvement Association (UNIA) recruited many members and inspired devotion among the West Indian employees of the United Fruit Company.[1] Mr. Paul is one of many people of his generation who were thrilled to see Garvey in person:

"I went to a few of Marcus Garvey's meetings. He came to Bocas [Bocas del Toro, Panama] twice, and I happened to go to a rally with my mother, but I was young. I only remember seeing this guy and knowing he was magnetical. I remember that. And his personal secretary, that girl had a magnetism in her. Those people really had something in them. Marcus Garvey was a thunder. He didn't need no microphone.

Those things helped to create a dream in about 90 per cent of all Negro descendants, the ones who became a part of Garvey's movement. My father retired early because he saw it would be a failure through the actions of certain leaders. He didn't like the deliberate hatred that was preached against white people because he said it was going to go from one extreme to the other. That was what caused him to retire. But he couldn't talk too much because people were fanatics. The people who had a little more education could see the danger of preaching hatred. Most of it was revenge against the white people that had oppressed them so long. In a sense it was used to capture the

---

[1] For more information about the activities of the UNIA, see Chapter 12.

mass of these people, but then in the long run it wrecked the Marcus Garvey movement because the white people had to get rid of Marcus Garvey because he really would overthrow the whole damn system."

United Fruit Company administrators feared that the Garvey movement would incite workers to revolt. They petitioned the presidents of Costa Rica and Panama to prohibit the circulation of Garvey's *The Negro World* in their plantations. They fired dozens of workers who were Universal Negro Improvement Association activists, and they pressured the U.S. State Department to revoke the visas of UNIA international representatives visiting Central America. The Company hired spies to infiltrate the UNIA and successfully pressured the president of Panama to have UNIA leaders arrested in Almirante.[1]

Paul Rodman is angered by the fact that most Costa Ricans believe black laborers were acquiescent within the Company structure. The year 1934 is often cited as the date of the first strike against the Company, organized by the national Communist Party under the leadership of Carlos Luis Fallas. But workers in the Company's Sixaola Division, most of them blacks, were organizing strikes as early as 1913 and suffering cruel consequences.

In March 1913, the Company imported 200 hispanic Nicaraguan laborers to break a general strike. When the Costa Rican government sent 150 armed men to Sixaola on Company boats to protect the strike breakers, angry West Indian strikers stormed the docks. One black worker was killed and many others were beaten. When the strike ended in April, all the strike organizers were fired.

The people of Talamanca remember the 1918 strike as the most violent; it left two workers dead and many wounded after three months of struggle. The strikers demanded a pay raise from ten to twenty-five cents (U.S. currency) per hour. The Company refused to negotiate with the black strike leaders and brought in hundreds of white strike breakers. Together with the Costa Rican police forces, the Company's strike breakers threw more than a thousand strikers and their families out of Company housing, burned their possessions, destroyed their vegetable gardens, and pursued them into the mountains where they had taken refuge. There, also, they burned the families' rough shelters and possessions and brought the strikers in under arrest. A British

---

[1] This and the following information on early strikes in the Sixaola Division is documented in Bourgois 1989.

delegation sent to investigate the 1918 strike, reported 168 cases of physical abuse and illegal detention at the hands of Costa Rican police and Company strike breakers.

The workers who returned to their jobs after the strike were awarded a 15 percent salary increase, but many didn't go back. Mr. Paul tells the story of the 1918 strike as he heard it from his father:

"The Company system was a plantation system, and the people were oppressed. In those days any type of movement that was organized to seek some form of benefit for the people was also repressed by the national government. The Company could always influence the government to suffocate any type of movement that was made.

Even so, the people organized several strikes before I was born. My father said they were striving for better pay and more liberal policies among the employees. Because as I have seen since I have sense, the Company dictated whatever laws they wanted. They pay you what they feel like and you work when they feel like and you don't work when they feel like, and there was no compensation. There was 14 hours a day work, there was no vacation, no hospital. Well, there was a hospital in Almirante, but it's only when you die that maybe you reach there. And there were times they just didn't give you work and that's that. So I think those people organized to try to get better treatment toward laborers.

But the Company always crushed the strikes. In fact, some of the population of Puerto Viejo is here because their parents had to run away or hide in the woods because they were strike leaders. Mr. Gale, Mr. Newton, around six or seven came into this area, hiding. They were people that could read and write and had communication with other leaders, so they were sought for, persecuted, and they had to hide away. They were not highly educated, but they were independent people. They were obstinate, hard-dealing people. They had a sense of independence, and it was hard to beat. I don't know how they got it.

Those people, they lived so hard a life that you wouldn't believe it. They run away from the Company, live in the woods and make farm without anything, alone. They didn't know Puerto Viejo existed, and they were only a few miles from here. Well, later they got to know everybody here. But, man, cho! When I got big and my father told me about those men, I just say, 'boy, that was really tough people.'

Now people are saying that the first strike against the banana company was in 1934. They're mad. Tell them I say they're mad. You had strikes before I was born and recently after I was born.

My father never participated because he was always saying it was not necessary to strike against the Company, it was better to use diplomatic pressure. My godfather was the same. Well, if everybody was like my father and my godfather, there would never be any revolutions."

In the Sixaola Division, as in its other plantations, the United Fruit Company leased many of its 28,202 hectares to independent producers who were called *arrendatarios*. In this way the Company passed on the risks of production to the *arrendatarios* while it enjoyed a monopoly on the marketing of their products. The Company generally exploited the fertile, freshly cleared land for the first ten years; then, as productivity declined, it leased the exhausted soils to *arrendatarios*. Bananas planted on exhausted soils are more vulnerable to disease and produce fewer "hands" per bunch, reducing their market value.

By 1929, after the Company had been exploiting Talamanca soils for twenty years, 71 percent of bananas exported from the Sixaola and Bocas del Toro (Panama) Divisions were cultivated by "independent" producers.[1]

Paul Rodman describes the life of an *arrendatario* in the Sixaola Division:

"My father leased three camps of Company houses and about 60 hectares of land where he planted bananas. The Company put all the risk on the *arrendatario*. I remember when I was a boy I would see up to 300 bunches of bananas, maybe 400, on the track line waiting there, and the Company didn't accept even 50. And I knew bananas better than any damn inspector because I grew up in that, and they were saying, 'too thin; too full', but you could see it was perfectly good banana. The proof of it is, you put the same banana out at the next port when the train is coming down and the cars don't full because they reject too much, and they would select 80 per cent of the same banana that they reject before.

The inspectors was paid to dump the fruit. They only wanted a certain amount and the production was ten times that, so they were dumping the fruit deliberately. A lot of banana inspectors in those days, some were killed, some were murdered, some were beaten by farmers. They just got mad. And the inspectors weren't Americans. They were Costa Ricans, some were Jamaicans, and they were paid a good salary to do it.

---

[1] Kepner and Soothill 1935: 273.

When disease bring down the banana production, they started planting cocoa with the same *arrendatario* system. You pick the cocoa, break it, bring it out to the track. And if you had 50 boxes of cocoa out there and the train don't come or the inspector don't accept it, you lose. The Company don't lose. They are only responsible for the cocoa once they put it in their boxcars."

In the 1930s, cocoa replaced bananas as the principal product of the Sixaola Division. "Panama disease" had reduced the profitability of the banana enterprise, and a great flood in 1935 destroyed the Company's plantations in the upper reaches of the Talamanca Valley, carrying away its bridges and warehouses. Whether the flood was an Act of God, the inevitable consequence of massive deforestation, or witchcraft perpetrated by the displaced Indians of the Talamanca Valley, it forced the Company to withdraw to the lowlands of the Sixaola Valley. It still operates there today under the names of its subsidiaries, Chiriqui Land Company and PAIS, S.A.

Paul Rodman comments on the ending of the era of Green Gold:

"The Company started planting cocoa in the early 1920s, when Panama disease was starting to infest the older banana plantations. So they convert them to cocoa. But they keep pressing farther and farther into the upper Talamanca Valley, clearing more land for bananas all the time. But they never really dominated the upper Talamanca. As fast as they could put a trestle in, the rivers would take it away. And it was said, and the people still believe it, that the Indians were capable of making floods and washing away the bridges. The flood in 1935 wrecked everything up in Talamanca, so the Company pulled out and came back down to Chase. And they planted cocoa from there right down to Sixaola. After the flood they never had another banana train. They leased most of the cocoa farms; that's how they avoided problems with the unions."

Looking back on the impacts of the United Fruit Company in Talamanca, Mr. Paul criticizes the Company more for what it didn't do than for what it did do:

"The United Fruit Company created a lot of problems that we are still living with. If that company in those days had tried to give some benefit to the area, I think today there would be more cooperation with other companies coming into the area. For the amount of bananas and cocoa that United Fruit took out of Talamanca, if they had invested even ten per cent of all their profits into developing the zone, the entire area would be well developed today. But they left nothing."

The 1935 flood washed away everything the Rodman family had in Margarita—house, farms, cattle, everything. After the disaster, Paul's father started planting bananas on government lands near Puerto Viejo, where he eventually acquired rights of possession.

But Mr. Paul's dealings with the multinational didn't end there. Many years later, he confronted the Company bureaucracy when he tried to get a pension for his godfather who had been on the Company payroll for 33 years:

"My godfather opened the road from Fields into Talamanca. He actually built, or helped to build, all the Company's railroads in the Sixaola Division. He and thousands of others gave a lifetime of service to the Company, and let me tell you how they treated him.

He was working in the Sixaola Division for 30 years, here on the Costa Rica side. Afterwards they transfer him to the Panama Division. When it come time for him to pension, he had been working three years on the Panama side. And when they gave him his severance pay, it wasn't even one month's salary. They only recognize his three years working in Panama, as if to say it wasn't the very same Company he was working for all his life in Costa Rica. And he accept it. That was his mistake.

I took the thing to the Colombian embassy because he came over on a contract from Colombia. They took down all the information and they guarantee that if I took him back to Colombia the government there would make the Company pay him every cent that they owe. But I would have to take him to Colombia, because they said the Company had too much power here in Costa Rica and it wouldn't be worth the fight. That was about 12 or 13 years ago.

The Company never give pensions. What they really did was repatriate some of the old workers back to Jamaica or wherever it was they sign the contract. Those men didn't know no one in Jamaica, they had nothing there, and they didn't live long because they were old and they couldn't live on what little the Company gave them.

Well, my godfather was old and didn't want to go to Colombia to die there alone. So I still have him here with me."

As late as the 1980s, a number of retired Company employees were still trying to get pensions from United Fruit. Even those who talk proudly about their years of labor with the Company bitterly resent the Company's indifference to their current plight. The great majority of Talamanca residents never worked for the Company. Those, like Paul Rodman, who did, thank God for having become independent of it. As Mr. Paul says, "I wasn't born to be a servant."

The Coal Mine

While the United Fruit Company was beginning to build its railroad into the Talamanca highlands, some Costa Rican businessmen were wondering if they could make themselves rich exporting coal from Talamanca. Mr. Mason tells how his adopted father, Joseph Hunter, accidentally discovered the coal mine for which the region Carbón is named, and the fate of the would-be coal barons:

> "My adopted father found a piece of rock in the Hone Creek river. He didn't know where it come from, but he was a judge here at that time. He put it on the papers in his office there to keep it down from the breeze. They always send an inspector from Limón, so when he come and check up the books he found that piece of stone shining and square from rolling in the river. The river bring it a shape that you would believe somebody did make it. And the inspector say, 'Well, Hunter, what kind of stone is this?' And he say, 'I found it hunting.' And the inspector say, 'But it don't look like a stone. It look like something else. Would you allow me to take it to San José and see what it is?' And he says yes. He think nothing of it.
> And the inspector took it to San José, and three weeks after there was a boat belonging to the government name of *Irazú* came there right in Joseph Channel load with officials, up to the brother of the President, Rafael Iglesia. There was his brother, name of Carlos Iglesia, that was Minister of Arms, and Dr. Castro, and Dr. Vilaski, that was the first and the oldest doctor in Limón, and some others. It was seven of them on the launch beside the crew. They want to see where he found that stone. And they went in the bush, and they brought enough provisions, tin meats and so on, to last for perhaps a month. And he said he don't know the direct spot, but he say we will go more or less.

And for three days they couldn't find it. And they made an attempt to kill him, threaten him to kill him because they say that he know but he don't want to show them.

But then he realize that he was coming down the creek when he found the stone, so he went back to that said creek. And when coming down the creek they saw a mountain, black, look like rock. But there was a slide, and the trees slide off the coal and leave it open. And when they look they see that slide. And they say it look peculiar, and going down they see against the bank of the river some black stones. And they carry all kind of equipment with them, you know. And when they dig it was blocks of coal drop down in the creek from the slide. Then they found it. That was in 1908. And they name that creek Carbón.

After they found it they was working on it for years and take sample from it. And then those seven men form a company to work the mine. They denounce seven thousand hectares from Suárez bridge right back to Sixaola River for obtaining the concession of the coal. And they build a road from Klines, this side of Hone Creek on the beach, back into the woodland, and they use cow cart, mules and horses to draw the coal from the hill. It came from the hill by man's back, as much as you can carry, fifty pounds, into bags. They get the Indians to draw the coal from the hill down to a certain place where horse can go, then from horse and mule back to the cart on the level land. From the cart they build a road to the Hone Creek river, and they put it in boat and land it at a place they give the name Puerto Cayuca, by Klines. And from there they cross the cow cart 'round and come and go on the beach by nights, come here and load it on a launch and take it to Colón. From Colón they ship it to England for a test. Was a Spanish company, all Costa Rican men. They were trying and trying up till 1918. They even start to build a dock at Puerto Vargas.

But the company forfeit because the people in England did say the mine is too young.

The manager of the Northern Railroad came here during the Second World War, was to lay a railroad in here from Penshurst to work the coal because they was getting short of oil. But they found that the war would soon over, so they didn't worry with it again.

And just a month and a half ago [January 1977] a white man came from Canada and say they have a company manufacturing the coal in dust, and he came here and get my information how to reach there. He say he was to return in a week's time, but he don't return up to now. And it is very easy now to work because we have the *carretera* [road]."

The Sinclair Oil Company

The Sinclair Oil Company of the United States was next to try its luck on the Talamanca Coast. First at old Cahuita, just south of Duncan Creek, and then near the present-day health dispensary at Old Harbour, Sinclair erected derricks and dug deep wells, searching for oil. They set up camps and kitchens for their own laborers and those they employed from the local population. Sinclair has the distinction of introducing the first electric plant to the coast and employing for the first time large numbers of coastal residents.

George Humphries was one of Sinclair's younger employees, and he tells of the company's activities at old Cahuita:

> "They did have an oil man in Cahuita, was working in 1920, named Sinclair Oil Company. They worked there more than a year, was drilling for oil. I worked for them too. I was dragging logs from out of the swamp. They did have a hell of a high rig, about seventy-five feet in the air, and a drill on it to drill down in the earth. They use wood, fire with wood, to make steam for run the machinery. So we young boys, about sixty or seventy of us, we go every day. They pay us by the day, one dollar and twenty-five cents a day, draw out the wood from the swamp. Have water and deep mud in there. They had men cutting wood out there, could make big money, up to ten dollars gold a day.
>
> Well, they treat us pretty good. They feed us. They have their camps built there. It was an American concern. Had motorboats there made two trips a day to Limón, carry the big boss up and down, carry nails and all them things. The launch named *Bertha*, very fast. Get down to Limón in about an hour and ten minutes. They feed us pretty good, three meals a day. Have a big mess hall. They have their own laundry place, water supply, they make their own ice, have a ice plant, and they run electric light from the plant there too. They have electric light strung from the rig there straight down to the camp, right along. They have three shift, some of the men go on eleven o'clock at night. They have light on for the men all night long through the coconut walk.
>
> They hire some men to catch kingfish for them, pay them a monthly salary. Them days you catch lots of kingfish. People from Cahuita carry lots of foodstuffs down there to sell, plantain, yam, all them things.
>
> Well, one night, don't know what wrong, the rig catch fire and burn down. From that they move their things out to Old Harbour, was working up Old Harbour there too. They drill down a couple thousand feet in the earth."

Mr. Johnson says Sinclair found not oil in Cahuita, but natural gas. The well, now sealed with cement, is on Mr. Johnson's property, but according to Costa Rican law, he says, "what is on the surface of the land is mine, but what is below is not mine. But I know how to catch it. I was learned by an Englishman from England, came here and look at it, and he showed me how to catch it. It's like a vapor of the clouds when you catch it into a bottle."

Mr. Johnson explains the fire that Mr. Humphries told about: "They use electric light working, and the electric bulb burst and the current flash like that and caught it on fire. And it burn up one man and burn down the rig. They get the man to the doctor, and he was saved."

"Boyse" Spencer says the fire burned for a week. "It was blazing from the well so they went out to get some pipes, connect up some pipes to lead that blaze out to the ocean. At night over here at the Bluff you could pick up a pin with the light of it, it was so bright, that fire blaze."

Work continued for a short time after the fire, Mr. Johnson remembers: "They begin to drill again, and they was drilling but they didn't get it, get to it. At a certain depth water come on them, but the gas still remain there, the gas still coming. And they stop, leave from here and went to Old Harbour."

Sinclair was unsuccessful in its oil search in Old Harbour too, but Mr. Mason says the company's campsite has brought him good fortune in later days:

> "The Sinclair Company start in Cahuita, and they move to Old Harbour in 1921. They built the first dock here, leave again in 1922. They lay a tram from this creek by my sawmill to O'Conner's pasture, and they pay twenty-five colón for each coconut tree that they destroyed. Made a place they call Location, ten hectares of woodland, and made their settlement there. They have camps for laborers, *bodega* [warehouse] and everything. At that time there was no diesel, everything was wood-burning. They make contract to cut the wood and bring it in by cow cart to where they was working.
>
> Right now I have ten hectares of cocoa right there. First I had it in banana, and then I make it into a cocoa farm, and I call that farm Oil Mine. And I get the most produce from all my cocoa farms from that Oil Mine farm."

## The Penshurst Banana Company

The company that made the greatest impact on the communities of Cahuita and Hone Creek during the decades between 1915 and

1948 was the Penshurst Banana Company. The United Fruit Company planted bananas in the Estrella River Valley beginning as early as 1910. Around 1930 two Englishmen, Galbraithe and King, and a Jamaican, Finley, made a deal to sell bananas to the Company at Bonifacio from plantations to the south of the Estrella River. From the Costa Rican government Finley, Galbraithe, and King bought a concession to land between the Estrella River and Tuba Creek, and they named their farm Penshurst. In 1933 the Penshurst Banana Company laid its first railroad track from Tuba Creek inland to the Bordón region. In 1935 it purchased an enormous concession on an inland strip between Cahuita and Hotel Creek. To service the banana plantations it envisioned, the company constructed a track

Deirdre Hyde

line from Tuba Creek and Hotel Creek, bridging the large Hone Creek river with the steel structure that serves until this day. Axe men and railroad gangs worked from Tuba Creek moving south and from a Puerto Vargas camp moving inland until the track was completed in 1936.

Mr. Fred Ferguson, of Cahuita, remembers the day the first "Puffin' Billy" engine steamed down the track from Penshurst:

> "I was a little boy, and I see a lot of people running, everybody running, and I run along with them. I don't know where I was running, but I follow them. And really, when I reach out not too far from the track I heard a little engine blow 'boop-boop-boop,' and the people was glad to see this engine. Crowd, you know. Anyone could come in Cahuita that day and steal away anything and go about his business. Everybody out there watching that little engine. That's the way it started."

The Penshurst Banana Company planted thousands of hectares of bananas along its track. "The whole of Hone Creek was in banana," Cyril Gray remembers. "Only my farm I still occupy, but all the balance of the land along the track was banana farm for the company, near out to the beach except where people had their coconut walk."

Mr. Leslie Williams, of Cahuita, known all about as "Mr. Sorrows,"[1] tells how the small farmers reacted to the coming of the banana company:

> "There were a lot of small settlers that cultivated on the hilly part of the land, because the company then monopolized the whole of the flatlands. The company used to buy bananas from the small settlers because the price of cocoa had gone down to nothing. Cocoa went down as far as four colónes to the quintal during the Thirties. So most everybody in the Cahuita area cut their cocoa farms down and they planted bananas and sold them to the Penshurst Banana Company at thirty cents [American dollars] per count bunch.

---

[1] Mr. Sorrows gives this explanation of the nickname by which his neighbors know him: "When I left my father's house, you know I was *triste* [sad] around, a boy not used to living on his own, and there was a man around, he used to see me sitting by myself and one day he said, 'But this boy I always see him around like a man in sorrows.' Yes, just like that. And from that day that name fasten on me."

That's one colón and twenty cents per bunch. The percentage of the banana that the company receive was very little because they used to reject the bananas a whole lot. Anyway, the people plunged through all those hard times."

Mr. Jonathan Tyndal is one Cahuita farmer who cut down his cocoa to plant bananas for sale to the Penshurst Banana Company. He describes the difficulty of making a living when the purse was in the hands of one company alone:

"We used to get thirty cents a bunch, and we could live, but Thursday, Friday you don't have no money at all, money gone, until you get a little check from the banana again.

They has a man by Penshurst, we call him 'estimator,' one that take the estimate and tell you how much to cut. He come and tell you they have a cutting such and such a time to be picked up such and such a time, and they want English fruit or German fruit or whatsoever it is. And you cut, and in eight days time you get the money. You had to go to Penshurst to get your check and cash it right there at the commissary.

The German fruit was what you call 'string bean,' that is thin banana, very thin, not too full, and the English fruit is a little more fuller. It's the same banana, but you cut the German fruit sooner, before it get big as the English fruit. When the thin fruit is cutting, it is better for you, the farmer, it easier to handle, it lighter, and you cut more. But it run down the farm a lot.

The banana spoil a lot of time. Sometimes you cut the fruit, but they tell you 'sigatoka,' they tell you different names, 'water-log,' 'squirrel mark.' And they throw away sometimes out of twenty bunches you may get twelve. They throw away eight, say it's no good. When they say 'water-log,' it looks like must be soak up water. When they say 'squirrel mark,' say the squirrel may walk on it and the squirrel's nail may juke [poke] it and it leave a mark on the fruit. They have more names for them I don't remember now, but it mean they don't accept it.

Sometimes the banana that they leave is pretty, pretty banana. And it rotten right there or you take to feed the pigs."

"You could call it no more than a hand-to-mouth living," Fred Ferguson says, and it got worse. Mr. Ferguson continues: "It happen that in the year 1939 I remember a man was living here named Goodwin. He was the first man I ever heard speak about war and that the nations was at war because Germany hit Poland and they gone to catch it. And I think in 1942 the buying of the banana had to be stopped because it was war time. They couldn't do no commercial movement on the oceans like how they had the freedom first, before the war. So the company close down, stop buying banana."

Selven Bryant says the bananas on the company's plantations were failing by 1942, giving the company little motivation to try to weather the difficult years of World War II. The company abandoned Talamanca and moved on to greener pastures, leaving the coastal farmers with useless fields of ripening fruit. Although private buyers continued to send launches to purchase bananas, without the company's train service transportation from farm to port was a problem. Most of the farmers cut down their plantations and returned to cultivating subsistence crops and cocoa. But many people, discouraged, left the area and never returned. Mr. Sorrows remembers:

> "When the banana company closed down, everybody start to drift away. The majority went to the Canal Zone to work during the war. From that time this zone went right down. The people that remain went right back to the cocoa. I remember in 1944 we had one of the most terriblest weathers, and in 1945 it brought an actual desolation to the zone here. It became real tough. There was a shortage of plenty things on account of the war and the bad weather. It destroyed all the young cocoa plants. Yet the people pressed onward and they kept trying. And in 1946 the cocoa price start to pick up, because the people could get as much as fifty colones for a quintal of cocoa."

The Penshurst Banana Company dealt a heavy blow to the people of the coast, from which they suffered for several dismal years. In the long run, though, the company inadvertently brought lasting benefits to the area. Mr. Sorrows explains:

> "After the Penshurst Banana Company went out, the lands that were cultivated by them in Hone Creek and in Penshurst, they had only concession to those lands, so the moment they were through they turn the land back over to the government, so small people were able to go into these lands and cultivate.
>
> The tramway also was turned over. The rails were sold out to another company, and they started to take up the tramway. But the people made a petition to the President of the country. They sent a commission to talk to the President, and he sent to investigate the matter. And he saw that it was necessary to keep the tramline because there was no other means of transportation for the people inside here. So the tramline remained for the benefit of the people."

The Penshurst Banana Company's track was converted first to a public tramline and finally to a ballast road. The long-range results of the company's activity in Talamanca were to open more land to cocoa farmers and to blaze the trail for inland transportation services. The coming and going of the banana industry also had a cultural impact on the coastal population: for the first time large numbers of Spanish-speaking Costa Ricans came into the area, and many stayed. Mr. Selven Bryant describes the social changes that took place in Old Harbour during the banana boom:

> "No Spaniard wasn't around in those days. Spaniard start to come in here around 1934. That time Finley open the tramline from Penshurst to Hone Creek, and they bring in Spaniard to do all the woodland work: line track, chop bush, plant banana. And those Spaniard come to Old Harbour because those days Hone Creek never had any shop. So when they get paid they have to come here to drink them rum and buy them foodstuff here, then go back to Hone Creek.
> After the company abandon the banana plantations in Hone Creek, then the Spaniard take up the land and start to move up and down here. But at first you only had Chico Ramírez was Spaniard, and he had to speak English because the Jamaican they don't know Spanish."

## Logging

Another company that exploited resources of the coast during the first half of the Twentieth Century was a San José-based logging company under the management of Guido Castro. Its site was south of Monkey Point along an uninhabited section of beach and swamp known as Gandoca. Although the people of the coast watched the big ships carrying the *cativo* and *cedro macho* (cedar) logs to Limón for years, they were scarcely affected by the company's activity. Few people lived in the Gandoca area until the logging company brought in workers, and residents today see little evidence of Señor Castro's logging industry. But in the early 1950s, steam engines ran on U.S. rails through two thousand hectares of forest there. One of Mr. Johnson's brothers served as engineer on a tugboat that hauled the enormous logs from the beach to the large ships anchored off-shore. Miss "Sis" at Grape Point remembers some fine dances that the Castro laborers enjoyed, but no one knows how much timber was extracted from the lowland forests of Gandoca.

The Tower

The foreign effort most puzzling to the people of the coast was the appearance in 1936 of the United States Marines off the shores of Cahuita's white-sand beach. Mr. Fred Ferguson remembers:

> "They anchor a ship a way outside on the white beach, and they go and come in small motorboats bringing whatever materials and equipment necessary. They say they want to build a tower up the hill there. Alfonso Brown was a young man in those days, and he help with that. They were here about three weeks. Everything they bring with them. They just built that big tower you see up the hill there and a little lighthouse out at Cahuita Point, and little by little the sea come in and wash that one away."

The people say the Marines left as quickly and unexpectedly as they came, without explaining to anybody what the towers were for. Everyone might have forgotten the incident except that the tower was there to remind them. And then in 1964, during the student riots in Panama, about fifteen soldiers from the U.S. Army appeared in Cahuita. Mr. Ferguson continues:

> "The soldiers rent that little place in front of Cana Tyndal. They buy some machete from Solón shop, sharpen them, and went right up to the tower. They knew all about it. Nobody show them. They went straight up there. They spent a few weeks here. They wouldn't tell anybody what they doing. They was pretty friendly. They walk down all by Sixaola, one almost drown in the Sixaola River, but they save him. And then they gone. Nobody know what they was doing."

The incident remains a mystery, but the tower still stands high on a hill, a two-hour walk from Cahuita through cocoa farms and bush. To hikers unafraid of heights it offers a sweeping view of the Talamanca Coast, from Limón to Old Harbour.

# 11. Transportation and Trade

During the years between 1915 and 1948, sea trade along the Talamanca Coast peaked and then began its decline, gradually giving way to ground transportation by tramline and train. Several companies based in Limón sent freight launches south to Cahuita, Old Harbour, and Manzanillo, their agents competing to purchase or carry the coast's produce. On any given day from a porch in Cahuita one might see one or another of these boats making its way along the coast just outside the white water of the reefs. Far out to sea, against the horizon, larger seafaring ships glided north toward Nicaragua and Honduras and south toward Bocas del Toro, Colón, and Cartagena.

Trading Ships

The earliest coastal trading boats were sailing ships like Maduro and Sons' *Vanguardia*. Mr. Johnson served as engineer on the *Vanguardia* for ten years, then for eight years did the same job for a Chinese tradesman, Alejandro León, on the *Cantón*, followed by twenty-two years as captain of the *Leonor* for a Greek-owned company, Mateo and Sons. On all three sailing ships turtling was the main business, supplemented by cargo and passenger runs along the coast during the off-season. Landings at coastal towns were made at the convenience of the companies, not as a public service to the communities.

Since cargo service by sea was so unreliable, coastal farmers continued to build their own dugout canoes to transport their coconuts, oil, cassava, yams, and plantains to Limón. But while they harvested their coconuts and "provisions" along the coast, the settlers were also expanding their farms into the hillsides and planting them in cocoa. The manufacturers of famous German chocolates were eager to import more raw material for their sweets, so the Niehaus Company established itself in Limón to export cocoa to Germany. Niehaus boats, the *Marta*, the *Energy*, and the *Santa Elena*, initiated regular runs to the Talamanca Coast, buying cocoa and carrying other freight and passengers.

Mr. Albert "Vincent" Guthrie was one of Old Harbour's early cocoa farmers who watched for the launch sails to "come 'round the point," signaling farmers to get their goods to the dock. Until the 1950s dried cocoa beans sold at five, ten, and fifteen colones for one hundred pounds, but Mr. Guthrie remembers one time when the price took a sudden and unexpected turn upward:

> "I give you a good joke. In the days when the cocoa price start coming up, around 1934 it was, there's two companies that used to come down here and do all the business. That was Niehaus, they were Germans, and the Limón Trading Company, that was American. So they had the launches that used to run down here. So this captain came down to buy, and the price going up to twenty colones for one hundred pounds now. That was plenty money, man. Twenty, thirty, till it reach to forty colones.
>
> So one Wednesday evening the Niehaus captain came in and as he leaving out again he say, 'Presumably I'll be back tomorrow, but if I come back tomorrow you can be sure the cocoa is going to sixty colones.' My, oh my! Everybody say, 'Cocoa at sixty colones? Could that ever be?' So everybody go home and think about it, because that would be too much money to spend!
>
> So it was Thursday around eleven o'clock. Those days everybody keep their eyes looking at the point to see if the sail come around the point, you know that launch coming. So everybody as they see the sails, they come down to the center to see what news this launch bring or what new faces come in. So when everybody came down they wanted to know if it's true cocoa go to sixty colones. The captain step off the launch and say, 'Anybody have dried cocoa? We'll pay them sixty colones a quintal.'
>
> There was an old Jamaican here that time, he felt so nice about it, he had a horse like everybody that time, and he say so all could hear, 'If cocoa go to sixty colones, I buy a gold teeth to put in me horse mouth!' And that was just an extra laugh for everybody now. So astonished he was to get so much money for cocoa. So that was a good time, but not long and the price go right down back to fifteen colones and less."

Mr. Rufus Hawkins, of Old Harbour, is a veteran of thirty years of sailing for the Niehaus Company. He and George Humphries, of Cahuita, worked together on the *Marta*, but of the seven-man crew of the *Santa Elena*, the largest pre-World War II vessel on the coast, Mr. Hawkins is the only member alive today. As he looks to sea from the porch of his house in Old Harbour, he remembers his career as second engineer:

> "We made one or two trips a week, just depends on how the freight going. And the weather. We leave out from Limón Monday, carry passengers and freight to Cahuita. It takes an hour and a half,

two hours. Just depends on how the current coming. If the current coming from the north, you come down quicker. If the current is from the east, well you got a little hard time to come down, but still you come. Don't take longer than two, three hours.

The *Santa Elena* was a real good sea boat. She had in two sixty-horse-power Atlas engine, one starboard and one port. So the two of them working same time. The engine, you could depend on them. They were all American-made. *Santa Elena* carry no sail—bare engine she have.

So we come to Cahuita, anchor outside of the Hole, and we use a small boat to come ashore with the passengers and freight. Then the sailors carry the goods to the shop or put it on the beach where the owners come and take it.

Then we go on to Old Harbour, take nearly the same amount of time. About two hours. Unload and maybe we sleep there a little. Then to Manzanillo, same thing, except now we're looking to come back, so we take on all the freight. Niehaus had two or three agents out along the coast buying cocoa, so the agent have the cocoa there and the people have their other produce. The mate, he check the goods when they come on board. Then he deliver that paper to the captain, and the captain turn in that paper to the office in Limón. They all go ashore, the captain and the mate and the sailors. But the engineer don't business with nothing more than work with the engine, so we stay on the ship.

So we come back now to Old Harbour, take freight and passengers and back to Cahuita. When the weather is real rough we can't land there."

Bad weather often prevented boats from landing at the Hole. Cahuita residents remember many long walks to and from Cahuita Point, their produce packed on horses and mules. Since little could be done to reduce the danger of the coral rocks at the Hole in a high sea, the municipal government in Limón built a dock at Cahuita Point in the late 1930s to ensure safe landings there. The dock, built of iron rails and floored with boards, lasted only a few years before the sea salt corroded the metal. Only a skeleton of it remains today.

Mr. David Buchanan, of Cahuita, had a lot of respect for the crew members and the farmers who loaded and unloaded the trading boats: "Seem like in those days people could not get tired, because those men would come lifting box and bag, and they would be there from say eight o'clock in the morning until all eight o'clock in the night, loading and unloading and, ¡que va! How we work so hard when we were young?"

Depending on the launches to carry passengers and freight could be a frustrating business. Mr. Buchanan remembers:

> "Sometimes we used to carry out the cocoa in the morning for the boat to carry it to Limón. We put it on the beast back, horse or mule, and when the sea's rough and evening come you either have to sleep with it out there or bring it back home because the launch not able to land with the sea so rough. So it can't take your freight.
>
> Sometimes launch would come here around midday taking freight. And if I'm going to Limón, I'd be there until around ten o'clock next morning waiting on the launch to load the freight. It must take all the freight before it take passengers. Occasionally it may take on one or two people before dark. And as long as six hours it could take from Limón to Cahuita; the motors very slow."

Mr. Jonathan Tyndal, of Cahuita, tells this childhood memory of launch transportation:

> "I remember once that I came here with my mother and I took sick here—fever. And they had a boat was running here by the name of *Almirante*. Maybe I was around eight years old, and they had was to take me from here and carry me down to the beach where the launch was down by old Cahuita. And they put me in the launch there, and the launch leave out in the morning and we never did reach Limón. We pass two nights on the launch out at sea, two nights. It break down and drift and drift and start again and run maybe two miles and break down again, just that way. Until some one of them decide to take the small boat and paddle it to Limón to bring parts for it. And that's the way we got to Limón. They had food on the launch."

Mr. Hawkins remembers times when his boat got marooned at Puerto Vargas for days waiting for the weather to clear until it was possible to continue the voyage.

> "We go right in at the bight in Puerto Vargas, it safer there, and sometimes we stay for days, up to fifteen days one time, till the weather get good. All about out there you see the sea breaking. High sea. You couldn't go out there at all. Was terrible them days. Was bad, bad weather. You don't see it rough as in those days now.
>
> When we get trapped there at Puerto Vargas some of the passengers go ashore and sleep in Cahuita 'cause they got

friends, and they sleep at their friends' house, who don't want to stay on board. And some stay on the boat with the crew. As long as you're passenger you get food to eat. But those were terrible times."

## The Bad-Lucky Captain

There were yet more terrible times when a captain couldn't find a place to take shelter from a storm or when he was too foolhardy to seek shelter. Mr. Johnson, Mr. Hawkins, and Mr. Humphries survived their careers on the sea without a mishap to mar their reputations as sailors, but there was one captain on the coast whose recklessness was legendary. After sinking four ships and putting another one ashoal, Juan Smith fled finally to Panama, and the residents of the Talamanca Coast breathed a collective sigh of relief.

"He was a bad-lucky captain," says Mr. Humphries of Juan Smith. "Very bad-lucky. He did like the sea work, but he was bad-lucky like hell, man."

Smith's first shipwreck occurred on the long reef circling Cahuita Point. Mr. Humphries tells what happened:

"Juan Smith was running boats along here for years. He was captain of a little boat, the *Guillermina*, and after he load up cargo at the Hole here going to Puerto Viejo with cargo and passenger, and he was playing with some girl on the launch, and the other sailors didn't pay any attention, and they got turned over right outside there that place they call Long Shoal. Sea lick them to hell. The sea was heavy that day, and they stay too near to the shore, the sea lick them. I think a little girl get drown but all the rest of the people get saved."

Mrs. Ida Corbin, then a teenager, was a passenger on the *Guillermina* that day. This is how she remembers the frightful experience:

"That time we always make coconut oil, and I was going to get the coconut in Old Harbour. The launch come, the *Guillermina*. We get on at the Hole to go to Old Harbour and we meet the accident by the reef. A woman drowned with the baby. She drowned. Oh Lord, I don't like to speak of it. She had on a lovely frock, then the sea take her away. She had her hand on her head and that towel, and when I saw the baby, the baby take long to drown. I saw the current carrying the baby out. And I was away out and one of the sailors called to me and said, 'Try to swim!' And I try to, because I can swim, you know. And I go up and I catch the baby, and the sailor go down and come up holding the baby. But he couldn't manage to hold it good, and the current, you know, the sea carried the baby out. It take long, oh Lord! I don't like to remember.

And the people on the shore in Cahuita, at that time down there had plenty houses and you see people up and down. Up and down. Until we see them shove off a canoe. And I get a cramp. And a gentleman say, 'Swim up to me!' And he said, 'Hold on to the wood!' And I catch a piece of wood and I catch it and let it go back. Catch it. Let go. And I go down back, and when I go down I could touch the rock below. I just underneath like that, so that everybody say I drown, but after I come up on a box. And when I look, I only see the fish and the sharks them chopping at the people them. And I start to sink. I go back down, and when I come up I come out near to the boat, and then I swim and I catch the rope. And then they come with the canoe.

And everybody get excited on the shore. Katherine, she cry and say, 'Lord, Ida drown!' And I say, 'No, no, no!' And they take time and shake me, shake me, and I start to vomit. I got on one of those big flower silk dress, and it torn up. The sailor understand them things, and he tie my head and say, 'Tie her good in the boat that she lie down with her head up,' and I feel terrible. I start to cry about the baby and the mother, poor soul. When I go ashore I faint. I didn't know myself and my mother and those people. And I hold my head and start to bawl."

Juan Smith had a second violent encounter with the coral rocks of Long Shoal, but without the tragedy of the *Guillermina* wreck. No lives were lost when he sent the *Leonor* ashoal, and the boat was pulled off the rocks before she broke to pieces. The bad-lucky captain removed himself to the Sixaola River where he hired on as a pilot for boats moving through the treacherous river mouth. There he sank three ships before he fled, swimming, to Panama. Mr. Hawkins tells the story:

"First time was on the *María*, he was carrying a load of sugar from Limón up the Sixaola to the [United Fruit] Company. In the morning he came in load with sugar, going in the bar. But when we look in the sea, the sea was pretty heavy, so someone said, 'But Juan Smith must be crazy this morning. What happen to him? Don't see how the sea stay? Why him taking a chance like that?' And he turn back out and gone right out to sea. And in a few minutes you see him wheel right back again. And as he wheel back now, she hit the bar. And I want to tell you how you could stay on the beach and see when the sea take her. Her stern went up in the air. And when we did see her again she was in two half on the beach. Everything gone. Every sack of sugar. I was right on the beach. And when Juan Smith come ashore he throw down himself on the sand like a man tired. I say, 'Juan, what happen, boy?' He say, 'I meet a hard wreck.' I say, 'Hard head, man, 'cause you see the sea was so heavy and it's a big load you have in.' Well, nobody drown on that ship.

Next time it was the *Cantón*, and Juan Smith was to pilot her through the bar mouth. After she was going in the bar, seem like the engine stop or the engine break down. And then she went to pieces there. One woman get drowned on her. The order from the government was that no boats was to go through that bar with no passengers. But the woman was a little hard-headed, and she didn't want to come off the boat. So it was the captain's fault, but it was her hard luck.

The last wreck he did make was in a boat we call the *Rakeback*. On that one a woman and four or five of the crew drown. They came up the river from Bridgefoot, but they came late. They start late from up there. Dark. And he missed the channel, then he turn back 'round, and the sea break on her broadside and capsize her. One woman, her son was living in Manzanillo, name of Julio Dixon. His mother drowned right on that bar. He come with his mother until they nearly get on the shore, but a sea come and break and knock them down and they part from each other. And he heard when the mother call, but he couldn't find the mother again because it was dark. And the mother drown. And that woman drift. And she drift away down to Bogue's Mouth. And one of the son was riding a horse by a farm down by Bogue's Mouth, and he saw in the surf a dead person up and down. So he get off the horse. He didn't know it was his mother neither. So he run down on the beach and there he saw it was his mother. He get men and carry her to Bocas to bury her."

Juan Smith swam from the wreck of the *Rakeback* to the Panama shore and didn't come back to Costa Rica till he was an old man. He met his death not on the sea, but in the street. Mr. Hawkins recalls, "A few years ago he was back in Limón, he couldn't see very good, and he was coming from the dock, going home, and a car bounce him and kill him. He died on the land, but on sea he was always lucky. He was very risky, take plenty of chance, but nothing ever happen to him on the sea. He always get ashore."

Despite the dangers, the delays, and the inconvenience of sea travel, the people of the coast had to depend on it to market their produce and purchase their goods. Trading companies in Limón thrived on their business dealings with the coast farmers. It was, as Mr. Kayasso said, "not Limón build Cahuita, but Cahuita did build Limón." The prosperity of the Niehaus Company, Maduro and Sons, Mateo and Sons, Alejandro León, the Limón Trading Company, and the United Fruit Company depended on the productivity of the Talamanca farmers as much as the farmers depended on the companies for transportation.

### The Niehaus Company and World War II

Of the Limón-based trading companies, the German Niehaus Company was probably the most powerful until World War II brought its business to an abrupt halt. Rufus Hawkins, a Niehaus employee for thirty years, tells the story of the company's collapse:

"Niehaus had a big shop right where you see the National Bank in Limón now. That whole block was for Niehaus until the war started. They had big ships carry the cocoa to Germany, bring back foodstuffs, furniture, plates, dishes, all kinds of wares they sell at the store.

I have a bed right here I bought from Niehaus when I was working for them. And I have that bed up to this day. Spring bed, came from Germany. Good good good spring bed.

That time the United Fruit Company had a big commissary right by the park there, and they used to sell stuff, too. But Niehaus used to worry them plenty because people always crave for the German things 'cause Germany always make some good stuff. Well, after Hitler take possession in Germany, the ship used to come out to Limón, a big passenger boat and also freight boat, and they used to fly a fire-red flag. So everybody begin to wonder, why these ship them fly that kind of flag? That flag mean war. Well, nobody didn't know what it is, but Hitler know what he was doing.

Well, afterward the war break out. Then around 1942 the *San Pablo* sink in Limón harbor. The *San Pablo* was a U.S. boat, used to run from Boston for the United Fruit Company, carry bananas. They say it's a German submarine sink her right against the Limón dock. Well, that night me and the subcaptain of the port was talking right in front the Arasty Theater, and we never hear when the first bomb went off. We hear the last one 'cause that one kill every light in Limón. The whole town was in darkness. They hear that one away in Siquirres. That one was heavy. So I take a walk next morning to the dock, and I see the *San Pablo* sink, half in the water, half out the water, lay down on her side. Many people died in that rush. Plenty men aboard there, and they all died.

Just after that they send a boat from the U.S. name of *Crusader*. She came out and bring men to weld up the side where it burst, and they float her and take her to Cristóbal. Well, from that she never come back to Costa Rica.

When they sink the *San Pablo*, the government take everything the Niehaus have 'cause they was German people. About three or four weeks after that, a ship came in from the United States, pick up all the German them. All those Germans all about in the bush here, Cahuita, hiding. Take up the whole of them, carry them up to the States to concentration camp. One morning I see the train come in from San José. Must be eight or nine coach and bare German aboard. And they went to Guatemala, pick up what Germans was there, and carry them to the States to concentration camp. They made a petition to the government for one man to come back because he married in this country and had children here. So he could come back. But the others couldn't come back till years afterward a few did come.

But the Niehaus treat me pretty good. All the crew in that Niehaus ship get good treatment. Get good pay and good feeding. After the *San Pablo* sink, the government take the ship over and it go right down. First thing they do was cut the pay. And the foodstuff was poor. I stay about two months, then I quit. Niehaus was German all right, but I can't give them a bad name. They treat me pretty good."

There's much speculation in Limón concerning the sinking of the *San Pablo*. Some say maybe the United Fruit Company was jealous of the good business its German competitors were doing in Limón. Could they have sunk their own ship and blamed it falsely on the German Navy? Or did the U.S. Navy sink her, say it was a German submarine, and thereby convince Costa Rica to strengthen its support of the Allied cause? The rumors are fed by the fact that the United Fruit Company crew members were safely on shore when the explosion occurred; only Limón dock workers were on board the *San Pablo* when she was struck. Whatever the truth is, the results were immediate for German businessmen in Limón: many were exiled and all their property was confiscated, including the Niehaus Company's two coastal trading boats, the *Energy* and the *Santa Elena*.

A Community Tramline

Though boats from the other Limón companies continued to sail the coast for two more decades, the people of the coast made use of the disasters of World War II to provide for themselves an option to travel and trade by land transportation. The World War that ruined the Niehaus business also closed down the Penshurst Banana Company, which had been operating its private train between the Estrella River and Old Harbour, transporting bananas. The company had never offered passenger or freight service on its tracks, and when its business closed down workers started taking up the rails, moving them out to a United Fruit Company abaca farm on the San José-Limón line. But the people of Cahuita were quick to protest. Mr. Johnson recalls the beginnings of the community-operated tramline:

> "We make a committee and we went to the President of the country and ask him to give us power to keep those tracks. We call to the company and they come back and fix the track, but they didn't do the thing right, and they leave it. People out here, we couldn't get help. Then I got the privilege from the Municipality in Limón to take those lumber off that old iron dock at Cahuita, and I brought it up here and fix up the bridges along the track. And I brought a man from Limón and the president of the Municipality, I invite him and we had a meeting here, and we form the *Junta de Tranvía* [Tramline Committee] to take charge of the tramline. Was me, David Buchanan, William Tabash, and Carlos Lam on the *Junta*. And we have men to work, keep the tracks good, fix the bridges. That was Frank Buchner and Lester Johnson do that work along with some others.
> And this is how we get the money to do these works: Each sack of cocoa that go out on the tramline pay two colones. The merchant that buy the cocoa is responsible for that. As he get the cocoa, he pay two colón each sack to the collector we have there for the *Junta*. And we take that money in the *Junta* and buy the materials for the tramline and pay three laborers to go out to do their works. We put collector in Old Harbour, one in Cahuita, one Penshurst, so wherever the merchant buy the cocoa, is there he pay the *Junta*."

In Old Harbour, Hone Creek, and Cahuita, enterprising individuals bought used freight cars from the company or built themselves wooden carts that could be drawn along the train tracks by mules. They agreed to a schedule and offered their neighbors passenger and freight service along the tramline between Old Harbour and Penshurst. For a while, Mr. Mason extended a service south of Old Harbour to the Cocles River with a cow cart.

Finally the coast residents had a reasonable alternative to sea travel. The land route was cheaper for passengers, at one colón from Cahuita to Penshurst by mule cart, and two colones from Penshurst to Limón by train, versus the six colones charge on the boats. It was hardly luxury travel, however. Cars fell off the tracks. Rain blew under the canvas "shed." Under the best conditions the nine-kilometer ride between Cahuita and Penshurst took two hours. And then in 1948 a flood on the Estrella River carried away the banana company's bridge. Until 1976 the people would have to cross the Estrella in canoes.

Nonetheless, the tramline was a great improvement for coastal transportation. Passengers, producers, mule-car operators, and merchants all cooperated with the community *Junta de Tranvía* through its two decades of service.


## "It Can Be Done"

This chapter concerning transportation and trade from 1915 through 1948 cannot be brought to a close without mention of the first truck to spin its wheels and grind its gears and get stuck in the mud on the Talamanca Coast. Mr. Sorrows tells the story:

> "There was a man here during the Twenties. His name was Herbert Wilson, and he was an agent for the Niehaus Company here. He had the ambition that something could be done here so he brought in a truck. Landed it from a boat. That truck used to work just in the Cahuita area because there was no way out. There was no tramway. They used it for hauling cocoa from the people's house to the Hole where the launch used to load the cocoa. People would dry the cocoa and have it stored up in the house and when they ready to sell, the truck would draw it from the house to the Hole. The remains of that truck is still out there by Carlos Vas' house.
>
> It was an ancient-days truck because it was a solid-tire truck, the tire was welded on. To start the engine you have to crank it. The man said that something can be done here so he put a sign on it say, 'It can be done.' The people look at the truck and say, 'It can be done.'"

Another man who had faith that something could be done on the Talamanca Coast was Augustus Mason. In the mid-1940s Mr. Mason got the idea to build a plane landing strip in Old Harbour. "I went to Turtle Bogue once and I see the plane base there, and I just imagine that something could be done here. And I come back and build that base by where you see the health dispensary. I made it with pick and shovel and cows taking out the logs. I spent eight thousand colones on it in the Forties. The first plane that land here was Vanoli plane. I forget what year, but it was the 20th of April. He land here without I give him invitation."

His faith intact, Mr. Mason waited for his plane base to prove itself useful.

Deirdre Hyde

The community tramline.

# 12. Community Life and Organization

Cahuita and Old Harbour were busy communities in the years between 1915 and 1948, supporting populations nearly as large as they are today. The Hone Creek area contained only a few farmers until the Penshurst Banana Company evacuated the area during the Second World War, leaving thousands of hectares of cleared land for new families to claim and cultivate. Grape Point, Manzanillo, and Monkey Point existed nearly as they do today, with smaller populations and fewer social organizations than their neighboring communities to the north. Gandoca came into existence in the late 1940s as the site of Guido Castro's logging company; most of the Gandoca settlers were—and still are—ladinos rather than blacks.

Community life on the coast was centered around shops, churches, schools, sports clubs, and the government office.

The New Town of Cahuita

In Cahuita the first shop established at the Bluff belonged to Dimesio Joseti, a Spanish man who sold out to a Chinese proprietor, Alejandro León, in 1922. Hilma and Alberto Lam now operate the business in the original location purchased by Mrs. Lam's father. A second Chinese businessman, Isaac Lee, located his shop adjoining the León property. William Nassin, a Lebanese butcher, started his career in Cahuita with a meat shop, establishing a larger store in 1918. His sons, the Tabash brothers, operate the establishment today. Another Lebanese, known as Mr. Lazarus, put up a business on the main street, later selling it to "Uncle Sam" Williams who operated it until his son Leslie (Mr. Sorrows) took it over. A Spanish man, Mr. Castro, moved his business from old Cahuita to the new town around 1920.[1]

In addition to these privately owned businesses, a local farmers' cooperative operated two shops during the 1920s, one at the present-day

---

[1] This account of Cahuita business history was given by Mr. Selles Johnson.

167

site of Solon's establishment, another down the Black Beach road, a path leading north from Cahuita to Little Bay. Mr. Sorrows, whose father was active in the cooperative, gives this account of the history of that organization:

> "The farmers in the Twenties formed a cooperative. They had two groceries, and they went on fairly good for a couple years. But the men who were on the administrative board hadn't good ability to manage them. They used to deal with the Limón Trading Company, and the business run bankrupt, and the Limón Trading Company took over their properties. And the Limón Trading Company had it functioning, they employed people to work in it, until the shops were finally sold out, one to my father, and the one up the beach, a Chinaman bought it. That went areef in the Thirties. My father was an associate in it. It had a cocoa farm, too. They paid people to work on it, and the income would go to the cooperative."

Through the international trade of the Limón shipping companies, the Cahuita shops were well stocked with goods that old-time residents remember with pleasure. Mr. Humphries works up an appetite remembering:

> "Them days Cahuita here, in the shops you get pig tail, pig nose, salt beef, all those things you get, butter. A woman there name Miss Castro, very nice Spanish woman, did a nice business there. You get codfish, real good codfish, about an inch thick. You don't see those codfish any more for years. Pig tail, pig nose, all them things we always get in barrels, salt beef, they always come from the States and from England. White codfish, clean and pretty, you can eat it raw. Very nice. We cook it with ackee."

The Baptist Church and St. Mark's moved to new locations at the Bluff around 1920. By then a Seventh Day Adventist congregation had established itself at its present location. Jehovah's Witnesses began meeting in the home of Ella Brown, whose house was later replaced with the present Kingdom Hall.


Schools: English and Spanish

The Baptist, Adventist, and Anglican congregations cooperated in offering space and partial financing for English schools. It wasn't so difficult in those years to find English teachers. Many qualified teachers had immigrated to Costa Rica from Jamaica. The difficulty was in keeping them satisfied in the isolated communities of the Talamanca Coast. David Buchanan explains, "In Cahuita you see the most of the parents were not able to find money to pay the teacher's salary. So the teachers would come and stay for a while and have to go. Every once in a while the people used to give the teacher what we call provision: yam and yuca and pumpkin, plantain, and so forth, for support. They could not pay her."

Parents organized school boards to hire and pay English teachers and to maintain the classroom in a home or church. A popular form of fund raising for the schools was giving concerts. Fred Ferguson remembers one teacher in particular who helped the School Board organize lively shows to bring in funds for the school. "There was one teacher, Mary Davis, she came from Twenty-eight Miles. What cause me to remember Mary Davis so much was because she always put on some real good concert. She could play piano and organ and guitar—I don't know what music that woman never play."

The Adventist and Baptist churches in those days had pedal organs, Mr. Johnson remembers, and Jamaican teachers like Priscilla Wier were well-versed in Shakespeare, so the concerts were sometimes events of sophisticated English culture. "The Church of England made plenty concerts those days," Mr. Johnson says. "They put on all kind of play, sell food and cakes, bun, bami,[1] ginger beer. They was lively people those times."

A long series of English teachers taught for a time in Cahuita and also in Old Harbour. "One teacher would stop, and the next one would come and take it up again," Fred Ferguson says. But there were times when one teacher left in mid-year with no one to take his or her place, with the result that a child's schooling was often interrupted. Some parents who were very concerned that their children should receive an adequate education became discouraged and relocated in Limón.

---

[1] Bami is a dry yuca (cassava) cake made by the old-time Jamaicans. Mrs. Adine Bryant tells how her mother made it: "First she grater the yuca and get a piece of flour sack and put the yuca and a little salt in that cloth. And she squeeze out all the juice from the yuca so it dry, dry, dry. After it come in a lump. And she get a sieve and she sieve out and throw away the coarse pieces. And she put some into a pot, a round pot, and make the pot hot and throw in a little salt. And she cover it up. And after it kind of steam, she put in a little more and she turn it over and leave it bake about fifteen minutes. So I see my mother do it. And it come round and thick, just like the bottom of the pot. That come from Jamaica. They eat it all the time with pear [avocado] or fish."

David Buchanan remembers:

"In 1933 my father sold a portion of his property and took us out to Limón so we could get a little English, because there were no teachers here. It was so hard and so difficult, and so I remember hearing him say he was going to sell out a portion. And he rented a house in Limón and put us there. We were there for many years. He send us to English school only, we the older ones. Afterward he send the younger ones to Spanish school."[1]

The government sent Spanish teachers to Cahuita as early as 1920 and to Old Harbour beginning in 1927, but the Spanish schools didn't win the confidence of the Afro-Caribbean people until years later. Joseph Spencer describes one problem faced by teachers from the Central Valley:

"Most of the time there was no Spanish teacher in Cahuita because the Spanish couldn't stand the climate. So they come and stay about three days, they get the yellow fever or malaria, and they go right back. There was only one Spanish teacher I remember in all those years who wasn't so sickly. He was the only one that spend a year out here in my days."

Selven Bryant talks about the early Spanish school in Old Harbour:

"In 1927 a Spanish teacher come here. Well, he just teach first grade. Every one of them come teach first grade. They come from San José and they couldn't stand the climate here, sometimes they spend three months, go away, next six months before the next one come. And all of them come teaching only first grade. Over and over and over till 1942 they start to teach second and third, and around 1945 they start to teach fourth and fifth, and afterward sixth grade. That's why the Cahuita people speak more Spanish than we could, because they have Spanish school all the time."

After 1930 they did have Spanish school all the time in Cahuita, but only first and second grades for many years. Mrs. Pearl Cunningham remembers:

---

[1] The English-speaking people of the Talamanca Coast refer to the govern-ment-supported public school as "Spanish school," as opposed to their privately financed English schools.

"Oh, yes, yes, we have Spanish school from I was small, from I have sense. But only two grades, first grade, second grade, first grade, second grade, first grade, second grade, like so. How long you can keep going first grade, second grade? So just a few people send their childen there. Everybody was English school, English school. Only since Figueres come and built that new school there, all the colored people send their children to Spanish school and English school."

The Universal Negro Improvement Association

An organization that was especially effective in promoting English education as well as cultural and social programs was the UNIA: The Universal Negro Improvement Association. Mr. Marcus Garvey founded the organization in his homeland, Jamaica, in 1919. Two years later he arrived in Limón on the organization's Black Star Line ship, the *Frederick Douglas*, to establish a branch in Costa Rica. Garvey was no stranger in Limón, having worked as a timekeeper for the United Fruit Company on the Old Lines in 1916 and 1917. When he returned he registered the UNIA with the government, published the constitution, and gave a well-remembered speech at the ballground in Limón. Marcus Garvey established a world-wide reputation as a leader of black people and a champion of human rights. The UNIA branches that were organized in Old Harbour, Cahuita, and Penshurst played a vital role in the life of these communities from the 1920s through the 1940s.

Mr. John Burke, of Cahuita, first joined the UNIA during his years in Cuba, later participating in activities of the Limón branch. He gives this explanation of the purposes and programs of the UNIA:

"In Cuba I joined an association called the Universal Negro Improvement Association. I was secretary there for quite a few months. That was in Garvey's days; he was the organizer. The idea was to organize the Negro people to have one substantial idea of who they are, where they are from. Because the facts had been hidden by the other people.

Garvey gave us a lot of lessons, let us understand the position that we were in. Because we were told in the early days that the colored people were very much inferior. So Garvey go and get the history from Africa, and then we find out that the Negroes were ruling the world before, but through their waywardness God turned them down. Sin came in, and they were taken away like Israel as slaves. That was how a certain amount of people came to Jamaica, Barbados, Trinidad, all around the West Indies. So Garveyism came in to let us understand more about ourselves, our people. And it really did help. It's a big history.

The UNIA only want to bring the people together to understand about their history and to expect a better future. They had plans for better education. Liberia was a substantial country in Africa where all the most intelligent Negroes went to get a certain amount of training. And they were building Liberia as the first independent republic. And it is the first independent republic in Africa. But in Barbados and Jamaica they had teachers trained in Liberia to give a better education to the colored children than what was being given by the other teachers before.

When I came here I attended several meetings in Limón. Mr. Mitchell was the president. They had instruction of the past history of the Negro people and plans for the future. Today a good amount of the people, this new generation, didn't seem to take much of that teaching. They got some of it, but they never had it as how we had it in the older days. Because, you see we suffered more with the white people in the older days, so then we were determined to have a way out, that we could have our own administration.

So under that strain the UNIA worked a lot. They had a school and they teach the same English and the history. Take like the history of the West Indies under the British control. The history that we got from England, you see, they give it their way. We got to make with a different one altogether for the colored people.

You know, from the early days some of the colored people never believe there was any equality with the whites. And Garveyism bring that matter in. They had a way of saying everything got to be 'yes, sir; yes, sir,' but you see Garvey let us know it wasn't necessary under that compulsory way. So to me and to the whole world, Garveyism meant that the rest of the African nations, after Liberia, were so organized that today we have thirty-two independent nations in the continent of Africa. That's the fruit of Garveyism. And now the United Nations cannot take any advantage because those thirty-two nations are voting, while in the early days it weren't so. And it's still going along hard because up to now there are two African nations still holding out the strain. But I'm sorry for those two nations. If they don't put up that old idea it's going to be destructive for them. South Africa and Rhodesia they are. Because it is said, God make all men equal. Garveyism came on the scene and opened that trail.

Garvey went up to the States and did wonderful work in the States. And there were some plots made up to get him back to

Jamaica, but when he return back to Jamaica he became a member of the Legislative Council. That help him now to force the law and the proper instruction for the colored people in Jamaica and all around, because the Association was all around different countries.

When I came to Costa Rica you could scarcely find a colored man in any kind of important position. Now and then you may find one. But the work of the UNIA in Limón with the assistance of the Costa Rican government make plenty changes. I never get the opportunity to have a talk with the last governor they have in Limón. I have it in mind, but never get the chance. I was to give him a word of encouragement that I live to see in the Province of Limón we had a Negro governor. It was something wonderful. And when I went into the post office in Limón, and I saw the young man there in charge of the post office, I said, 'Very good!' I could see the improvement of Garveyism along with the assistance of the Costa Rican government. And in many other departments. I'm pleased to see it."

Mr. Selven Bryant remembers the establishment of the Old Harbour branch of the UNIA:

"You have men come in from Limón, and afterward they form a branch with president from right here, and secretary, treasurer and all. Practically all the families around was in it. They was trying to unite the people, get all the Negroes together, say they was fighting to go to Africa, to go home back, for they claim that Africa was the home of the Negroes. But they didn't succeed in that part of it. But you had about two men come from Africa here visit all the UNIA branch."

The large UNIA Hall in Old Harbour is still standing, although the branch is inactive today. Mr. Mason recounts building the UNIA Liberty Hall in 1922:

"That was the first board building in Puerto Viejo. All the lumber they cut with a hand saw and drag by men, women, and children by night and day, from the woodland to build that building. For about fifteen years the UNIA was strong in Old Harbour. It was through the UNIA we get English teachers here and they form a school board. We always wear the UNIA uniform. The colors of the flag was red, black, and green, so we make tie, shirt, dress out of those same colors. We were always marching, have Scouts, give concert. Now we realize it was something great."

Old Harbour people say Miss Daisy Lewis was one of the greatest singers and actresses to perform on the Liberty Hall stage. "What a voice that woman had! How I used to love to sit and listen to her sing!" says her neighbor Clinton Bennett. Today, at the age of sixty, Miss Daisy nostalgically remembers the concerts and plays that she enjoyed in her youth:

"Anytime a program coming out, we put a notice at the shop here and send some to Cahuita and Manzanillo, inviting the people them. In those days, they had to walk or come in boat if the sea is good. But it always be crowded. When the people hear a program, they is coming!

Sometimes we win prizes for the best singer, the best musician. Once I played the organ and I won the prize; I won two books. Mr. Roper had an organ at his home and I went there every evening at 4 o'clock to practice. I had to work in the farm in the day, and sometimes I come out late, and then I had to run and practice. But I love music, and I was interested. And the little that I get, I grasp it. The piece I played came out of religious books: *Children Hozanna* and *Choral Praise*.

In those days, when we are going to have a dance, a group of boys here always be the musician, such as Vibert Myrie play the trumpet, Dudley Waite play the guitar, Clarence Patterson play the drum, and we had this great man Mr. Lewellyn from Hone Creek and sometimes he comes to accompany on the clarinet. We had sacred concert and we had rag concert. Rag concert is a joke, just to make people laugh.

One of the best piece we always have was the parson. The Baptist minister, his church was full, and the minister preaching and telling the people them not to do wrong things. But meanwhile he's preaching, some people come in on the other side of the stage away from the church, and they start to dance with a sweet music. And one of the church members gone over to them. And so on and so on, and when the parson look, only one member leave in the church. Everybody take off and gone to the dance. Total, the music get sweeter and sweeter, and when the parson look, the one member gone. And after, him put down the Bible and him take off him gown and him start to dance. The people always like that joke.

One time we made Noah's Ark. We had to get a lot of cardboard to make this big boat. And then we had some very strange animal, ugly animal, all kinds, and everything by pair. So they all going in the ark, and as they go they all make sounds: the horse going 'neeeeigh,' the pig going 'ugh, ugh,' the cow going, 'muuuu, muuuu.' Oh, the people love that. And everyone have on his costume, mask, tail and all, and we walk on we knee. A lot of children have to act in that for the small animals.

And when everybody get inside now, the door close. And the rain start to fall. Somebody outside pouring water! And the rain can't stop. And then the people come around, some of them with their babies, begging, 'Lord, have mercy on us. Master Noah, open up the door and take us in.' It was a little solemn, too, you know. You see all the people all outside begging. Some of we try to tear down the ark. We try to perform it just how we read of it in the Bible. And after, we just throw down ourselves around the ark. We were dead people. And then they draw the curtain."

Miss Daisy Lewis lets coconuts dry in half-shells to sell as copra.

In addition to its cultural and educational programs, the UNIA wanted to demonstrate that it could make real the dream of black people of returning to Africa. The organization's ships of the Black Star Line docked in ports throughout the Caribbean and welcomed the people on board. Mr. Mason remembers a time when the *Frederick Douglas* made a stop in Port Limón, and people were invited to go on board to take a look. He says he met the captain of the ship, "a black black man named Cockburn. He was the first black captain sailed over the ocean."

175

Mr. Humphries, who was working on the docks in Limón at the time, also remembers the ship's stay in the port:

> "They did have a big place for the UNIA in Limón. They sell the ticket there for the people to go look on the ship. People come all in from the country. Train make special excursions to bring them in. All the day you see people on the docks there looking at the ship. I think it stay there for one day and then it went down to Bocas. I hear when it get to *Almirante* they just throw a rope off the boat, they didn't even use winch, the people alone them haul in the ship to the dock. They was so glad to see that ship. They claim the ship was to go to Africa."

In Cahuita the UNIA Hall was located on the lot where John Burke now lives. It was the site of many concerts and meetings, sometimes serving as a classroom for the English schools. The UNIA also operated a grocery store in Cahuita for a number of years.

The popularity of the organization declined in the 1930s when Marcus Garvey was experiencing legal difficulties in the United States. Although the Limón branch remains active, the organization no longer functions along the Talamanca Coast.


Midwives and Snake Doctors

As the years passed it became easier to transport sick people from the coast to the hospital in Limón, but the business of keeping coastal people healthy remained largely in the hands of midwives and snake doctors. Some of the midwives, like Joseph Spencer's mother, had received nurses' training in Jamaica. Mr. Frankie McLeod, of Cahuita, remembers an old woman that everyone called Mother Rob, who tended pregnant women in the Cahuita area:

> "Mother Rob was a woman that was studied. She had books that she was dealing with. I used to visit Mother Rob's home, and all the time you see her studying. If woman wanting to give birth and could not, Mother Rob is certainly sure that she know what to use that that woman give birth. She was a old lady. She went away back to San Andrés, I guess. There's one herb that's a famous herb that I always see the midwife plant in their yard. It is called pennyroyal. And this thyme that we use for cooking."

Mrs. Adine Bryant, of Old Harbour, remembers Eunice Dixon, the midwife who tended her when she was bearing her children. She says,

"Those old days, midwife was the doctor. Nobody go to Limón to doctor. The midwife have a way how to sound you. She have pills called Indian Root pill. You have to take that a certain amount of times, certain months. And at a certain month you take some castor oil. If you not feeling good she come and tell you how that baby set and tell you what to drink and how to do. When you take that Indian Root pill you have good time for have the baby, you don't have no trouble, and the baby born healthy.

When you feel pain you send and call for the midwife, and she come. The mother, sister, good friend may assist her. And about five days after the baby come, she give you a dose of castor oil and black beer. You don't see that black beer anymore. The bottle have a bulldog on it and an English cork, band down with wire, and when you open it you hear it make a noise, 'pluuuumm!' And then now you have to drink wine to build up the body.

The midwife stay nine days while the mother in bed. She cook and wash and tend to the baby, make hot bath for the mother. And then after nine days she finish and she charge twenty-five colón. In those days it was much money.

The midwife, as she look at you, she can tell if you making baby. And she tell you what kind of baby, whether boy or girl. And when she look at the afterbirth she know how many more baby you to have."

Mrs. Bryant's husband, Selven, talks about the effectiveness of the Old Harbour snake doctors, claiming that their skill was superior to the methods doctors now use in Limón to treat snakebite:

"These days you have to go to Limón. Everything change. Those days there was no way out, so you just dead or get better. Just like snakebite. Look how many people now go to hospital and dead for snakebite. And in those early days nobody dead for snakebite. You have three good snake doctors 'round here, a man name of Nathan, and Johnson Deen and Francisco Downer. Don't care what kind of snake bite you. They have their bush they give you and something make you to vomit up that poison, and nine days you well again."

In the Cahuita area, Edward Masters gained a great reputation as a snake doctor. Mr. Jonathan Tyndal tells how Mr. Masters cured snakebite with a "Belgium Stone":

"Edward Masters used to cure a lot of people from snakebite. He know a lot of bush remedy, and also he had a little stone, they call that the Belgium Stone. When the snake rip you, you put that stone

177

on there and it hold, it stick right there. And he give you medicine to drink, and when you see that stone drop off, you are free.

He put it on my foot. One of them black tommy-goff [*tamagá*], a bad snake, bite me. I was working down Black Beach cutting banana, and I step over a log and it hit me on my foot. And I ride the mule and I stop by Masters, and he put the stone on it, and I come home. The stone stay on about five days. It's a little stone about an inch in length and it black. But you got to keep it into a glass of milk. He give me bush to drink and tell me what to eat: roast plantain and soda biscuit, drink black coffee, don't use no sugar nor salt. He told me that I wasn't to have no argument with no woman at all. Don't let them come look for me.

But one day a woman come to the window there, and I sit down on the bed, and she was there speaking with me. I never feel bad, and she was there around fifteen minutes. And after that I feel my head just going that way, and a bad feeling take me. And it look like she did know, and she leave same time and went away. When snake bite you, you not to let woman see you nor nothing. It's funny.

But I know snake bit a man once in the bush. At that time the women them used to go into the bush to break the cocoa, so they went out breaking with that man on his farm. And the snake bite him. And after the snake bite him he run going to the women and the women say, 'No, no, no, no! We not to speak to you nor nothing.' But him say, 'But no one is here now. You got to help me. Help me now to tie this place.' And they tie it and then he come out."

Festivities and Holidays

Through the 1950s the people of the Talamanca Coast organized many forms of community entertainment that have since disappeared. Only the older people still remember celebrating the traditional Caribbean holidays of Easter Monday (the Monday after Easter Sunday), Slavery Day (anniversary of the abolition of slavery in the British colonies) and Harvest. There were also ocasional concerts and plays as well as gatherings every Sunday which were known as Pleasant Sunday Afternoons. Mr. Paul Rodman reflects on these social activities:

"The Jamaicans had a tendency to organize themselves in groups for cultural reasons. They had fraternal meetings and singings and all kind of thing. We had schools and churches that give concerts all the time, and educated people would come from Jamaica and they would have competition between the different villages in plays, Shakespeare, recitals and singing groups.

Among our people there were many that were interested in seeing to it that culture was sustained and maintained as far as they could. And they try to advance. At this moment, I would say we are behind the achievement that was made up to the late 1940s.

Concerts were Saturday or Sunday night affairs. It would be songs or dancing or plays. And we had Pleasant Sunday Afternoons that were semi-religious programs. There would be hymns and plays with biblical themes. These things were organized by people in the community with the teacher and some other women that would come in like social workers. There was one woman in Hone Creek, Cahuita had a few, some were UNIA people, and they would train the people in singing, plays, everything. All the people would come together in the schoolroom evenings and nights and practice. That was the only diversion we have.

You had quite a few people who knew music. Most people had organs—pedal organs—in those days. They were cheap to buy, and families had pride in buying an organ as soon as they had a girl child, for it was considered mostly for girls. But you had a few boys who could play it. In those days if you had a girl child and didn't buy a sewing machine or an organ, you could lose your wife! The organs were old, but they were making a lot of nice music.

We performed a lot of plays that dealt with English history. They were directed by Mr. Cranston and the teacher before him, a colored man from Cambridge, England: Mr. Chambers. He made a lot of drama from English history, all those kings: Georges and Edwards, and hell, he used to get me mad. He made me act as King Edward once, and I didn't like King Edward nohow because I had to write so much essays about King Edward that I'd get mad. And Shakespeare, he used to love him, too. Teacher Cranston, also.

On the Pleasant Sunday Afternoons you had recitals and singing from school children—solos, duets, choruses—and then the big people used to participate, too. You had women would sing and men would come up and give a recital in their own primitive way, but anyhow they did something.

You had a guy here, Mr. Barnard. He could play a singing saw, but he could only play one tune on it: Rock of Ages. So he was famous for the first ten times when he play it on the Pleasant Sunday Afternoon. Then, after-ward, everybody know what he was going to play, but still everybody listened to him."

In those days, Holy Week was a solemn, sacred holiday; special services and programs were held in all the churches along the coast. But the day after Easter Sunday was known as Easter Monday, and it was a great day for merrymaking. Mr. Selven Bryant remembers:

"On Good Friday some of the people went out to Limón, where they always make procession in the streets. Then on Easter Sunday they have special service in the churches, where the children recite. And they always have a program at the UNIA Liberty Hall; everybody sing and recite.

But the fiesta come on Easter Monday. On that day you had cricket match, baseball game, you dance the May Pole, play bull's-eye, make picnic. And you always had horse race on Easter Monday. Say the race is here, then the men from Cahuita, from all along the coast, they ride they horse down here the Saturday, rest off Sunday, and then the race is on Monday. And afterward they make dance. Easter Monday was a big fiesta, man.

They have a big cooking: rice and beans and soup, and the food was cheap, fifty cents a plate. About four or five women go together and cook. They kill cow and get the bones and make soup, and cook up the meat and yam and cassava. They make ice cream in the bucket and sell, and everybody eat."

Mr. Selven also recalls celebrating Slavery Day:

"Slavery Day, when slavery abolish in England, that was a fiesta day. Eating and drinking, kill cow and pig, have horse race, cricket, everything. That day England turn over all the islands, give them their freedom, no more slaves.

All Jamaicans celebrate that day. But they don't keep it up no more. We don't even remember it again; it just abolish. 'Round in the Sixties it die out. It was just the old Jamaican them was keeping up that, and the young set just don't worry with it again."

Miss Daisy Lewis describes the traditional Harvest festival:

"We always celebrate the Harvest in the churches and in the UNIA. It is in December month, when you have the cocoa crop come in. Everybody bring in the best, the biggest fruits what they have: plantain, banana, coconut, sugar cane, yam. But you bring in the biggest, prettiest ones. And you carry it and leave it on the rostrum. In the service now everybody give thanks to God with hymns and prayers, and then the next day is the selling of all the fruit. We use the money to help the school or the UNIA or something that the community need."

Mr. Cyril Gray remembers how Christmas was celebrated in Old Harbour and Hone Creek:

"At Christmas, some of the homes keep dance, merrymaking. In the old days when I came here, is from house to house dance. There wasn't so much people, and everybody were friends. No one was thinking himself better than the other. We come to your house and we eat and we drink and go on to the next house and we eat and we drink. For the Christmas and New Year, go to church, come back and dance again and eat and drink. That was the habit of Old Harbour people from here right to Hone Creek. Used to live good, live loving. But today you are living with fear. Of late, you have a dance, you have to get a policeman. In the old days, no. Everything change now."

Horse Racing

The decades before World War II were a great era for the sportsmen along the Talamanca Coast. Competition in horse racing, cricket, skitlolly, and baseball drew crowds of spectators on Sundays and holidays. Excursion boats carried teams and their fans from their home communities to the site of the competition. Women prepared great pots of "rice and beans,"[1] buns, sweets and ginger beer for the picnics that followed the sports matches. Dance bands from the communities or imported from Limón played Caribbean tunes long into the night.

The horse racers of Cahuita chopped out a nine hundred-yard path through the coconut walk between Kelly Creek and Duncan Creek for their race track. In Old Harbour races were run right along the sandy beach. Champions from the Talamanca Coast competed on race tracks throughout Limón Province and even in Cartago. Trading and breeding and training and doctoring horses were serious and time-consuming matters for the great horsemen of the coast. From Cahuita they were Selles Johnson with his champions Caribbean, Sir Edward, and Surprise; George Humphries with his pride Sonny Boy; Naman Temple with Scamp; and David Kayasso with his mysterious Indian-named Walpa. Old Harbour horse racers included Selven Bryant with his Bell Boy and Whitewater; Edward Myrie with Noel; William (Paul) Rodman with Milkman; Hunter Klines with Kid; and Nelson Douglas with Escape. A formidable Manzanillo competitor was Francis Hudson with his two horses, Rabbit and Shamrock.

---

[1] Jamaican-style "rice and beans," also known as "rice and peas," is a traditional dish of red beans and white rice cooked together with coconut milk.

Mr. Johnson tells about the races and his own methods of caring for his famous horses:

"We commenced to have races here in 1939. They were over the creek there, we had a race track that was nine hundred yards. I had three horses. One was the name of Sir Edward, one Surprise, and the other one Caribbean. The Old Harbour people they brought theirs and we had races. We always charge two colón for the games. There was music too, from Limón. We had dances and other things, and you bet your money. All those money from betting, we take out twenty percent for the race track. I get that money and I pay laborers to keep the track clean.

Just across Kelly Creek where the race finish we had a big booth area where we keep the dance. It was an open spot, and they make booth there. We sell *fresco*, we sell food, we sell everything. Holiday! Every Easter Monday we did have horse race and big fiesta. You had a good time there. You had music. That's why we charge two colón for everybody that goes over, because we have to pay the musicians too. So you go over and bet your money, and somebody else win your money, and that's the way it goes. And then you eat and drink and dance and enjoy yourself. Excursion come in from Limón, Siquirres, all about, people coming to the race. Plenty of people. And dance the whole night, you see.

We had good times, good times. And I took my horse and go out to Siquirres and run him. I win! I lose too, but I win too. And in Cartago they had a pretty track, round. You start here, circle the track. You got a hill to go up and then you turn, circle 'round and come back. They had big houses and everything. You could take horse and lock them up in there. The feeding come to him, you only pay, you know. And everything comfortable. And all that place was destroy. They had a big disaster with the volcano, destroy up everything. But before that it was a very good place.

My horse, I use them for work. They not just for sport, you know. I tell you straight. Sir Edward was the greatest horse on the tramline. That horse was the greatest horse. Him pull anything. The name Sir Edward did fit him.

Surprise was a little horse I bought in Penshurst, and he fell into a cave once, and got his foot there half broken. And I bathe him, care him, rub him. I have a little idea about medicine. Until I got him better. And then a fellow had a horse down in Old Harbour and come here, asked me if I want to give him a run. I say, 'Yes, I'll give you a run.' And I took the horse out here, and the horse beat him so bad that I went home and think about it. And then I began to feed him. You know you got to feed him and care him, brush him and everything. And the next week a Chinaman come with the next horse and ask me to give him a run. I say, 'All right,' and I beat him again. Then I think that horse is a good horse. So I call him 'Surprise,' and I begin to care him more.

You got to bathe them every day, bathe them in the sea. And then you come and rinse them off in the creek, and you come home and you brush them. You give him his corn. You cut grass and you get it clean and you have him in stable. You don't let him go in no pasture. You keep him in stable.

Then you snuff his nose with vinegar. You rub his head with vinegar too. Then you use the brush to shape him. You look at him direct. He mustn't have no big belly. If you see him have belly you brush him, it cut down the belly.

And you give him punch in the morning. You beat the egg properly, you put a little brandy in it and milk, and then you give him it every morning, and that help him.

When the race come on now, you got to be different. Then you go to the drugstore and you buy your medicine. You got to buy eucalyptus, essence of peppermint, oil of cinnamon and the nutmeg. The day of the race now, you want him to get good wind that him can go. You take the white of the egg and you beat it, beat it, beat it till it foam, and you add drops of that peppermint, eucalyptus, cinnamon and nutmeg, drop, drop, drop, three or four drops, and you give it to him and he drink it, and you give him a good rub.

The next thing is doping him. That's an extra one. You buy the dope at the drugstore. White dope, they call it. It's a powder. And then you put it in the bottle with some whiskey and you shake it up. Some people use water, but I use whiskey. It's better. It cut the dope a little. Bare water is very dangerous.

And they have a thing for rubbing the joints of the animal. They use egg white, with good vinegar, a little turpentine, oil of white. But the drugstore hardly want to sell everybody that thing, oil of white. It's a bad thing. If I rub it on my horse and I get ahead, you can't beat me. It's a strong liquid. You can't get them thing now. They don't carry them.

But a Jamaican man the name of McCray had a drugstore, and he always sell it. But you had to go there and tell him, 'I'm going to run a race,' or he don't sell it. You say, 'But man, I running race, man,' and he say, 'All right, then I sell you.' Then now you clean the horse down properly, you rub all his joints here, you touch him behind his ears, and touch his shoulder. It keep the animal loose, you know.

You give the horse the dope just when you're going to let him go, at the track. If you give him before, he mad on you. Before you're going to start him, you got it in your little bottle, and you lead him down to the track to start. You open his mouth just as they're going to call the start of the race. They always have a man there to start them. And you put it into the mouth, and you let him wash his mouth, and then you let him go, and that send him along. But remember when you done with him, see to it that him don't eat a blade of green grass, because that will kill him. You got to purge him now, after that dope. You get salt physic and then you purge him, and the next day you can feed him again.

If I believe your horse is faster than mine, that's when I dope my own, and I beat you, you see. Nobody knows that I do it. The others, them do it too, but nobody tell you. But afterward I found out that dope kill the horse sinews, make the animal overrun. We find out the joints become big because him overrun. It not so good to use, and afterward I didn't use it again.

Well, we can't do those things again. Where we did have the track, that coconut walk is in government control now. They are declaring it National Park. It grow up in bush now because since the government have it, the people them don't worry with it again."

## Cricket

The decades of the 1920s and 1930s were the great years of cricket in Limón Province. All along the train lines, the United Fruit Company communities sponsored teams, and the people of the coast joined in the province-wide competition. Mr. Gray talks about the sport he loves:

"I like baseball because I can't do better. I don't like football. It's dangerous. But my fancy is cricket. We had our ballground right up there where the plane base is. We go all about and play. Guabito, Limón, Siquirres. You see, you look at the umpire, they like a parson. Two umpires, they stand up like parsons. They wear white gowns, you know. Once you had a German man came here and he ask, 'What the hell those is? Are they parsons?' I say, no they are umpires. He says, 'How you mean?' I say they are the judge for the game. We import those uniforms from Jamaica. Cricketing finish from when football take up in Limón. The government take it away. Change the cricket ground to football [soccer].

But Old Harbour team was big. Every time we have a game here we have excursion launch come in from Limón. Dance day and night. Bring a bands from Limón. I like it. I like to look at the baseball and the basketball, but my fancy is cricket. But the young people not interested now. All they are interested now is football. There are just a few places now they keep up with the cricketing: Trinidad, Australia, a little in Jamaica.

Bob Bernthal

Mr. Cyril Gray

The money we take in from the dance, we use that now to fix the ground and to buy the gears; we have bats, glove, and everything. And in case ever a player becomes sick, any accident or anything, we able to help them with that money.

Say tomorrow we are going out. Today then is practice and make selections, and tomorrow we gone all up to Bataan and play. Preparation is made for us there, you know, eat and drink, everything until you leave. The only thing that they don't pay is your fare. And when that team is coming here now to play us, we make preparation, place to eat and sleep two nights. The night when they come to play, next day play and the dance that night, and then they go.

Oh, I love even to see a picture of a man standing with his wicket and his gloves, see his legs and his bat in his hand. Oh, yes, I like cricket."

Deirdre Hyde

In Cahuita, cricket matches were played at the present-day ballground, a lot purchased by the Limón Municipality for the purpose in 1920. Manzanillo organized a team, and for years every Sunday meant cricket and picnic in one community or another. Rivalry between the coast teams was strong but good-natured. George Humphries tells the following story of an excursion from Cahuita to Old Harbour for a cricket match, declining to guess whether the Cahuita fans were victims of a joke or an accident:

> "We used to have a launch called *Energy*, one name *Santa Elena*, and we always get them to run excursion. Come here, Old Harbour, Manzanillo, all them place, to make picnic. It was a better time than now. They charge us three colón a head. The launch come from Limón load with people for the excursion.

One time we make an excursion to Old Harbour. Don't know if they made a mistake or what. They cook very good, but somehow they throw this thing called castor oil in the rice and peas. And, boy, when the night the excursion leave back, I myself did purging like hell. Everybody purging. All Luther, everybody get a bad belly that day. Leave Old Harbour about four in the evening, and when we get back, next day we couldn't do no work, man, we meet hell from that rice and peas, man."

## Baseball

Gradually cricket gave way to baseball as the favorite sport in Limón Province. Mr. Sorrows explains the reason why cricket died out during the 1940s: "The gears that they used to play cricket could not again be so easily obtained on account of the war, because all those things used to come from England. So it became difficult to get the gears, and cricket disappear around here in the early Forties."

Fred Ferguson remembers his first view of the new game, baseball, in Cahuita:

"When I was a little boy we never know anything about the baseball game. Everything was cricket. Around 1937 they made a baseball team. The first name for it was Navy, and they invited a team from Limón, that was the Cubs, they were strong players. And they gave the Navy down here 28-1. First baseball game I ever see in my life. Then you had the Yankee Band from Limón in those days, they play real good music. And they made placard, an Italian in Limón make those placard, and it say, 'Come to the Golden Shores of Cahuita. We will have the Yankee Band playing.'"

Mr. Zephaniah Palmer, Cahuita's "lover of baseball," organized and managed Cahuita's first successful baseball team, Liberty. The players formed a club with rules and regulations, dues, and responsibilites, and Mr. Palmer built a clubhouse for the team's meetings and social functions. "Frankie" McLeod talks about his days as a member of the Liberty team:

"The name of that team was Liberty. Mr. Lexburn Walker was captain, and they had me subcaptain and field marshall. We went on fine. We go out and play with several teams from the outside and gain victory from them, which is very strong teams.

In starting we takes contract to clean people's farm so we could accumulate an amount of money to make our start in buying our first set of gears and uniform. Mr. Skinner, he is a tailor, and we buy a roll of cloth for the pants, and Mr. Skinner is the one that made the uniform, right in Cahuita here. We chiefly use bluejean for the pants, and white *marina* shirts [T-shirts], and we put the initial on the back and on the front. We use tall socks to catch the end of the pants, we call that style of pants knickers. They join the socks. Then we use baseball shoes, a shoes that is prepared for the baseball players.

And we pay a monthly dues. And then we give functions by making excursions, getting people from Puerto Limón to come down with launch, and we keep dance, sell foodstuffs and liquor, and then we accumulate an amount of money, and we keep that in the treasury so that whatever we are short of, we can buy from that same money. We could afford to pay to keep the ballground clean at all times.

At first we use one of Miss Gatha's house for clubhouse, one room. And then after we start to improve, Mr. Palmer go and make a clubhouse over on the other side where he have the Sands Restaurant now.

I play with the Liberty until in 1941 I went off to Panama to work in the Canal Zone for the war. After I returned from Panama we went on playing, but most of the team members they differ, so Mr. Kayasso made up another team by the name of Fearless. And we sold out the gears to that club because the majority of our players went away to Bocas del Toro and other parts when the war was on.

The Fearless did good, but not as in the days of Liberty. Liberty was a stronger team and more active players. We purged the Liberty club by throwing out the players that would not keep to the rules. We had twenty-four rules so that they can't do anything contrary. You know, sometimes one may get irritable on the diamond and may use a loose expression. There is a law that he would be throw out for three months or six months, like that.

But it was only the Cubs that was sure. The Cubs was the best team that Limón had, and you could say the best in the country at that time because you know it's only the Negroes play baseball. The Spaniards wasn't playing much baseball those days."

## Cahuita's Music Man

Mr. Palmer's clubhouse became a center of community merrymaking during the 1940s and on through the 1950s. Every Saturday night they cleared the floor for a dance, and Mr. Sylvester

Plummer, Cahuita's self-taught music man, set up his band. Mr. Plummer, who still plays his homemade electric guitar on his porch to entertain friends and neighbors, talks about his development as a musician and the lively old-time dances at the clubhouse:

"The first thing I started to play was a mouth organ, harmonica they call it. I get it from Limón when I was a boy. And from the harmonica I started guitar. I start first just by a friend begin to show me a few positions on the guitar. But then I imported lessons from the States. I make my own guitar and violin. And I practice violin until I begin to play by myself, just by my mind. I never had a teacher. It cause many people to wonder because I never went to school to learn those things. I do many things of myself and by correspondence from the States. Until I learn to make electric guitar. I always went along with friends who could play, and they teach me and I do better from that. Those days boys were interested in music. I made about four violin to sell, and I make guitar, about five of them, and tenor banjo.

And when it come to Christmas season, we boys that play music we go from door to door before daylight, play music and sing songs. And each party would open the door and entertain us with drinks and cakes and things like that. We bring in Christmas morning joyfully those days.

Mr. Sylvester Plummer

And now nothing like that. Year after year we do that, and the people very much appreciate our visits. We play all kinds of songs. We have enjoyable times, but not again. Those days were more loving. People were more loving. We go from door to door and just have a jolly time. But everything change. Just change of times. The world change, Nature change, everything change. Your mind change, my mind change.

I used to have my own bands here, and my bands consist of violin, tenor banjo, guitar, and drum. There were six of us make up the bands. Mr. Cunningham, he was my guitarist. Mr. Mike, he was my guitarist, too. The others, they all dead now.

You have dance most times once every three months, a special dance. We bring in the musicians from Limón, have a really good dance.

But every Saturday night we have a practice dance, and my bands play for that, by Mr. Palmer's clubhouse that was there. It was a big place. And all the people come to practice, because you dance a special way. Not like how these people dance, when you dance anything now. Those day you have to learn to dance.

Those tunes were strictly by order. You dance quadrille, waltz, what you call *pasillo*, swing, blues, different ones. I used to play all kind of music. You had six figures, first figure, second, third, fourth could be anything, a blues or fox or something else, but strictly the fifth figure is the quadrille. To dance those kind of dance you got to form by set. Eight into a set, and they spin around and they make the proper motions. They got to practice that. I don't dance it, I was strictly a player. Selles Johnson was professional dancing quadrille.

Those days were more livelier than now. Now is more modern but is very bad for this. In my younger days there were more people for sport because there were few Jehovah's Witnesses, and Adventists was very few. And all the people just for sports. But now there is a difference because you have thousands of Jehovah's Witnesses around and Adventists, and they separate themselves from those kind of life, so great sports go down."

## Set Ups and Nine Nights

In addition to their regular celebrations for Christmas and Easter Monday, their sports events, concerts and dances, the Afro-Caribbean people of the coast gathered together for consolation and encouragement whenever a community member died. The night of the death is the "Set Up," followed nine days later by the "Nine Night," when the whole community keeps vigil at the home of the deceased until dawn.

Set Ups and Nine Nights are not mournful affairs on the Talamanca Coast. The purpose of the Set Up is to do honor to the dead and give comfort to the family; the Nine Night is more lively, a gathering to joyfully send off the spirit of the dead and to rejoice in the togetherness of the living. As Christians, the coastal people have faith that the Christian dead find an end to suffering in Eternity. Their customs of keeping Set Ups and Nine Nights are rooted in African tradition, but few people today are conscious of this.

Before the road to Limón made it possible for funeral arrangements to be handled by a mortuary, all the preparations for burial were made by the family and friends of the deceased. The day that a community member died, his family and close friends gathered to wash, dress, and prepare the body for viewing at the Set Up. A carpenter constructed a simple wooden coffin, and a member of the cemetery committee contracted someone to dig the hole in the burying ground. Church members arranged for a funeral service the next day. Someone was dispatched by launch or mule cart to contact relatives and friends along the coast, and in Limón, and provide transportation for them to come for the burial. Because it was impossible to preserve the body long, all these arrangements had to be made very quickly.

As community members learned of the death, they put aside their plans for the day to be present at the home of the deceased. Women cleaned and cooked for the guests who would stay awake all the night. Men brought bottles of rum or homemade liquor, draughts and dominoes and decks of cards. Church members brought their hymn books. Musicians brought their instruments.

Through the night of the Set Up women served food and coffee from the kitchen. In the main room people gathered to look upon the body of the dead. Others sang hymns, talked, told stories. Outside the young people played games and the men played dominoes or draughts until the sun came up.

A mule cart would arrive at the home to carry the coffin first to the church for the funeral service and then down the path to the burying ground. All the people walked behind the coffin, carrying cut flowers to place upon the grave.

Nine nights later the people gathered again at the home of the deceased to celebrate the Nine Night much the same as the Set Up.

Miss Mavis Tyndal describes these traditional practices:

"These customs started from the real old-time Jamaican people. If it's even a little baby die, they will have the Set Up in the house that night. They will bring the liquor, they will have different drinks, coffee, tea, chocolate, and they will bake their bread, especially Johnny cake[1] they use for Set Up. They will sing and play their dominoes till morning light.

After they go and bury the dead, nine days after they keep the Nine Night. They come also and they bring liquors and drinks, and the women serve soup and so forth until twelve o'clock, always twelve o'clock they serve black coffee, tea, chocolate. And they sing and play dominoes and cards until daylight. It's just a memorial, it show appreciation for the family, to cheer up the family.

Some of the old-time people have a custom to put a table in the corner, spread a white tablecloth and a mug with water and a glass, and they say during the time up till the Nine Night that dead person come back and drink that water. That's a old-time custom. They also have a custom that the bed that the person die on, they spread it clean clean with a white sheet, and they leave it there, nobody go on it and soil it. And they say after the Nine Night now the next day they will go and see how it look like a person was laying down there, like the bed kind of mash down from the person on it. But then after the Nine Night everything like that is forgot, and somebody else can go sleep on that bed.

They have a next thing, on the Nine Night they take one bottle of whiskey and sprinkle it in the four corners of the house where that person die.

They say that's just to get the spirit of the person away from there after the Nine Night, so it doesn't come back.

They have also a custom that when anyone die, they go and buy a bottle of perfume, and they throw the whole of that bottle of perfume on the dead, on the body. And there are times later that they smell that same kind of perfume, and they say it's that person come around again. I've heard that many times. Up to last week I heard that saying. They do it so that anytime later that dead person come around, they will know. Even after years, that

---

[1] Johnny cake is a biscuit made with coconut milk. Mr. Selles Johnson says the original name was "journey cake," because the biscuits were the perfect size for carrying for lunch on a journey.

same scent can come around and you will hear someone say, 'Well, my aunt's spirit was with me because I smell the same perfume that I use on her when she die.'

Some people live with a fear inside of them that the dead will stay around the house. And they will do anything they can to get that spirit out of the house. They have a thing by the name of horseshoe. They always stick it over the door. They always put a ruler over the door, or they burn out their houses with incense. And they find that the spirit doesn't appear to them again. Some even go to a priest, and the priest give them something to wear and keep out that spirit from the house.

For me, when a person is dead, he is dead. But Satan exists. And Satan will transform himself into all different things to make people afraid. So it's not the person that die, it's the spirit of that person Satan transform himself into. But there are some spirits that are fierce ones, very fierce, and you can use many thing to get it out. Satan has plenty power.

But this system of the Nine Night is from the old-time Jamaican people, until even in these younger days they still keep up with it. Because I say after things is changing, knowledge increasing, they would done away with that. I thought maybe these young ones would forget about it, but they are still with it. It's a thing that will never be done away with. Here now in Cahuita the people doesn't set up with a baby dead, nor have a Nine Night for a baby. But down the coast, in Manzanillo, if it's even a baby, everybody is coming to have the Set Up and the Nine Night with big drinking and everything. It's just a cheering up for the ones that left behind.

They have riddles, Anansi stories, jokes and things like that. Some of the riddles they are hard. Take for instance, I remember a lady that came up with a riddle like this:

> I know a man, in hair he walk,
> Ten detectives went for him,
> Sentenced to hang him at Naily Park.
> What it is?

And everyone keep guessing and guessing, nobody couldn't answer that one. And she repeat it, but nobody couldn't answer it. So she says, 'I going to tell you what it is. The man in the hair he walk, is the lice in your hair. Then ten detectives went for him are the ten fingers scratch the head to get out the lice, and they find him and sentenced to hang him at Naily Park. Naily Park is the fingernail you pinch the lice with!' Now, that riddle was hard! And everybody started to laugh.

Again she went and she said, 'Guess me this riddle: water stand up.' Everybody wondered, 'What is this riddle, water stand up?' Nobody could guess. She said, 'Water stand up is sugar cane!' And a lot more she mentioned. So on the night of Set Up and Nine Night you find all these things, jokes and riddles, and that help the time pass and the people feels happy."

## Tales of Anansi the Spider

It was at Set Ups and Nine Nights that the coastal people listened to the old-timers tell riddles and stories that had been passed down through generations of Afro-Caribbean families. Lacking radios and books, storytelling was a natural form of entertainment.

Deirdre Hyde

194

The art of storytelling involves not just remembering a story as it was told before, but amplifying it with the vitality of the storyteller's own personality and imagination. A good story survives through generations because it has been adapted to suit the environment and experience of each new generation. And so it happens that the people of the Talamanca Coast tell stories that originated in the communities of their African ancestors.

The oldest stories in the world, in all parts of the world, probably originated from the need of human beings to explain the world around them, to assign a kind of order or rationality to natural phenomena, and to pass on this understanding as a lesson to the next generation. The stories survive through centuries when they are successful in explaining the mysteries of the natural world, or when they successfully reflect essential human traits in a manner that is both entertaining and enlightening.

The stories about Anansi the Spider that originated in West African villages many centuries ago survive yet in Africa and anywhere in the world where African people have migrated because they accomplish these two necessary functions of a story. They offer an explanation, however ludicrous, of natural phenomena (Why do monkeys live in trees? Why do tigers run wild in the bush?), and they illuminate ever-lasting elements of human nature (greed, trickery, revenge, cleverness, justice) in such a way that lessons can be learned through laughter.

The modern stories of Brother Anansi and his animal comrades have changed during centuries of retelling as the African peoples passed through years of enslavement and migration in the West Indies and the American continents. The animal characters remain the same, but their personalities and activities change as the life experiences of the story-tellers change. The sixteenth century Anansi of an Ashanti village sings and plays a drum. The twentieth century Anansi still sings, but he plays a violin. The sixteenth century Ashanti Anansi plots for the rewards of the tribal king. The twentieth century West Indian Anansi schemes for the riches of the white landowner.

The stories of Anansi the Spider are classic in their morality: cleverness wins out over superior physical strength, and the lowly spider makes fools of his powerful enemies as long as his cleverness surpasses his greed.

During this century, Anansi stories have been recorded and published throughout Africa, the West Indies, and the Americas.[1] The people who tell these stories on the Talamanca Coast, however, have

---

[1] Costa Rican versions are found in Anglin Edwards de Scott 1981 and Duncan 1975. For Jamaican versions, see Sherlock 1954; for African versions see Appiah 1966.

not read them in books. They have inherited them through centuries of oral tradition, passed from one generation to the next.

Mr. Joseph "Boyse" Spencer tells three Anansi stories which he likes to call "belly-full" stories, as he explains: "That mean to say, well, I got a good stomach full, I have nowhere to go, and so we plan these stories to tell the children and the neighbors and friends around that we will help pass the afternoon. We call them belly-full stories, Anansi stories, nonsense stories. The people remember them from their old parents, and you have some that just make them up, too."

## Brother Anansi and the Riding Horse

"Well, I'm going to tell you something about Tiger and Anansi. Brother Tiger was courting Tacuma's daughter. Two daughters Tacuma had, then Tiger fall in love with them. Well, Brother Anansi also fall in love with the daughters. So now, Anansi visit Tacuma's home. He been trying to court the girls, and the girls tell him that they was in love with Tiger. So Anansi say to the girls, 'You mean to say, you can love a man like that, and he's my father's best riding horse?' Well, the girls say, 'But we never know that!'

So now Tiger come to pay his visit, and the girls say, 'We don't have nothing to do with you because you Anansi's father's riding horse, and you can't do nothing for us.' So they had a big talking.

Well, Tiger get annoyed because him is a hot man, and he went to Anansi and said, 'Anansi, what a thing you could do like that, cho!' Anansi said, 'What is that, Brother Tiger?' Tiger say, 'You go to them girls and say I'm your father's best riding horse!' Anansi say, 'No, Brother Tiger, me?' Cho! I couldn't do a thing like a that, sir. I couldn't do a thing like a that. You mean them girls so wicked, they go and tell a thing like a that? No, Brother Tiger, nothing like that.'

Brother Tiger say, 'Well, Anansi, you have to go and prove it now.' Tiger get hot, you know. 'Well, Anansi, you have to go and prove it.'

'Yes, Brother Tiger, I will, Brother Tiger, sure. I will, but I sick. I sick, and I can't walk to go so far.'

Tiger say, 'You have to go. You have to make it possible to go.'

Anansi say, 'Yes, Brother Tiger. But I can't walk, cho. Can't walk at all. If you carry me, I go, but I can't walk.'

Tiger say, 'Well, if I have to carry you, then I will carry you.'

'Yes, Brother Tiger, I will go,' Anansi say. 'But cho, my belly, my belly, Brother Tiger. I can't go again. My belly, Brother Tiger.'

Tiger say, 'Well, Anansi, you just have to go.'

'Well, Brother Tiger, if you carry me I go w'you. But you know, Brother Tiger. Me is a man me like to sit down in something that I can sit on top you, Brother Tiger. If you get a little something called a saddle I may can sit down 'pon it, Brother Tiger, me sit down 'pon it, and me go.' Tiger went and get the saddle.

'But Brother Tiger, it look hard, you know. You can get a little something they call bit, me go then, you know, Brother Tiger. Then me go w'you.' Tiger went and him get the bit.

Anansi say, 'Well, Brother Tiger, you can get the little thing they call stirrup, put up on the saddle, so? Then I can rest me foot. Then we can go. But I gots to rest me foot because you know, my belly, Brother Tiger, my belly!' Tiger went and him get the stirrup. Then Anansi saddle up Tiger and they going down the road.

And when Anansi see the house now, him take the whip and him touch Brother Tiger to the side. 'Anansi! What you doing there?' Anansi say, 'Brother Tiger, a fly hitch me up, I go for chase it off.' And him go a little further and touch Tiger again. Tiger say, 'But, Anansi! Come on, behave yourself!' Anansi say, 'Brother Tiger, but you know there something on my foot.'

And going, going, going until them get near the house now, Tacuma's gate, and Anansi take the whip and him lash Tiger wild and jump the spur on the Tiger's belly so the Tiger jump and get shame and run in the yard now. And Anansi sing:

> See me, Anansi coming down,
> See me, Anansi coming down,
> See me, Anansi coming down,
> Down down down down!
> See me, Anansi coming down,
> See me, Anansi coming down,
> See me, Anansi coming down,
> Down down down down!

Anansi prove now that Tiger was his riding horse. So the tiger get wild, and from that day until today the tigers run wild in the woods, and Anansi get all the girls."

## Brother Pigeon's Birthday Party

"Monkey is a man have a lot of energy, like to jump and prance and play a lot. So Anansi was invited to Pigeon's birthday. Pigeon have a party. So Anansi say, 'Brother Monkey, I invited to Pigeon's birthday party. But, you know me, I don't like to go alone. I would like you to go with me, and we could have a good time there.'

Monkey say, 'All right, Brother Anansi. We'll take a walk over there.' So them go to the party.

When him get in to the party now, Monkey have a lot of style, and him start dancing with all the girl them, and none of the girl them want to dance with Anansi. And Anansi say, 'Well, Brother Monkey, if I did know you going to take away all the girl them, me never come here at all, cho!' And Monkey started dancing with the girl them and him keep right on dancing.

Well, Anansi go and get Tiger to come to the party. And Tiger and Monkey never move good together, you know. So when Tiger come to the party now him say, 'But stop. Monkey, what you doing here?' Monkey say, 'Anansi bring me here, sir.' And Tiger gets rough with Monkey and him make a fight, and Tiger a big man now, and Monkey run up into the treetop, and from that day until today you don't see Monkey come on the ground. Monkey live in the trees. They jump from one tree to another. Up to yesterday I saw some in the coconut walk there, won't come down to the ground. They still jumping."

## The Pigeon and the Crayfish

"There were an old lady who had a corn field, and she visit the corn field every day. Well, the Pigeon like the corn very much, and he invite Crayfish to go and have a feed off this old lady's corn. But Crayfish say to Pigeon, 'Brother Pigeon, I don't have no wings. I can't go because you can fly and me no.'

Well, Pigeon say, 'Brother Crayfish, I will lend you some of my feather.' So Pigeon pick out four feather and stick them into Crayfish, and they fly to this little corn field. And they feed and feed and feed on the corn until they find that their belly were so full that they fall asleep. Well, they sleep and they sleep and they sleep.

Pigeon woke up before Crayfish, and him say, 'Well, them feathers is mine. I'm going to take away my feathers and leave Crayfish here.' So Pigeon took out the feathers and stick them back in his wings and fly away and leave Crayfish. Well, Crayfish was there sleeping until finally Crayfish wake out his slumber. And he wondering what to do. He see a stone, and he was wondering if he could go up on that stone, make one jump and jump into the river that was under the stone. But he try to get up on the stone, and he slide down all the time and can't get up there on the stone. And when he look he see the old lady coming.

Crayfish start to sing:

> Good morning, Nanna, oh,
> A pigeon bring me here,
> Cu blan, cu blan, cu blan!

Well, the old lady, she hear the song, and she begin to dance. And she dance and dance and dance. And the Crayfish was singing the song over and over again, wondering if he can get this old lady to put him up on the stone. And he sing,

> Good morning, Nanna, oh,
> A pigeon bring me here,
> Cu blan, cu blan, cu blan!
> You put me on the stone,
> Me sing me song fi you!

And the old lady dance and dance and take up Crayfish and put him on the stone, and the Crayfish jump in the water, 'oooooPluuuum!' And from that day the Crayfish live on the rocks, because that was the only way he could get away from Nanna."

There are many versions of Anansi stories that involve wingless animals who borrow feathers to fly. The next story is told by Mrs. Pearl Cunningham:

## Anansi and the Blackbirds

"Three Blackbird used to go over an island to feed, while Anansi was up and down hungry, didn't have nothing to eat. And one day the Blackbird said to him, 'How are you?' Him said to them, 'Bad,' because he is hungry. They say, 'Well, we get feeding over there on an island have a big apple tree.' Him say, 'Well, I would like to go over there, but I don't have no feather. I can't fly.' So they take out three of them feathers and stick them into Anansi and him fly out and go over there. And when him reach to the island and see the apple tree them, the Blackbird couldn't get none to eat. Every one them go to pick, Anansi say, 'That one is mines! That one is mines! Don't trouble that one!'

Well, you hear them cry, the bird them hungry, but they stay and pretty soon when Anansi's belly was full him drop asleep. Now the Blackbird take out back them feather and fly away and leave him.

So every day him get up and him eat the apple, eat the apple, until the apple was done now. He have nothing more to eat, and him was hungry again. But him don't have no feather now to fly over back. And as he look down him see the sea. Him say, 'How am I going to get home back? Well, I'm going to drop me bag, and if the bag float, I will float. But if the bag sink, I will sink.' And him drop the bag and the bag sink. And him take off him hat, and drop the hat, and the hat float, so him throw down himself now and him sink to the bottom, was right into Alligator's house.

And Anansi say, 'Brother Alligator, long time coming I want to look for you and I couldn't reach, and now I just come.' And Alligator was so glad. And him say, 'Yes, Brother Anansi, come, eat and drink. And I want you to learn the children and teach them.' And Anansi say, 'Yes, Brother, me can do that.'

So Anansi start to teach the children them, and make noise and everything, and every day him start to eat up one kid. The next day him eat one, and eat and eat till him eat up the seven children them. And when he eat them off done, him don't have no more children now. It's him alone now in the school, making noise that the Alligator would believe that was the children them making noise. And when him see that it look too bad now, him decided to go on home.

So Anansi tell Alligator that him ready to go and look some more books to come back and teach the children them. And Alligator get a boat now, and Anansi get ready and get in the boat, and while the men paddling, going on to shore, Alligator go and look for her children. And when she don't see one of her children she start to bawl, 'Bring back Anansi here!' And Anansi say same time, 'Pull fast to the shore because storm and breeze!' Alligator call, 'Bring back Anansi here!' Anansi say, 'Pull fast, pull fast, storm and breeze!' And the sailors pull fast and pull fast until when him reach on the shore, him jump out and say, 'You foolish brutes, you! She say to bring me back, and you see that you land me ashore.' And the sailors was Kingfish and Mackerel, and them never go back to the river. Them go in the sea and them stay in the sea because Alligator is vexed with them now."

Mr. Walter "Gavett" Ferguson tells a different ending to the same story.

## Brother Anansi and the Alligator

"It happened that Blackbird was very fond of Brother Anansi and they always go and bring apple and bring it to Brother Anansi. It happened that one day Anansi never feel so pleased, although he was receiving some benefit from them, but he say, 'Cho, you are too selfish, man, you're selfish.' They say, 'Why?' He say, 'You always find apple and you don't carry me and show me the tree, man.'

So they said, 'But you cannot go there. The tree is in the midst of a river, and it's only birds can reach there, Brother Anansi.' 'Cho,' he said, 'but suppose each one of you give me three of your wing feather, me can go, man.'

So they consider, yes, yes, it is reasonable, so they consult each other and they all give him three wing feathers. But now he got more feather than they did, because it was quite a group of them, and Anansi flew off to the apple before them. And he reach before them. He had a bag, and he started to pick and throw in his bag, and he started to eat until his belly was big. And when the Blackbirds did reach, as they saw one apple he say, 'Don't touch that one, that one is me own.' As they saw another one, he say, 'No, no, no, don't touch that one. Me saw that one before you.'

So the Blackbirds sat down and never interfere with Anansi anymore. But then Anansi fell asleep with his bag around his shoulder. So they said, 'You know what? Let's go play this guy a trick.' So they take back all their feathers, and left him alone on the limb.

And when he awake, he find that he had no feathers, and the deep water was there below him, and he said, 'What I going do now?' Him say, 'Well, if I drop my bag, and it float, I must float too.' So he drop the bag, and the bag floated. And he say, 'O.K. I going now.' And he pitch down in the water, but he started to sink, but he grab the bag with him, and he went down to the bottom of the river.

Alligator was just coming to devour him, but Anansi went and greeted Alligator, and he said, 'My own cousin! Alligator! Long time I did want to come see you, and I couldn't reach until now. All kind of atrocity on the road, and this and that.' Alligator say, 'Well, you are lucky. I never know we are cousin, but since you say so, come on.'

So Alligator took Anansi inside and they ate and drink and so forth. But finally the quarters was too small for all of them to sleep, so Alligator took Anansi over on another bank where he had one hundred eggs, and he said, 'Well, you can sleep right here. But be careful. I have one hundred eggs here, now don't interfere with them.'

'Oh, no, Brother Alligator, I not going to trouble them.'

So when Alligator went back to his quarters, Anansi start to eat the eggs. He had three days there, and he ate ninety-nine eggs and leave one.

So Alligator called to him from over the other side, 'Brother Anansi, this morning is the morning that you going to go back home. And I'm going to send two boatmen with you.' Anansi say, 'Thank you, Brother Alligator, thank you.'

But Alligator suspected, maybe this is a stranger after all. Maybe he make way with the eggs. So he called to him, 'Brother Anansi, count those eggs for me before you come over.'

'Sir, the eyes of the master fatten the calf, sir. Stand up there and see them.' So Anansi took up the egg and say. 'One, Brother Alligator,' and he put back the egg and pick up the very same one again and said, 'Two, Brother Alligator,' and he put back and pick up the same one, until he did that one hundred times.

Alligator said, 'Well, you is good.' So he call for the boatmen to cross him over the river. But Alligator still had a doubt. So as the boatmen leave out with Anansi, Alligator say, 'But you know, better I take a run across and see what happen here.' When he go he saw one egg. So he run back to the riverside, and he call, 'Bring back Anansi home!'

But one boatman was dumb and one was deaf. The dumb one really heard, but he couldn't speak, and the deaf one don't hear at all. Anansi bawl out to the deaf one, 'Pull on fast, pull on fast! Storm a come! Don't want one cousin fi dead 'pon sea!' And they start to pull and pull until they reach Anansi home.

Well, from when Anansi reach, Blackbird cut off all communication with Anansi. They was good friends, but they aren't friends again."

Here is another Anansi story from Mr. Gavett:

## Anansi and Sister Tiger's Soup

"Brother Anansi used to be an intruder to Brother Tiger. He was lazy, and he never care about working. So he always go over to Brother Tiger and say he is sick, and they always give him something to eat. Because Brother Tiger is a working man, and he always have a full store of provision.

As it happened, Brother Tiger finally tell Anansi, 'Well, I can't put up with this no more. You got to try to do something. I cannot maintain you any further.'

So Anansi went away, and he went down by a riverside, and he picked up some stones. Pretty little stones. And he carried them to Sister Tiger, and he said to her, 'Sister Tiger, I tired of bother you. But I get some beans, man, real real vitamin beans, man. When you cook this it give you strength.' So she was so glad about it, and she said, 'Let me see. But these beans are tough, Brother Anansi!' So he say, 'No, Sister, you don't know better. You bring a little flour, bring a little piece of corned pork, bring a little yam and onion and all them things, and make me cook a big soup for you, and you will see how it nice.'

So she did bring all these things and give it to Brother Anansi. And Anansi did make one big pot of soup, and everybody enjoy the soup.

And that's the way Anansi live off Tiger. Every day he carry a lump of those stones and poor Sister Tiger never know better. So he strain off the stones, fix up the soup, and live off Brother Tiger."

Mrs. Velita Parker, of Hone Creek, tells this tale of Brother Anansi, Brother Tiger, and Brother Monkey:

## Brother Tiger and the Well

"Once upon a time, Brother Tiger fall in a well, and Tiger call to Brother Anansi to help him out the well. And Anansi said, well, him don't have any tail. But Monkey have tail, so Monkey better to help him. And him call Monkey.

When Monkey come, him pull out the Tiger, but when Tiger come out him so hungry that he go to eat the Monkey. And Anansi say to Tiger, 'No, Brother Tiger, not so. You must hold up your hand and say, "Praise God."'

That mean now that when him hold up him hand and say, 'Praise God,' Monkey get away and run gone on the tree. That's why Monkey live on the tree till now."

In Mrs. Parker's story Anansi befriends Monkey, but Mrs. Pearl Cunningham tells one in which Brother Anansi sacrifices friendship for profit:

## No Thief Backra Sheep

"They had a white man, a man have plenty sheep, and Monkey used to eat the sheep. And the man's looking and looking and him try to find out and him could not find out who was eating the sheep. So him give out a reward and say, anybody that tell him who is eating the sheep, him will give him the reward, let him be overseer over his property.

And Anansi did know it was Monkey was eating the sheep. So now them have a dance and they invite Anansi to the dance to play the music. Him have a violin. And Anansi invite Monkey to come with him and play the drum. Monkey say, 'But me don't have no clothes to wear.' So Anansi have the skin of a sheep, and him give the skin to Monkey to put on for the dance.

Then now when him start to tune up his violin, him sing with the violin tuning,

Thief thief thief thief,
Sheep sheep sheep sheep!
Thief thief thief, Backra
Sheep sheep sheep sheep!

And them went and started to play, them start the music, and Monkey have on the sheep skin, and Anansi sing,

All the time I go tell Brother Monkey,
No thief Backra sheep,
All the time I go tell Brother Monkey,
No thief Backra sheep!
Thief thief thief thief,
Sheep sheep sheep sheep!
If you think I lie, make I tell you,
Monkey have the skin on to show you!

So the man get on to him and find out was Monkey thiefing his sheep, and him run the Monkey to the trees and take Anansi and give him to be overseer over his property.

## The Problem of Citizenship

During the 1920s the Costa Rican government began sending delegates to Old Harbour and Cahuita to serve as local authorities. The people referred to these men as "judges," but since life was for the most part peaceful, judges were rarely called upon to arbitrate judicial matters. Some of them took an active interest in community problems and needs, helping to organize the people to dig drainage ditches or repair streets. Some set up businesses or made farms and functioned in their official capacity only when called upon. Some became members of the community in every sense; others kept a distance between themselves and the local populations, waiting for the good news of a transfer to the Central Valley.

A most important function of the judge was to register newborn children so that they could become Costa Rican citizens. Until the 1940s, children born in Costa Rica of foreign parents retained the nationality of their parents. Theoretically, upon coming of age they could apply for naturalization *por opción*; in practice, however, there were many obstacles to naturalization of black people.

Few first-generation immigrants chose to change their Jamaican, Colombian, or Nicaraguan citizenship through the process of naturalization. But once the settlers realized that they had found a home in Costa Rica, that their wandering was over, most of them wanted their children to claim citizenship in Costa Rica. So the outing to register new children's names with the *agente de policía* was an important event.

The hopes of the Afro-Caribbean parents were often frustrated. They spoke little Spanish, finding it difficult to make themselves understood to the judge. If they wanted an English name for their child, the judge would not be able to spell it. Finally, a number of judges took up the practice of choosing a Spanish name for the child, regardless of the wishes of the parents. Many of the English-speaking people gave up when they received *cédulas* (I.D. cards) with unknown or badly misspelled names, deciding not to bother any more with citizenship.

Mr. Selven Bryant describes frustrating encounters with the Spanish-speaking judges of Old Harbour:

> "You see, in those days when you go and register the children, the Spaniards, they never know English. Then all those name was English name, and some of the Jamaican people can't write to write it down. So the judge just write how it sound to him. That why

Paula Palmer

Mr. Selven Bryant

205

plenty of the people don't register, because when you send it to the registry, the registry send it back spelled all wrong, and the people just take it and throw it down. Sometime the name you register is not the name your family call you. Lot of mix up, like my name. They spell it Celvin Brayant, but I spell it Selven Bryant. Then they have my name in the registry Brayant Brayant. All the rest of us is Brayant Stevenson because my mother is Stevenson. But I don't carry my mother's name at all through some mistake.

Around in the Thirties a judge came 'round here named Santiago Acosta, and him now start to give the children them Spanish name. That why you see plenty of the colored people have Spanish name. When you go to register he just give you Spanish name because the English give too much trouble in the registry. One of my sister name Cornelia. Him is who give her her name. The next brother named Nicolás. That judge is who give him that name.

The Spaniard sometimes just write what they feel because they don't know the English. And some of the judge them don't know to read and write neither. The Jamaican who know to write, they write out the name on a piece of paper and give it to the judge, and then it go all right if he can even copy. Then you have a judge later who could read and write Spanish good and speak English nearly, Goyo Ramiro. So he give the children them Spanish name too, and kind of cutting out the English name. The people maybe don't like it, but they just have to accept it."

For black West Indians, there were legal as well as linguistic barriers to attaining Costa Rican citizenship. Beginning in 1862, Costa Rican laws prohibited the immigration and settlement of people of the "African and Chinese races." Costa Rican authorities did not enforce these laws on the Talamanca Coast. Perhaps the geographic and social isolation of Talamanca and its reputation as an inhospitable, unhealthy place protected the region's black immigrants. Exceptions to the immigration law were also made to permit the importation of thousands of West Indian laborers to build the transcontinental railroad and to work for the United Fruit Company. But Afro-Caribbean workers were seen as a foreign—and temporary—workforce; they were not viewed by the Costa Rican public as potential fellow citizens and neighbors.

The 1927 census recorded 18,000 blacks in Limón province, almost all of them "foreigners." At that time there were 2.2 foreigners for every Costa Rican citizen in the region. Many of the outnumbered hispanics resented what appeared to them to be preferential employment of blacks by the United Fruit Company. As unemployment increased nationwide during the years of the

Depression, Costa Rican workers pressured the Legislative Assembly to institute employment quotas favorable to (white) Costa Rican citizens.

Although many of these appeals and subsequent legal measures were couched in nationalistic language (Costa Ricans versus foreigners), the underlying sentiment was often racist. For example, 543 white citizens in Limón addressed the following letter to the National Assembly in 1933:

> ... We want to address ourselves especially to the Black problem, which is of the utmost importance, because in Limón province there exists a situation of privilege for this race which is manifestly inferior to the white race to which we belong. It is impossible to coexist with them because their bad customs don't permit it: for them neither the family nor the honor of women exist, and they live in disgraceful promiscuity which puts in danger our families founded in accord with religious precepts and good Costa Rican customs ...
>
> That is why we come ... to ask the Constitutional Assembly to put an immediate end to this humiliating situation in which a race inferior to ours comes into our own country to invade our countryside, our cities and our homes ...
>
> It should certainly be possible to dictate a law to prohibit the immigration of blacks and the granting of citizenship to them, because they are a race inferior to ours.[1]

Since the law of 1862 already prohibited black immigration and settlement, the racist appeal of these Costa Ricans was in keeping with the ideological and political context of the times. It gained further legislative support in 1934, when the United Fruit Company negotiated a new contract to transfer its operations from the soil-exhausted Atlantic region to virgin lands on the Pacific coast. The Companion Law (Decreto No. 31) to the 1934 Cortés-Chittendon agreement instituted employment quotas favorable to Costa Rican citizens and prohibited the employment of black workers in the new Pacific plantations. Article 5 of the law reads:

> In the works associated with production and exploitation of the banana industry, preference will be given to Costa Ricans who will enjoy... the same advantages and prerogatives of employees and workers of other nationalities.

---

[1] Archivos Nacionales, Sección Legislativa, No. 16753. Translated from the Spanish.

> For office and [machine] shop personnel, [banana] enterprises will employ at least 69 per cent Costa Ricans ...
>
> It is prohibited to employ, in the Pacific Zone, colored people in such works [the banana industry].[1]

Although a few Costa Rican politicians energetically opposed these racist measures, the administration of President León Cortés (1936-1940) enforced the color ban on the Pacific plantations. In Limón, the new employment quotas forced the Company to lay off many hundreds of black workers. During the Cortés administration, blacks were barred from the public baths in Limón; seating in the public theaters was segregated, and the nation's only mental hospital refused to admit blacks.

The people of the Talamanca Coast were well aware of the racist climate that pervaded the nation during these years. John Burke, of Cahuita, remembers being denied lodging at Limón's Park Hotel. Martin Luther was refused employment on the United Fruit Company's plantations in the Pacific Zone. But at home in their coastal villages, they were buffered by their isolation and comfortable as the numerical majority and as well-established farmers. Says Selven Bryant, of Old Harbour: "The color question, well, you know it always exist. To be frank, it exists today, same way. Out here on the coast, nobody come to molest us, but nobody was giving us any assistance neither."

The first opening of opportunity for blacks seeking naturalization as Costa Rican citizens came during the Calderón Guardia administration (1940-1944). A Limón newspaper reported that during the first six months of 1942, more than 3,000 blacks in the province presented their requests for naturalization.[2] But only people who were able to pay lawyers' fees were successful in naturalizing. Selven Bryant and two of his brothers made the long trip to San José, where they had to stay a week, paying room and board as well as lawyers' fees, to get their naturalization papers. Other blacks born in Costa Rica indignantly refused to naturalize. Mr. Eddie Patterson, of Old Harbour, is one who insisted that the government should recognize his right to citizenship by birth. It was a long wait. In 1967, nineteen years after his first application, Mr. Eddie was recognized as a Costa Rican *por nacimiento.*

---

[1] Koch 1981: 291.

[2] Koch 1981: 299.

It would not be until after the 1948 Revolution that the color ban on employment in the Pacific would be lifted, and blacks would be fully integrated into the political life of the nation. By that time, three generations of Afro-Caribbean families had been born and raised on the Talamanca Coast, most of them retaining the nationality of their pioneer ancestors. The prevailing attitude among them was expressed by Albert Guthrie, of Old Harbour: "I know where I was born, so why I want to worry with lawyers and papers? They only take your money. Stay away from those problems, because it's only problems, you know. Just live good and don't worry with it."

Suffering the Second World War

It was through the radio that the coastal people first heard rumors of war in 1939. Mr. Sylvester Plummer brought the first radio to Cahuita in 1932. It attracted huge crowds to listen to British broadcasts of cricket matches and the Derby races, but the most popular broadcasts were Joe Louis fights from the United States. "I don't know why the floor didn't fall through those nights," Mr. Plummer remembers, "so many people in the house." In Old Harbour, the only radio was at the shop owned by Ramón Acón. Mr. Selven Bryant tells how he and his neighbors followed the news of the war:

> "During the war of '39, every night the people went out to Ramón Acón's shop to get the news. The radio was inside, and Ramón alone listen to the news, and later he come out and tell us how the war is going.
> What happen, that radio work with a car battery and sometimes the charge was very low. They had was to send it to Limón to recharge it and sometimes it don't reach back for up to eight days. So, since you could hardly hear the broadcast, Ramón sat close by it listening and then he come and tell us."

The war years were terrible on the Talamanca Coast for a number of reasons. First, the United Fruit Company moved lock, stock, and barrel to the Pacific, abruptly cutting off public services and leaving thousands of black men and women unemployed. The Penshurst Banana Company abandoned its business, leaving the coastal farmers with useless fields of bananas. A great number of able-bodied young men left the coast to work as contract laborers in the Panama Canal Zone; many of them never returned to their homes in Talamanca. As sea trade declined, the shops quickly emptied their stores of foreign products with no imports to replenish supplies. The coast suffered shortages of flour, sugar, medicines, and cloth. And then heavy rains hit the area in 1944 and 1945, destroying the newly planted cocoa trees just before they were ready to bear.

Fred Ferguson talks about the war years in Cahuita:

> "It was a terrible time in Limón because there was no flour, and an extra demand come on corn to make tortillas. And no sugar. No needle. No thread. You know, everything coming from outside, and the war stop the trade. About four years we were without things. Some people used to send little vital things from Panama to their parents here. No condensed milk. Nothing at all. Some of the sugar-milling machinery wanted replacement, and the only replacement parts could come from the United States. So no sugar. Even some of the people down here went out in the bush and got cane and they wring the cane, mash the cane with a hard spike, and then wring the juice out of it and boil it. Then get some bush and put in that cane liquor, and boil it so it taste like you boil a bush tea and sweeten it with sugar. Not even sweeties was in the store.
>
> When trade begin again after the war, everything we was getting that time was much inferior to what we used to get before the war, and up till now it is inferior.
>
> There were a lot of things that you could get over on the Panama side on account of the Canal Zone. People used to run contraband. You know John Bull. He used to go over the River Sixaola, and people sell things and he bring them over and sell them here. But not by the bridge there, to avoid the guards. Clothing and medicine, embroidery thread. So many things. People would go all down from Bluefields, Nicaragua, to Colón in canoe for contraband items."

Mr. Jonathan Tyndal remembers making a trip to Bocas himself just to get four pounds of flour. He remembers using wild honey to sweeten his coffee until the honey ran out.

Of the contract work on the Panama Canal during the war years, George Humphries says:

> "In this last war lots of people went down to work in the Canal. They beg you to work. Plenty people make contract. A couple of us went down on our own. They take contract from all Colombia, Venezuela, because they had plenty of work. All kind of different work. I was working on docks there, loading ships, all

kind of work. They building house, big buildings and hangars for the plane base. Colón have ten docks, and sometimes every one of them filled up with ships in the war time, load with cargo. Working day and night to unload them ships. They carry cement, steel, lumber, zinc, all kind of material. They had workers all around, day and night, making fortifications for the war purpose.

You hear a plane up in the air, you get under a shelter they have there. Soldiers all about, big guns. Sometimes you have blackouts in the night, all lights stay off, you can't smoke a cigarette neither. When the work slow down I come home back, and soon I hear the war stop. I liked over Panama. Made good money."

## Revolution

Not long after peace was restored in the world, war came to Costa Rica. In April 1948, José Figueres Ferrer led a revolution whose success was to have a major impact on Limón and the Talamanca Coast. The new government that don Pepe established would be the first Costa Rican government to respond in a positive way to the needs of the Afro-Caribbean population on the Atlantic coast. The determination of the coastal people to build schools and roads would be met by cooperation on the part of the government; the ban against employment of blacks outside the Atlantic Zone would be repealed; and gradually the people of the Talamanca Coast would begin to take part in Costa Rican politics, exercising their rights as citizens. There would be difficulties and disappointments, too, attending the assimilation of Limón into the Costa Rican political and social world; a loss of the cohesive identity of the Afro-Caribbean people, confusion, and a conflict of cultures. But there would be no turning back to the days of cultural homogeneity and political isolation. Talamanca was to be claimed by Costa Rica for better and for worse.

But in April 1948, the coastal people had no idea of the significance don Pepe's revolution would hold for them. All they knew was that guns were firing in the streets of Limón, the train was stopped, the docks were closed, and there were rumors that soldiers were on their way to Cahuita. The young men of Cahuita had no interest in fighting a war for or against anyone. Jonathan Tyndal tells what happened:

"A lot of young men out here were making jokes and frightening each other. A rumor did come over that they are coming here to take up the young men to carry them to fight. So all of us run that night.

Maldo came here the night around ten o'clock. 'John! John! They coming! I just see a gang of them coming up here!' And I was laying down. I kind of wake up out my sleep. I was a little foolish. I jump up, draw on my clothes and run out, because I had a plan that if they really come for us, I'm going to run for the boat. And after I shove off the boat it's Bocas I'm going to. And Maldo come and call me so sudden, same time I jump, run down where the boat is and shove off the boat, and we was going.

I said, 'But Maldo, wait now. We can't go like this. Only we two alone. There's plenty more boys would like to get away too. Let's haul up the boat here and see if we can go back and sneak in easy and see who of them we can carry.' Him don't want to come back. I say, 'All right. You stay here in the boat, and I going back.'

We was down at the point. So him remain there, and I come back. And when I come I look around and I see none of the boys them. And I look and I see some of them over on the beach there, hiding. I see some of them in the pasture, I see some of them go over on the tramline. So I tell them, 'Who want to go, come with me. I can carry five.' Well, them say, 'Let we wait and see when daylight what really happen.' I say, 'That's the best thing.' But when daylight, not a thing like that. We stay out in the bush the whole night, the whole night. But still some of the boys believe it, that there is someone coming to look for us, so some still remain in the bush hiding.

We down here didn't care who did win because we were just living. And at that time we didn't used to vote. We didn't business with it at that time. A few of the colored folks in Limón used to vote, but we down here never used to vote until 1952."

A number of coastal residents were witnesses to the taking of Limón by José Figueres' troops. Mr. Selven Bryant recalls:

"When the Revolution break out in Limón, I was there. That time my mother living in Limón. I was going out from her house to get the train to come home to Old Harbour. So when I reach by the Park, going to the station, I hear gunfire in the Park, but I didn't pay it much mind. I reach the station, buy my ticket and go and sit in the train, and when I look on the Aduana [customs] building I see a man up there with a rifle on him back. And still a few shot firing in the Park. So I say, what kind of business is this?

When the train leave out now, it come down by the crossing and it turn back to the station, and it leave out again. And people start to come off the train. I say, well, I not coming off. And when the train reach the crossing now, you see man coming with rifle on them back and they start to shoot the train. And the driver kick up a speed, man, and him never stop till him reach a place called Santa Rosa.

When I reach Bananito, I see some man line up to go Limón. I say, 'Revolution in Limón!'

When I come to Penshurst I see some more, and I say, 'Revolution in Limón!'

And I walk it from Penshurst right to Old Harbour and tell all the people, say, 'Revolution in Limón!' and everybody get scared.

And after that, no more train from Limón, no launch for about eight days. Anybody coming this side to get away from the fighting, they had was to walk it."

The 1948 Revolution would be the last political event in Costa Rica from which the people of the Talamanca Coast could hide. From then on their destinies would be influenced, as never before, by the workings of the government in San José.

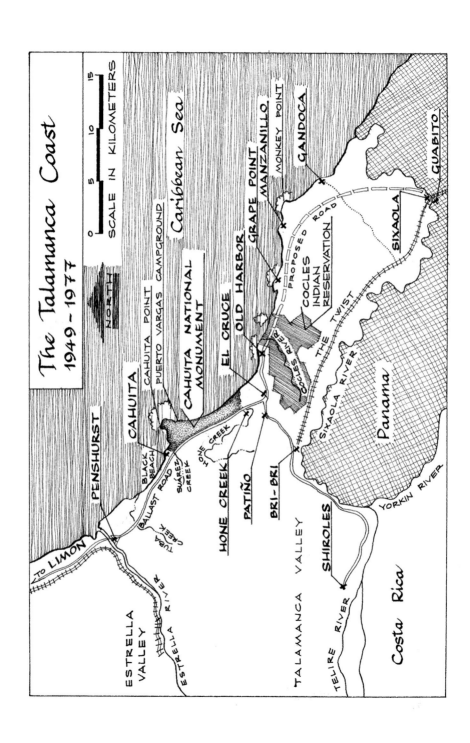

The Talamanca Coast
1949–1977

SCALE IN KILOMETERS

0    5    10    15

NORTH

Caribbean Sea

PENSHURST

CAHUITA

BLACK BEACH

(BALLAST ROAD)

SUÁREZ CREEK

HONE CREEK

CAHUITA POINT

PUERTO VARGAS CAMPGROUND

CAHUITA NATIONAL MONUMENT

EL CRUCE

OLD HARBOR

GRAPE POINT

MANZANILLO

MONKEY POINT

GANDOCA

PROPOSED ROAD

COCLES INDIAN RESERVATION

SIXAOLA

GUABITO

COCLES RIVER

THE TWIST

SIXAOLA RIVER

Panama

PATIÑO

BRI-BRI

HONE CREEK

SHIROLES

TALAMANCA VALLEY

YORKIN RIVER

TELIRE RIVER

Costa Rica

ESTRELLA VALLEY

ESTRELLA RIVER

TUBA CREEK

To LIMON

# The Third Generation

## Citizens (1949-1977)

"Now is when we have to be fighting most of all ...
to protect our community, our property, our way of life."

Mr. Alphaeus Buchanan

# 13. Entering the Modern World

Since 1948, Cahuita has experienced the most rapid and extensive development of all the coastal communities. When the area around Cahuita Point was declared a National Monument by executive decree in 1970, Cahuita began attracting national and international attention as a tourist area. It has also become the center of activity for government ministries and development programs serving the Talamanca region.

A quick glimpse of Cahuita today will illustrate the dramatic changes that have taken place since the Revolution.

A Preview: Cahuita, 1977

It is Semana Santa (Holy Week) 1977, and a visitor from the Central Valley has come to enjoy the four-day holiday at the Cahuita National Monument. The shops in Cahuita comply with government prohibition of liquor vending for the prescribed period. For weeks the population has been preparing for the rush of tourists who have never heard of Easter Monday, the old-time Jamaican holiday. As a matter of fact, few children raised in Cahuita have heard of Easter Monday.

Our visitor steps off a bus after a one-hour ride from Limón that costs him less than the four-hour trip by train, canoe, and bus cost local residents two years ago. He arrives in a village of cheerfully painted laurel wood houses perched on cement posts, roofed with zinc sheets. The wide streets cough dust when the tourist vehicles pass, or splash mud, depending on the weather. Jukebox music blares from the central bars—Spanish salsa, Jamaican reggae, an occasional old-time calypso tune, North American rock and roll. In a circle young boys whirl gigs (spinning tops) in the street, taunting each other in a creative mixture of Spanish and English boy-talk. Behind them, on the porch of Tabash's shop, the overflow crowd from the bar lounges on benches, beers in hand, lethargic from sun and drink. Miss Willel sits in her customary spot at the corner, selling bags of fried plantain chips out of a green-painted kerosene tin.

Movement flows south down Alfredo Gonzales Flores Avenue toward the beach. Fast-talking Ticos from the Central Valley carry their blaring transistor radios and ice chests bulging with Coca Cola and

Palo Viejo. A pair of bearded, sunburned gringos toss a frisbee over the heads of their surfboard-toting companions, nearly colliding with a cocoa farmer who is wearily guiding his horse toward home. A young boy balancing a broad, blue plastic basin on his head approaches a couple of tall blonde women in halter tops and jean skirts.

"Patty? You want patty?" he calls.

"What's a patty?"

"Meat patty. It have cow meat and plenty pepper."

"Oh no, we don't eat meat; we're vegetarians!" they say, walking on toward the beach followed by a slowly sauntering group of floppy-hatted local men, at ease in their hometown, amused by all the activity of the tourists.

Our visitor joins the flow toward the beach, smelling Miss Rachel's banana bread baking in her outdoor oven as he passes, hearing the Buda Band practicing its electric music for tonight's dance at the bar. At the Park Service hut by the entrance to the beach he takes a litter bag offered to him by the guard, stuffing it into his plastic PanAm bag. And there before him lies the blue-green Caribbean, rolling in across turtle grass and pirate ships and rawa ranches, but all our visitor can see are the hundreds of bathers and picnickers occupying the shore. Canvas tents dot the coconut walk—there will be no horse race this Easter Monday—and tentless travelers are busy constructing their own shelters from palm branches, leaving dozens of young coconut trees stripped, some dying. Everywhere bathers are drinking coconut water, heedless of the fact that the coconuts are a cash crop, cultivated by the local farmers whose fathers and grandfathers brought them here when the coast was woodland.

Our visitor returns to Cahuita where he has reserved a hotel room at Mrs. Lam's, complete with running water and electricity. He drinks beer at an outdoor canteen, set up for the long weekend by Turrialba businessmen. He buys a beach hat from a Limón vendor and a shell necklace from a Cahuita school girl. For dinner he goes to Miss Bertha's house, where he enjoys a plate of traditional Jamaican rice and beans with curried chicken and a cabbage salad, listening to Johnny Cash on the record player. He has to make up his mind how to spend the evening. Dancing to the Buda Band at the bar? A movie at Mrs. Lam's theater? Shooting pool? Joining the local men for dominoes on the porch of Miss Gatha's fresco shop?

He decides to take a walk around the town. A modern four-room cement block school proudly exhibits the Costa Rican flag. An Education and Nutrition Center is under construction across the school yard, and there is a large zinc-roofed court with a stage. A Salud Rural jeep is parked in front of a cement block dispensary with a sign on the door: "Consultation Hours," flanked by posters offering information about venereal disease, alcoholism, and birth control. Next door is the headquarters of the Guardia Rural with a list of letters received last week: English names, Spanish names, Chinese names. A lighted sign on the porch of a new frame building reads: Banco Nacional de Costa Rica. There's a public telephone sign at Mr. Sorrows' shop, and the porch wall is covered with tacked-up notices: "Donate To The Red Cross Ambulance." "Open Forum Sunday On The National Park Debate: Come To The All-Purpose Room At The School, 3 p.m." "MONGE" on a green and white political banner. Bus schedules. "Banana Cutting Tuesday." "The Cahuita Baptist Church Invites You To The Easter Sunday Program, 3 p.m. Everybody Welcome."

Bandanaed women and white-haired old men nod and murmur "all right" from their porches, watching the sun set as our visitor passes. They won't be telling Anansi stories tonight; they're listening to a radio.

Three decades of history remain to be recounted to show how the Talamanca Coast developed between the discouraging years of the 1940s and the confusing but more comfortable years of the 1970s.


Don Pepe Takes A Look

The changes in Talamanca were heralded by José Figueres himself, who came to visit Old Harbour shortly after fighting his successful revolution. No high-ranking Costa Rican politician had visited the Talamancan shores since President Alfredo González Flores was marooned in Cahuita quite accidentally. But Figueres came because his political sense told him Costa Rica would have much to gain by developing the resources of Talamanca. He came in a ship operated by an American company that was taking up the black sand from Old Harbour beaches. Mr. Mason remembers playing host to Don Pepe:

> "Don Pepe came here for the first time on the last ship they sent for the sand, the last trip the company made. It was about six in the night when they arrived. And when he was leaving, about three in the morning, he said, 'I appreciate the reception. I came here by night and I am returning by night, but I have to return to Puerto Viejo sometime soon, that I can know the place by day.'
>
> It was soon after the revolution but before he became President, about 1949. When they came it was twenty-eight

of them, all officials, and I made a banquet for them. We had
a bands of music, Vibert Myrie from Grape Point play a
trumpet, and we had several other pieces of music, and we
receive him out the boat with music and a banner and march
him here to the banquet and march him back again to the
boat with music.

And he return very short after he become President with the
Loffland Oil Company in a small square rig, the *Ardilla*. She
make from Limón to here in one hour. And they went up to the
first well that they going to dig at Patiño."

Obviously, Señor Figueres was interested in the commercial
potential of the Talamanca area, as evidenced by the activities of the
American companies. No one on the coast knows today exactly what
the sand company was searching for, but it occupied a stretch of beach
for about a year, sending off enormous quantities of black sand to the
States. Mr. Mason recalls:

"That sand company was two American guys, John
Livingood and another one. Somebody send them out for a test
on the sand. They put a tramline on the beach, and a launch,
invasion launch, came ashore, and they run the sand right on
from a tramcar when the sea was calm. And when the sea was
rough, they anchor off-shore and hire boats to carry out the bags.
They stay here about a year. The boat take out to Limón about a
thousand bags of sand every day."

The sand company was the first to make use of Mr. Mason's plane
base in Old Harbour. "They pay me twenty-five colones for each
coconut tree, and eighty coconut trees we destroy to improve the base,"
Mr. Mason remembers.

The Loffland Oil Company

Soon after the sand company left, the Loffland Oil Company appeared on the shores of Old Harbour with a concession from the government to extend the old Sinclair Company's search for oil. It was to
visit Loffland's first oil well at Patiño that Pepe Figueres made his
second trip to Talamanca.

Mr. Mason recalls the initial activity of the Loffland Company in
Old Harbour. "They came in the early Fifties. They bring this barge
you see in the water there now from the Canal Zone with a big

tugboat, come and sink a foundation and use it for a dock. They had big boat coming in here. The dock was longer than what you see now, but the sea knock off a piece of it when it rot. Loffland work here about three years. I rent them the plane base and that area around it. All the camps, *talleres* [mechanic shops], warehouse, everything was right there."

To facilitate their search for oil in the Talamanca interior, the Loffland workers began building a road from Old Harbour inland, the first road for motor vehicles on the Talamanca Coast. When they completed the first stretch from Old Harbour to their first well at Patiño, they split their work parties into two groups, one to work the well, the other to continue the road inland to Fields (now Bribri) and eventually as far as Shiroles.

Of the oil that the Loffland Company found in Patiño, Mr. Mason says, "It was so clean that you could take it just like coconut oil and rub it in your hands. It smell nice. And we light it and it burn." But after years of work and the incredible expense of road-building through the woodland, the Loffland Company decided "the oil wasn't commercial enough and they remove out," Mr. Mason says. The Gulf Oil Company would come in 1960 to try once more, but they only stayed about eight months and said they found nothing of commercial value.

The Loffland Oil Company left behind it a serviceable plane base, having spent seventy thousand colones to improve it, according to Mr. Mason. For several years a private aviation company made regular landings in Old Harbour to pick up passengers en route to Sixaola or Limón. Mr. Cyril Gray remembers the "little plane that used to land here three times a week, carry just four passengers. As long as there is space for passengers, it come. First it was thirty-five colón per head. Finally it just didn't want to come, refusing to land here. They say the base not licensed and this and that." New houses line the unused air strip today.

According to David Buchanan, the modern names for many of the creeks in Talamanca were chosen by the surveyors and engineers working for the Loffland Company to map the route for their road. Whereas the original settlers gave their own names to the creeks to denote property boundaries, the *petroleros* selected names according to their own whims. Mr. Buchanan recalls, "I remember talking to one of the engineers for the oil company, and he told me about Hotel Creek and the different creeks. Why they gave the name Hotel Creek is because it is there they sat down and ate their lunch, so it come to them like a hotel. The engineer told me that."

Building a Road

By far the most important legacy of the Loffland Oil Company in Talamanca is the road it built from Old Harbour to Fields and beyond. Mr. Mason became the second private vehicle owner on the coast when he imported an International truck from the United States, set down on the Old Harbour dock by a Loffland ship in 1952. Mr. Mason was then in the unique position of being able to provide transportation for passengers, crops, and building material between Old Harbour and the communities of the Talamanca interior. His first business deal was with a Cuban company that wanted to buy cedar logs. Mr. Mason hauled the cedar from Bambú to the Cuban ship docked in Old Harbour. It was the beginning of a twenty-five-year trucking career for a man who had spent the first thirty years of his life walking Indian trails.

For the rest of the population, the Loffland road inspired hope that their tramline, which met the road at a junction known as El Cruce, could be replaced by a road from El Cruce to Penshurst. It was the Cahuita people who took the lead in requesting government financing for the construction of the road.

From the days of the UNIA and the earliest English and Spanish schools, the one committee that had served the community consistently was the School Board. In the late 1930s, when the Spanish School expanded to offer all six grades of primary education, the teachers organized a *Junta de Educación* with specific responsibilities and authority granted by the Ministry of Public Education. Lacking any other organized community association with specific links to government offices in San José, the people naturally turned to the *Junta de Educación* to put through their request for a road.

Mr. Sorrows, then vice-president of the Junta, tells how the committee first made a successful bid for a new school building and used the school's inauguration ceremony to get the road underway:

"In the year 1953 we made a petition, asked the government to get interested in the road from Patiño up to Penshurst. We invited the Minister of Public Works, who was Francisco Orlich in Figueres' government. He came in to inaugurate the school during Figueres' first term as President of the country.

The petition was made through the School Board, of which William Tabash was the president. Your humble servant was vice-president, Ben Scott was the treasurer, and the English School teacher here at the time, named Ebert, was secretary, and some other people. We were without a school then and we were making petition constantly to the Ministry of Education, and we never get any result.

Finally we decide to get a school somehow because the one we had was going to ruin. So myself and William Tabash formed a commission sent by the *Junta de Educación* to Limón to talk to the president of the Municipality, who was at that time Hernán Garrón Salazar. And he immediately formed a solution for us. We invited the Municipal Board here, plus the governor of the province, and they promised us a school. Of course we had to contribute. We went around and got contributions from the people, and the Municipality in Limón put the balance, and they built us a school with two classrooms.

For the inauguration of the school we invited the President because there was so much necessity, that we invited him that he would see and offer something. But he couldn't come, so he sent his Minister of Public Works. All that was Garrón's effort. And Mr. Orlich came, and he saw the condition. We took him part way down on the tram, and he promised us that when he went back to San José he would take it up with the Cabinet and see what can be done to get the road.

And it wasn't six months afterward the road started. The first section came from Patiño to near the place called Punta Caliente. Then from there the next government take it to Comadre. Then from Comadre to Cahuita, and the last from Cahuita to Penshurst, that last part with a contractor name of Juan Rafael Sánchez."

It may sound quick and easy the way Mr. Sorrows tells it, but the construction that began at El Cruce in 1953 wasn't completed to Penshurst (22 kilometers) until 1967.

When Pepe Figueres came to view Loffland's oil well at Patiño, the construction was bogged down, literally, in mud. For the next thirteen years the people would petition each incoming government, at four-year intervals, to allocate sufficient funds to complete the road. The result was that each government gave some money to the project, enough to move the road through a few more kilometers, and when the money ran out the people had to wait until the next government came in to file their next petition. In the meantime local farmers joined the construction crews as voluntary workers, putting their own time and muscle into the project, resolving not to give up.

And they gave money. Alphaeus Buchanan remembers:

"When the road was to continue from Hone Creek to Cahuita, don Hernán [Garrón] was president of the Municipality in Limón. And he came here, and in one day the people of

Cahuita, Penshurst and Hone Creek contributed twenty-eight thousand colones in cash besides around six thousand colones in offers, to pay for the interest and the bonds that they were going to use as a loan to build the road. And those were the dark days of the early Sixties when cocoa was selling at only fifty and sixty colones a quintal. The people would give money, give time, go and work to build the roads."

The old tramline was taken up section by section as the road construction progressed. In the early 1960s, when the road was finished between El Cruce and Comadre bridge, just south of Cahuita, travelers from Limón would ride the train to Penshurst, take a canoe across the Estrella River, bounce along on a mule car to Comadre, and then (what a pleasure!) board a bus to Old Harbour.

The first Talamanca bus was shipped in by David Bryant of Hone Creek, who operated it between Fields and Old Harbour and whatever point the road construction had reached. While construction work was in progress, travelers walked through the mud, across piles of ballast and around machinery between the end of the tramline and the beginning of the road. "It was very rough," remembers John Burke. "We suffer that hardship for many years. But it is so said, after the storm there comes a calm. And so, the road was completed to Penshurst [in 1967]."

Here's how Mr. Burke finishes the story of land transportation from Talamanca to Limón, bringing us up to the present time:

"But then for nine more years we had the crossing of the River Estrella. That was another terrible go. It give me heart beats when I had to go across there on those canoe with my wife Blanca, because she was so nervous, you know. I'd say to her, 'Take it easy, man. Look, all the people going across and nothing happen. You'll go across like them too.' But anyway, she was a bit nervous that way. Until, Hallelujah! It was so said they're gonna string up the bridge! Blanca never did live to see that much. And that's how it is today. We can get the run from Cahuita right to Limón and after Limón on to San José all in the same day. So the improvement is wonderful—wonderful!"

The contracts to construct the road did not include building the entrance stretch from the road to the town of Cahuita, nor did they include the maintenance work on the completed sections or within the towns of Old Harbour and Cahuita. Members of these communities turned out to do road work, understanding that no one would do it for them, accepting as their fathers and grandfathers had that when something needs doing you go out and do it. Fred Ferguson tells of Cahuita's volunteer road construction crews:

> "Everybody who had a horse or a mule would bring out that beast to draw stone from some part to fill up some mud hole. Was every Friday they did agree to do that work. I remember George Humphries was a very active man in that work and this same Mr. Burke. Is so they make the road from the crossing in to Cahuita, that sort of a Y, and right down to where the police is now. Who don't have a mule, well you give labor by help to pack those stone and shovel and throw dirt, because it was mud. Just a few people decide to do it, and everybody roll out every Friday to work."

Selven Bryant talks about similar efforts in Old Harbour:

> "You have a bridge to build, everybody come together to fix that bridge. Up to a few years ago whenever this *carretera* get bad, people get together and go in the woodland and get logs and bring them out. Mason saw lumber, and we become the engineer to build the bridge them. We used to build Hotel Creek bridge and those two bridge going into Old Harbour. Yes, the people do it.

Bob Bernthal

Construction of the bridge across the Estrella River at Penshurst, completed in 1976, finally linked the Talamanca communities to Limón by road.

One man spend a lot of money to keep up that road from Bambú coming out here, Tonio Villalobos. He have to come here for his merchandise, so he just have to fix the road himself."

In the mid-1950s, the people of Old Harbour and Cahuita formed *Juntas Progresistas* (Committees for Progress), whose main tasks were to organize volunteers to repair and maintain roads. Alphaeus Buchanan gives this account of the formation of the *Junta Progresista* and its work in Cahuita:

"It was a new law that we had that communities could be forming into *Juntas Progresistas* to work along with the Municipal Board at the community level to solve local problems. So all over the country we had *Juntas Progresistas*. They function just like the Municipality, and the people would contribute whatever they could afford. And they would do any local projects like building bridges, schools, dispensaries.

The *Juntas* were elected by the communities. In Cahuita, Leslie Williams and William Tabash were in the *Junta*, I myself was president for a term. The project we did in Cahuita was that culvert over by Miss Coleman there. We were to get some money from the deputies.[1] We call that *partidas específicas*, but we never got those moneys because of political reasons. It's hard when the deputies don't take such an interest. Mr. Buchner was the overseer, the director of that culvert work, because he had a lot of experience. He used to work with the government as a foreman. The people volunteered their labor, and we built it ourselves. The little truck I had did all the drawing of stones and materials, the sand and everything. That was the only truck in Cahuita then."

Mr. Buchanan tells about Cahuita's second truck, which he brought here thirty years after the original "It Can Be Done" arrived.

"That truck came in 1955. We brought it across the Estrella River in three boats. We put three boats together and tied them, put some planks across, and then I drove it right on, and we poled it across the river. And we put up some planks to mount it on the burro cart, and one mule pull it right in to Cahuita."

---

[1] English-speaking people refer to Costa Rican legislators as "deputies," deriving the word from the Spanish term *diputado*.

Mr. Buchanan was so anxious to use his vehicle that in the years before the road was completed to Cahuita, he would mount the truck on a mule car, urge the mule to the end of the tramline, roll out the truck and drive to his property near Hone Creek, returning to Cahuita the same day by the same procedure done in reverse. It could be done, yes, but only by the very determined.

The Cocoa Economy

As it always had been on the Talamanca Coast, the primary motivation for seeking improved transportation was to market the area's produce. As the farmers returned to planting cocoa after the dismal years of the Forties, and as the population of the area increased, farms spread farther up the hillsides, extending greater distances away from the buyers' markets at Old Harbour, Cahuita, and Penshurst.

To get their cocoa to the Hole and Cahuita, for instance, a farmer would carry it in sacks to the tramline, load it on a mule car, drive the mule to the Cahuita crossing, then load it on a horse to transport it through the streets of Cahuita to the Hole. There it would wait for the launch, sometimes for a week if weather prevented landings. The people of Cahuita finally requested and received help from the government to build a public *bodega*, or storage shed, at the Hole, so the farmers could leave their cocoa overnight without being concerned about rain damaging it.

The *bodega* served its purpose until the road, completed to Penshurst, put the latter-day launches like the *Moderno* out of business. The *Moderno* was last seen on the Talamanca Coast in 1967. By that time it was running mainly to Grape Point and Manzanillo, where no road competed with its services. When the *Moderno* ceased its Talamanca trips, Mr. Maxi, a Manzanillo shop owner, took over the job of ferrying the southern area's agricultural produce to Old Harbour, where it was transferred to trucks. Mr. Maxi still runs his dugout motorboat between Manzanillo and Old Harbour today, while he and his neighbors wait for the road to reach them.

Cocoa farmers, who struggled through the difficult years of the 1940s, were rewarded for their perseverance in the early 1950s, when the price of cocoa started rising. Encouraged, they sought ways of sustaining their good fortune by circumventing the middlemen, the Limón trading companies, that bought Talamanca cocoa at one price and sold it abroad at a much higher price. To do this, the cocoa farmers organized a cooperative, *La Cooperativa de Productores de Cacao del Atlántico* (COOPROCAL), and began exporting their own produce.

Mr. Sorrows describes the "gigantic" success of the cooperative:

"In the early Fifties, a lot of farmers got together in this area here, and they formed a cooperative. It started to go along fairly good. The fellow who assisted most in organizing the cooperative so good was a fellow name of Johnny Humphries. He belong to right here in Cahuita, but he worked for the United Fruit Company quite a while, and he had a very good idea of accounting and so on, so he helped to arrange the cooperative. Another fellow who took a good part in it, too, was Conrad White from Limón.

That cooperative went up gigantic, and they bought a small launch. I think that launch could carry maybe two hundred sacks of cocoa to Limón. The launch was the

Ripe cocoa pods grow directly from the trunk of the cocoa tree.

Paula Palmer

*Cooprocal,* the organization was named COOPROCAL. They did well. The exportation was great. In fact, all the other local exporters had to stay aside whilst the cooperative went ahead because all the big producers took share in the cooperative. And there went the mass of cocoa. But it was gigantic. I think that cooperative used to export eighty to eighty-five percent of the cocoa in the Atlantic Zone.

While the cooperative was working strong, the farmers got more money for the cocoa because they would get an initial price of approximately what the other exporters would pay for a quintal of cocoa, and then when the cocoa was exported they would get a dividend. It obligated the other exporters to pay the maximum prices. Because they still have people who sold them cocoa because there were some people who did not join the cooperative. So the cooperative obligated them to pay a better price to everyone.

The best year for the cocoa farmers was 1954. At that time the cooperative was in its swing. We had a very good year with season, good year with the crop. Cocoa went to a peak of three colones per pound, or three hundred for the quintal. That was the most the people had ever got for cocoa. But then the cooperative begin to fail.

As the time went by, I don't know what scheme the exporters used, but the cooperative went to pieces. It started to fail in '56, if I'm not mistaken, '56 to '57. And the bank came in because Johnny and Conrad left or they were fired, and then the new management came in and the bank started to administrate the cooperative. But a lot of the farmers were afraid to support it. A lot of people became disinterested because they figured they would not get any benefit in the hands of the bank, so they didn't support it, and it failed. After it failed it owed a lot of money.

But before the cooperative went down they bought a bigger boat, that one came from the United States, second hand. It was too big along the coast here because it couldn't get enough freight to support it. I think they finally sold it.

A group of the initiators had to be responsible for the indebtedness of the cooperative. They had a lot of properties, and all was turned over to the bank. They had a cocoa dryer. And I think those men may be still indebted to the bank.

The only way the farmers can have a better opportunity for their produce is if they can get together and export it like any other producers in Costa Rica, such as coffee, cane, cattle, and so on. But I can say that the people are so scared that I'm afraid they would never try to organize another cooperative."

Selles Johnson says the people of the coast will never forget the year 1954, when perfect cocoa weather and a smoothly functioning cooperative rendered the best profit ever for the farmers:

> "1954 was the blessedest year we ever have. Everybody talk about that time. Never a year like 1954 again, no more. 1954 was the blessedest year here. Good dry times, we didn't have much rain. Now and then a little rain, but not too much. Good sun, but not too much. The climate was just all right. Everybody getting plenty plenty plenty cocoa, plenty coconut, everything was plentiful for all the people."

But in the years following the demise of the cooperative, it became increasingly difficult to make a living on cocoa production in

Mr. Fred Ferguson breaks a cocoa pod.

Talamanca. Arnold Hanbelamt came to Cahuita from San José in 1961, hoping he could make a better living for his growing family as a cocoa farmer. "But really," he says, "it never work out so." Mr. Hanbelamt explains how world politics affects the Talamanca cocoa economy:

Stirring cocoa beans as they dry in the sun on Mr. Cana Tyndal's barbecues, a young Cahuitan learns the business of cocoa farming.

"We bought two farms. The cocoa crops were excellent, but the price was awful. I remember it went down to sixty colones a quintal, then it went up to eighty-five colones a quintal, and we thought we were getting a top price, and then it went down back again. Until a long time it went up to one hundred and twenty colones, one hundred twenty-five colones, and back down.

Life was really rough in those days. As soon as the crop was off you were broke. The money you make off the farm working real hard never last to keep you working on the farm for a season. There was a year when things went worse, too. Even Mr. Plummer with fifteen hectares of cocoa had was to go out to work in the refinery in Limón when they just start building up. That was around 1966. The crop of cocoa was always good, but the price was very low.

The problem was Guyana used to produce quite a bit of cocoa, as Brazil, Ecuador, Colombia, Mexico, and Puerto Rico,

231

so they had an abundance of cocoa all around. And the Soviet Union and Japan wasn't competing in the cocoa commerce. The United States had a monopoly in the cocoa market. Then you know that problem, if one of these small countries would do business with a socialist country, the United States can cut their loans or something. So they just have to keep in business with the United States. It's just in the last eight years since we really start doing business with anybody who would buy. That's when the price started going up, in 1970. And now the price never go back down, just keep increasing. So you can make a living now.

The other thing that is in our favor now, it seems that bananas pay more than cocoa if you plant it in large scale. So you have a lot of countries that had cocoa farm that cut down their cocoa trees and plant bananas. So the cocoa got scarce, and the price went higher. Colombia, Ecuador, Brazil, and I hear African countries are producing bananas now in large scale.

I had to know these things because in the Sixties I felt the pinch."

## The Regional Association and the Alliance for Progress

It was the economic "pinch" of the early 1960s that motivated the initiation of political organization in Talamanca. Mr. Alphaeus Buchanan discusses the beginnings of the Regional Association that served as the community development organization for Talamanca from 1965 through 1969:

"The Regional Association started as a result of the low price in cocoa in the years '64 and '65. I think it started from '63. But it worsened in '65 like it had never done before. The price went right down to forty-five colones for a quintal, or forty-five cents for a pound. People were getting hungry here. Some of the poorer people that work on the farms, for instance, were eating just bananas and salt. Things was really sad.

In those days it was very dark for farmers. Nobody could help nobody. The banks had no interest in helping the people because the banks do everything on a commercial level, and if you can't pay, you can't get any money. So how could we pay when we weren't getting any prices for our cocoa?

I was going to Siquirres one morning to talk to some Nicaraguans who were paying a little more for cocoa. So when I went to the station in Limón, I met a group of politicians who were going in to San José to have an interview with Daniel Oduber, who was then Minister. So they invited me to go with them.

While talking to Daniel, I asked him if, as Minister of Public Relations, he don't think something could be done to help us with the price for cocoa, and he said no, because the situation was so bad in the market that the best thing we could do was to cut down the cocoa, plant bananas and plantains. So he didn't give us a solution. I thought it was all a crazy idea to tell farmers to cut their cocoa, plant plantains and bananas, and don't tell them well, we're going to finance you until those crops come about. Well, we didn't take it serious, because our parents did it before, and they had to plant back cocoa.

So we left, and I asked my friends to accompany me to the United States Embassy, and we met Mr. Lobit, Hugh C. Lobit, which was the Third Secretary of the Embassy. And we told him just what we had told the Minister. And we asked if the Embassy couldn't do something about the prices up in New York. He told us it was very difficult, and the only thing he could advise us was the same as the Minister said, diversify our products.

Well, I told him about our other social problems, and he said if you need help you would have to request it through your government because it would have to be a government-to-government concern. So I told him, if you can't help us directly without our government intervene, let's forget that I came here to you. Because we know our government isn't going to do anything for us. So he was very much concerned when I told him that. And he said, 'O.K., I'm going to give you all a visit.' And it wasn't one week after that he was here. He and his wife and another man from the Embassy. And we talked, and he was convinced.

He told us it was going to be a hard fight because the people in the Alliance for Progress think that the people of the Atlantic Zone is a useless people, you can't do anything for them. But he was going to give it a try. And he did. He left San José and came here every week to meet with us.

That time there was no road from Penshurst. You had to come through all that mud in mule car, mud splashing in your face, sometimes the cars they wreck with him. He would work with us, encourage us.

So when he came, he told us to organize ourselves into a Regional Association, and then they would help us. At that time they had another Regional Association in Guanacaste. But that one was financed and almost managed by the Alliance for Progress. But he told us he wanted a different type here, where the people would do the work and the Alliance for Progress would finance. And effectively it was like that. We had it organized the 12 of September 1965, and the Alliance for Progress gave us all the materials we needed, and we would do the labor.

We put up a telephone system here. We made a ferry over the Estrella River, the Peace Corps cooperated with us. We had a ferryboat over the river to bring over trucks and everything.

They gave us a cement mixer. The Municipality has it now, working on municipal projects. We made a series of culverts between Bribri and Bambú and coming down this side. We even started to build the Catarata bridge. The Alliance give us all the materials. We never had any cash from them. And then we, the people, did all the work, all the administration. Mr. Lobit came back any time he could to help us, encourage us. They finally fired him, got him out, because he was so aggressive in fighting for us. And he went to Viet Nam, and there he lost his life.

Lots of the American people kicked up against the Alliance because they said they were giving away the American money. But that wasn't true, because the Americans were getting things from us—our cocoa—at less than cost, actually. So they were only giving us back a little of what they got from us for nothing."

Alphaeus Buchanan served as president of the Regional Association in Talamanca, with representatives on the Board of Directors from all the participating communities—Cahuita, Penshurst, Puerto Viejo, Sixaola, Bambú, and Amubre.

"We did wonders," Mr. Buchanan says, remembering especially the enthusiastic cooperation of all the people of Talamanca who participated in the telephone project. A fifty-cent charge for each call provided funds to maintain the wires and poles until the Regional Association collapsed and the Municipality declined to continue the maintenance effort. More than a decade would go by before the national telephone service would install its first public telephones on the coast.

It was the Regional Association that arranged for the first nurses to come to Talamanca. The Board's requests to the Ministry of Health for a doctor in the area were consistently refused. Finally, the American Embassy contacted the Mennonite Mission, which sent the first volunteer nurse to Old Harbour in 1966. From the Alliance for Progress the Regional Association procured two electric plants for the nurses to use in the health dispensaries at Old Harbour and Fields, and a station wagon to transport the nurses to outlying communities. A report of Regional Association activities states that within fifteen minutes of its arrival in Cahuita the station wagon was dispatched to carry a sick child to the health dispensary in Old Harbour. The Mennonite nurses continued to serve the people of Talamanca until 1976.

Through the determination of its leaders, the cooperation of the Talamanca communities, and the collaboration of the Alliance for Progress, the Regional Association achieved great success in the four and a half years of its existence. Its most difficult task, according to its president, was to get the cooperation of the Legislative Assembly and the appropriate ministries in San José. Finally the Board's frustration with the unresponsiveness of the Costa Rican government led to the collapse of the Regional Association. Mr. Buchanan tells what happened:

"We had gotten from the Deputy, Hernán Garrón, one hundred thousand colones, fifty for the Regional Association, twenty-five for Old Harbour, twenty-five for Cahuita, for development of the area. So we had decided to use the money to buy two dump trucks. Then we were planning to ask the Alliance to favor us with a loader so we could use these trucks to maintain the roads that were already in existence. The oil company had built the road from Old Harbour all the way to Shiroles, and at that time the road this side was complete as far as Comadre bridge. So we decided to use these trucks to maintain these roads, because the government had no maintenance equipment inside here after the company moved out with their own.

But some deputies saw to it that the Minister didn't give us that money, so we lost the one hundred thousand colones. And I went to San José, and I fought with the head office of the DINADECO. And I told them that according to law they were the ones that should defend us. They were responsible for talking to the Minister and seeing to it that he gives us our money. Two weeks after I talked with them, they wrote me and told me that we wouldn't get the money.

So I call a meeting with the other members of the Board, and I told them that for the last four, almost five years, we've been spending our money out of our pocket, the money we should be using to educate our children, to build this Regional Association, and now that we try to get a little help from our own government, and they refuse us, it show that they have no good intention for us, and what we really doing is government work. So I'm not going to spend any more of my children's money doing that work. All those sacrifices we the leaders of the Regional Association made, and all the work of the poor people who couldn't afford to give even a colón but they work, planting all those telephone posts, building culverts, drawing rocks and dirt for years. So we said, if government help has failed us, why continue? So we resigned, and from then the Regional Association went down."

Political Participation

Beginning in the 1950s, Costa Rican political parties started recruiting members in the coastal population. Before 1953, the first year votes were cast in Talamanca, it didn't occur to coastal people to ask for help from the national government, but gradually through the 1950s and 1960s, they began claiming their full rights as Costa Rican citizens.

It was the *Junta Fundadora de la Segunda República*, established by the victorious Revolution of 1948, that opened the way for some 14,000 West Indians in Limón province to gain Costa Rican citizenship. The first step toward exercising rights of citizenship was obtaining a *cédula de identidad* (I.D. card). In spite of the facilitating legislation, it wasn't easy to get a cédula. Mr. Clinton Bennett, born in Limón in 1926, recalls:

> "It was hard to get a cédula in those days; not like now when they come here and take your picture and do everything for you. I remember when I was to get my first cédula after the Revolution, it was through a lawyer, Carlos Silva. You had to get a lawyer to be able to get a cédula! And even then, when I got it it said, 'Costa Rican by naturalization,' even though I was born here.
>
> But once don Pepe became president, the Liberation Party said that black people born in Costa Rica had as much right to citizenship as whites. It was only then that we could get the cédulas that said, 'Costa Rican by birth.'"

It helped, claims Mr. Edwin Patterson, if you promised to vote for the Liberation Party. Cédulas came through promptly for those who registered as party members. Others, like himself, met bureaucratic and economic obstacles. It took him nineteen years to obtain recognition as a Costa Rican by birth.

The first voting in Talamanca took place in Cahuita in 1953. "People from Limón came out here to form committees that year," remembers Mr. Clinton. "Each party had its representatives. They made their propaganda and they took their people by launch to vote in Cahuita." People were not able to cast their votes in Old Harbour until the 1958 elections, and the first voting day there ended in tragedy, as Mr. Clinton recalls:

> "The voting went along normally. We had to carry the votes to Limón by boat. According to the law, the voting booths open at 6 a.m. and close at 6 p.m., and the counting goes very slowly. Around 11 o'clock that night they finished counting the

votes, and a launch was anchored out to sea waiting to take the votes to Limón.

But just then a big wind began to blow and the sea got very rough. Mr. Vincent, don Juan Salinas, David Montegue, Paul Rodman and I set out with the votes into a little canoe to reach the launch. But a huge wave overturned the canoe and we all fell into the water. When I came to the surface I saw the canoe turn over. Mr. David shouted to me, 'Grab onto the canoe!' So we tried to hold on, but every wave that came in hit us so hard—plaaaaaf!—that we dropped into the sea again.

Finally I was so exhausted, I said to the others, 'Boys, I can't hold on any longer. Don't worry about me. I've made up my mind to die right here. Better you save yourselves, because if you keep worrying about me you're going to drown.' And I let go of the boat.

But Mr. David called to me, 'No, no, no, no! You can't do that!' And he grabbed me and threw me on top the canoe. And when I couldn't hold on any longer and was about to let go again, I heard the motor out on the launch start up. We were all yelling, 'help! help!', but it was night and nobody knew what was happening to us. There we were drowning, and nobody knew it! Until finally the people on the launch, it seems they heard us calling and they came to save us. When I heard the motor start up, it gave me hope, and somehow I found the strength to hold on till the rescue.

So the launch came up and pulled us aboard; all were saved except don Juan Salinas. The poor man had already gone down. We searched and searched but we never saw him again, we never recovered the body. Not even his clothes did ever wash up on the beach.

Well, we lost the votes, of course, but we had a copy of the count on shore, and when they hear the story the officials in Limón decide to accept the copy."

Mr. Clinton never again set foot in a boat, but he remains active in politics. He reflects on some of the important changes in the political situation of black people since the Revolution:

"Before 1948, there was a lot of discrimination against black people. Blacks were barred from important positions in Limón that were held only by whites. After 1948, all that changed. When José Figueres was president, we even had a black governor in Limón, Luis Bermúdez.

Before 1948, the government in Limón was actually controlled by the United Fruit Company. You could say the

Company was stronger than the government. Whatever the Company said, it became the law of the land. The hospital was belonging to the Company. All the big businesses were belonging to the Company. The banks were only for the rich. Before 1948, a poor man could never get a loan from a bank, because there was a clique of rich people that ran the banks that time. After they nationalized the banks, they opened their doors and a poor man could ask for credit."

Another important step toward full political participation was taken in 1970, when the cantón of Talamanca was established, with municipal headquarters in Bribri. Talamanca residents now elect their own municipal representatives [regidores], who are charged with managing public services and development in the region.

Arnold Hanbelamt, who became a member of the first Municipal Board of Talamanca, elected in 1970, explains the motivation for creating an independent municipality in the area:

"Until 1970, Talamanca was part of the Central cantón of Limón province. Progress was really slow around here in those days. To get a road inside here, even to build three or four hundred meters of road, you had was to go into Limón, put in your petition, maybe you sit around there the whole night and nobody pay you no mind because they was looking after Pueblo Nuevo or some place around Limón. So the Municipal Board in Limón never pay much interest if somebody come in there from Cahuita. Maybe if someone with influence from here, a large cocoa buyer, maybe Buchanan, Alberto Lam or Tabashes, maybe if they go to the Municipality they try to help them out, but otherwise it was really tough. And usually we never had no representative neither. They usually nominate someone from Limón to represent the Talamanca area. So they never have much interest, and they never know the place neither. So we pushed a program to have an election to make a new cantón."

William Tabash became the first president of the Municipal Board of the new Cantón de Talamanca, with members elected from all the principal communities in the area, from Tuba Creek to the Sixaola River. The projects that Mr. Hanbelamt helped put through for his home community, Cahuita, during his four-year term, included construction of the health dispensary, the office of the Rural Guard, and the Casa Comunal, a building designed for community meetings and programs, now rented to the Banco Nacional de Costa Rica.

Transportation was still a primary concern, and the responsibility for road maintenance now rested in the hands of the new municipal government. Mr. Hanbelamt remembers one year when "we had was to spend all the Municipality's money on the road. Then Puerto Viejo had a big slide out in 1972, and all the money we had to spend on that part of the road, up about a quarter of a mile from Hotel Creek. The road was in a terrible condition in those days. Every four or five months a bridge went down, and everything was mud."

One of the great longings of the people of the coast was for electricity. In each community a shop owner or two operated noisy, unreliable generators for their own use, occasionally running lines to private homes, but at very high prices. After the shops closed for the night, the communities were in darkness. Mr. Hanbelamt, who now works for ICE (Costa Rican Electricity Institute) as manager of the electrification program in Cahuita, tells of the struggle to get public lighting in Cahuita:

> "Electrification was one of the first projects started in 1971 by the Municipal Board. It started out with very little funds, about two thousand colones. The governor of Limón donated some funds to the Municipality of Talamanca to buy a motor plant. And from then on we started looking financing to get a bigger motor and we keep going up till we had something like one hundred seventy-five thousand colones. Reynaldo Maxwell that time was Deputy, and he tried his best to get us some money through the Legislative Assembly until afterwards they turn over part of the program to the ICE to study a plan for the plant, lines, and so on. And the study lasted so long that inflation catch us. The price of the diesel oil went up, so it affected everything. It went up to something like three hundred seventy-five thousand colones. So the whole program, to have everything finished, it cost something like six hundred and fifty thousand colones. It took us two administrations to get the light. Alphaeus Buchanan did a lot of political work outside to get the project through."

The lights in Cahuita were turned on finally in October 1976, with a great community celebration to commemorate the event. Contributions from local residents provided a complete meal and drinks for a delegation of political dignitaries, including Vice President Dr. Carlos Manuel Castillo Obregón, who were invited to take part in the festivities. The campaign to provide electricity in the remaining communities of Talamanca continues.

Maintaining a Culture:
Protestant Churches and English Schools

While the people of Talamanca were learning the skills of political organization, first through their *Juntas Progresistas*, then the Regional Association, and finally the Talamanca Municipal Board, they were also advancing their own interests through churches, schools, sports, and social clubs. All of these institutions suffered during the terrible decade of the Forties. By 1950 the people were ready to get them going again.

The Church of England, St. Mark's, never recovered from its membership drop during the war years. But its few remaining faithful joined John Burke in his effort to put new life into the Baptist congregation when he arrived in Cahuita in 1949. Mr. Burke, deacon of the church, tells how the group managed to build a new Baptist Church where it stands today on the Black Beach[1] road:

> "When I came here in 1949, there was no Baptist Church in Cahuita, and I walk all around and get the old-time Baptists organized. We had service in that same shop that Mr. Sorrows has now. The old man Samuel Williams, Mr. Sorrows' father, gave us privilege there. There was a gentleman at Tuba Creek, a colored man named Steven Williams, one of the richest colored men in Costa Rica, and he was deacon of the Baptist Church in Limón. I invite him down here one day, and when he saw the situation he decide to build us a little church. He put up sixteen thousand colones for the purpose. That was in 1953. And now we got Sunday School, morning service and evening service, and prayer meeting Monday nights."

The Jehovah's Witnesses pooled their offerings in about 1952, by Fred Ferguson's reckoning, to build the Kingdom Hall where services are still held today. "They was putting up little savings from long time," Mr. Ferguson says, "and the brethren built the Hall themselves."

The Seventh Day Adventist congregation remained strong on its original property in Cahuita. During the 1950s and 1960s it was the Adventist Church that provided the English school, a successful

---

[1] In recent years Little Bay north of Cahuita has come to be known as the "Black Beach," taking its name from its black sand in contrast to the "White Beach" south of Cahuita within the National Monument.

program that claimed the enrollment of about ninety per cent of the community's children, according to Mr. Delroy Fennell, who was a student there. Mr. Fennell remembers:

> "The Seventh Day Adventist school went on for years in Cahuita. It was the strongest one. Teacher Hibert Cox fought a lot. He had active part in the Spanish school board, so they didn't give him such a hard time about teaching English in a Spanish country. He didn't have much problem. He could help the Spanish teachers with the kids. Because of English he had a better communication with the kids, and they had more confidence in him. So he could help the Spanish teachers get on better with the kids.
>
> Out here the Spanish teachers understood the bilingual system of the town, and they never really interfere with it. They weren't so much oppressive. Even most of the Spanish teachers tried to learn some English to communicate with the kids, and some of them left here speaking English after a while, so I guess it actually help them a lot."

Mr. Fennell attended classes at both the Seventh Day Adventist English school and the Spanish school in Cahuita for several years, then moved to the city of Limón where he found a different attitude among his Spanish teachers. In their government-supported zeal to establish an identity as Costa Ricans among the Afro-Caribbean people of Limón, the Spanish teachers rightly considered language as a key. Without fluency and literacy in Spanish, the West Indian descendants in Limón would never be able to make their way in Costa Rican society. By 1950 most English-speaking parents agreed that their children must attend Spanish school and develop full competence in the language of their country. But they were not prepared to give up the English schools that they had supported for generations, the schools in which their own language, literature, songs, and values—their own culture—was taught. And this is what many of the enthusiastic, but unsympathetic Spanish teachers asked them to do. Mr. Fennell describes the conflict this way:

> "You could be going to Spanish school, and during recess they wouldn't like to know you be speaking English with your classmates or colleagues. They used to say it's prohibited to speak English. In a certain way it was a benefit to us because we didn't know that much Spanish, and we already had the English from the home. But I really saw the oppression of the English education, and that was bad. Some of the English schools had to

close up, but there were still private lessons. The government gave a lot of problem.

I remember in the Fifties while I was going to the government school in Limón, there were many times in the classroom I heard teachers ask the kids, 'Is anyone in this class going to English school?' And if anyone of the kids get up and say yes, he probably get a note to send to the parents to come talk with the teacher. And those note most of the time was to notify the parents that the kid shouldn't go anymore to the English school. Sometimes they say that if they went to the English school they would have to stop coming to the Spanish school."

The issue of languages in schools was, and is, a symptom of a general conflict of cultures that is built into the nature of Limón Province. On the Talamanca Coast the Afro-Caribbean settlers first experienced the conflict in their dealings with local judges who couldn't spell, or wouldn't spell their English names. For decades black people were not welcome in the nation's Central Valley or on the Pacific coast where the United Fruit Company offered jobs. Later came refusals for much-needed government aid on local development projects, which the coastal people viewed as racial slights. Then when the coastal people were making their own efforts to provide Spanish schooling for their children, their English schools were threatened. As their relations with government agencies, ministries, and political parties increased in importance, the coastal people even felt pressed to deny their Protestant religions, finding it easier to get through the Costa Rican bureaucracies with documents that claimed Roman Catholic baptism.

These conflicts were felt on the Talamanca Coast because the people were beginning to see themselves as Costa Ricans, needing and desiring a place of equal standing in the Costa Rican society. They were voting. They were participating in *Juntas de Educación*. They were forming *Juntas Progresistas* in compliance with Costa Rican law. They were meeting with ministers and deputies. They were paying taxes. They were doing these things willingly, enthusiastically, yet they were beginning to see that to become Costa Ricans they might be asked to compromise their Afro-Caribbean identity.

Most black parents want their children to benefit from both Spanish and English education, but the coastal communities have not been able to continue to provide private financing of English schools. In Manzanillo the English school dissolved when the first Spanish school was built in 1961. In Old Harbour, Teacher Cranston still gives private English lessons, but he is an old man now, having taught

English in Old Harbour since the days of the UNIA. In Hone Creek the first Spanish school was built in 1959, according to Ivan Watson, who was instrumental in the establishment of Hone Creek's *Junta de Educación*, but no English classes are offered there. In Cahuita, parents organized the most recent English school in 1974 and kept it going with help from the U.S. Peace Corps through 1976. Their petitions for assistance from the Ministry of Public Education to continue the program have been denied to date, leaving them with a classroom full of unused library books and instruction materials.

In 1974 the Ministry of Public Education enlisted a Limón educator, Miss Eulalia Bernard Little, to coordinate a commission to study problems in education in Limón Province and offer its recommendations to the Ministry. The commission developed a *Plan Educativo de Limón*, whose recommendations included:

(1) Give special training to educators in Limón concerning the evolution and historical, ethnic, cultural and economic realities of Limón Province, to develop in the teachers a better social sensitivity so that they may improve their work in the province.

(2) Reform and enrich the existing plans and programs in Limón education to be in harmony with the social, cultural, and economic necessities of the region.

Paula Palmer

Afro-Caribbean children benefit from Costa Rica's free, universal public education, but will they lose their Afro-Caribbean identity and culture?

(3) Support the philosophy that the Limón community should be as much as possible a truly bilingual society by using both Spanish and English in all levels and types of instruction, considering that English is not only one of the most important media of international and commercial communication, but that it is also a cultural reality of the Caribbean population in Limón.

(4) Develop audio-visual materials in all subject-matter areas based on the physical and human characteristics of the Atlantic Zone, with the intention of creating an identity among the students with their own environment.[1]

To maintain a vibrant Afro-Caribbean culture in modern-day Costa Rica, schools and other public institutions will have to incorporate the unique historical experience, customs, values, and needs of black Costa Ricans into their programs and plans. As their social reality changes, the Afro-Caribbean people themselves will also be reflecting on the significance of their culture and identity, as Alphaeus Buchanan does here:

"For black people, one custom that we must work to maintain is our language. Right now most people speak English in the home, so the children grow up learning it without any study. But since we don't have English schools anymore, many children never learn to read and write English. As they get older they feel more confident speaking Spanish because they go to Spanish schools, and they speak less and less English. What a strange thing it would be if one day nobody spoke English here on the coast!

We believe that education is essential for our children. We want our children to have opportunities that we didn't have as young people. Some of them could become lawyers, journalists, doctors, mechanics, professors, and those who want to be farmers should be better educated in technical matters than we were.

But recently we have begun to realize that education is tearing our black children away from their cultural roots. The education our children are receiving ignores the history of Talamanca, it ignores the scientific, historic and cultural values of our region.

---

[1] *Programa de Estudio de La Situación Educativa de la Provincia de Limón, Proyecto de Plan de Ejecución para el año 1975*, Ministerio de Educación Pública, febrero 1975.

Look, biologists come here to study the coral reef, but our children don't have any idea why the reef is important, because they don't find that in their textbooks. Anthropologists come here to study the Indians, but they don't tell us what they learn about them, and we are neighbors of the Indians and we don't know anything about their culture. Linguists come to study our English dialect as if it's something interesting and important, but in the schools the Spanish teachers tell our children they speak 'bad English,' so instead of being proud to be bilingual they feel ashamed.

It's not that we're ungrateful to the government for all the schools they have built out here and all the teachers and books they send; we appreciate that. We have to admit that *we* have the responsibility to educate our young people about our own history and culture.

Our customs like our love of dancing and our cooking, they haven't changed, although it's true that some of the young girls aren't learning to cook the way their mothers did, and their mothers could certainly cook. You will never taste our real old-time dishes because nobody is cooking like that again.

But, you know, modernization brings its advantages and its disadvantages. That's just normal. A society is always evolving. I'm sentimental, sure I am, but you can't fight against nature, and it's natural that times change. What do you gain by holding on to an absurd sentimentality?

There are important things we don't want to lose as a people, things that are worth working to maintain. One is the feeling of community unity. Our ancestors were slaves. They were badly mistreated and it's only logical that when you are mistreated you band together with others who are suffering the same abuse. Automatically you feel close, you feel brotherhood. Our ancestors came to America marked by their history as slaves and here they also suffered many injustices, so they were always united in their suffering. Black people feel like one big family.

That feeling of unity isn't entirely lost. I would say that integration has brought about many changes, which is logical. The white race has started accepting the black race as equals, and black people are more receptive now to white people, too. What is happening here is that the circle of unity is growing, and for me that is very important. What I mean is that here in Talamanca there's not just going to be unity among black people, but among Indians and blacks and whites. We are all *Talamanqueños*. We are all human beings. And that unity as human beings is really important."

## Sports

While the people of the Talamanca Coast were becoming more engaged in the serious issues of education and politics, they continued to make time, take time, for sports and entertainment. Cricket was to be seen no more after World War II, but baseball thrived for several years, then softball came into fashion, and finally Costa Rican football (soccer). Mr. Sorrows, of Cahuita, sums up sports history of the last three decades:

"The Estrella Tropical team started in Cahuita in 1950. That was about the best baseball team because we started to compete in the provincial league. We had players from Puerto Viejo with us. I was one of the foundation members, Mr. Palmer was the manager. He became very interested in the team. He made a nice clubhouse there for them to keep their meetings. He built a new building for it. They used it for dominoes, draughts, dances. He spent a lot of money on the team and that clubhouse.

We had an ace pitcher, Stanley Cunningham. He was so good that a Limón team take him away and he played with them. He was in the National Selection for a while. There was a very good second-division team from Limón, was called Enterprise. But we gave them a hard time with Estrella Tropical. Took the championship from them in 1951. Those two teams, the Enterprise and Estrella Tropical, when they were on the field would draw more crowd than any first-division team. Used to play real good. Estrella Tropical went back in the league in '52, they lost out, played in '53 and '54, then in '55 the game started to go down, until the late Fifties when they started to play softball.

We arranged a softball league here when Gene and Larry Popejoy came in. Gene was serving with the Mennonite Mission. He was a gigantic worker, boy. And Larry was in the Peace Corps. The softball league was comprised of Old Harbour (Los Leones), Hone Creek (Aguila), Penshurst (Sabaneros), and Cahuita (Thunderball). We had two successful years of league games, in the early Sixties it was. The league functioned for three years and then it dwindled. Two good competitors, that was Thunderball and Leones. They had real attractive games. Every week we move from one place to the other. One week have two games in Cahuita, next week two games in Hone Creek, and so on. It was beautiful. The first year we started with three teams, and in the second year we had five. One came in from Manzanillo. Board members for the league came from all the different towns. Every once in a while we would make a selection and play against a team from Limón.

Football came in right after. They had a league for the whole Talamanca region. They had a team from La Celia, Volio, Penshurst, Cahuita, Hone Creek. That lasted only two years, too. Since then they never organize a league."

Today in Cahuita local men and visiting Americans will revive softball for a couple consecutive Sunday afternoons, using Mr. Sorrows' collection of gloves and bats. When word passes through the streets that there's a ballgame on, the people turn out to the ballground still, matching what they see against their memories of Cahuita's Thunderball and Estrella Tropical. The five members of the recently elected District Sports Committee are just beginning their task of organizing a new football (soccer) league in Talamanca. The game has changed as the years have passed, but the sporting spirit is alive and well.

Music and "the Clarinetist"

For music in the 1950s the people of Cahuita turned to Walter Ferguson, better known as "Mr. Gavitt," and his band. Dances were held at Mr. Palmer's new clubhouse (replacing the orginal one he built for his Liberty baseball team) and in the large dance halls that had been annexed to the Tabash and Lam shops. The quadrille maintained its popularity during the Fifties along with Caribbean calypso, but Spanish styles were gaining ground as well. The people enjoyed dancing bolero, pasillo, guaracha, and rumba.

Like Sylvester Plummer, Mr. Gavitt is a self-taught musician. Mr. Johnson would say he was born for music, and no matter what else he does, music would be his delight. This is Mr. Gavitt's account of his development as a musician, from mouth-organ to pedal organ to guitar, and finally to the clarinet:

"It was my older brother had the mouth organ. I was little, and one day I pick it up and try it. It never run a week before I started to play a song on that mouth organ. And my brother himself started to admire me playing it. And after that he buy himself another one and he give the old one to me.

When I begin to grow bigger, I used to sing and I used to whistle. They used to call me 'Clarinetist' because when I whistle you believe was a clarinet. Then I used to play organ by Mr. Cox. But first when I was very small I used to play piano with my aunt in Limón. I played piano by ear. So my mother said, 'You know, I

Paula Palmer

"The Calypsonian," Mr. Walter Gavitt Ferguson

going to send you to Mr. Cox to learn organ.' So she buy a book, a very nice book, and when I had the first week with Mr. Cox, he said, 'I don't know how you have that head. You is the first one I see who don't give me no trouble.' He give me an exercise this evening and tomorrow evening I play it. But I never like it. Because of the pumping.

I was to play by Mr. Cox five o'clock to six o'clock. And afterward I went by Mistress Tabash, they had a shop there, same old-time shop, and they had a guitar there on the counter. And I took up the guitar, and Miss Tabash say, 'Bring back that guitar here! Put it back!' I felt shamed because plenty people heard. So she said, 'Poor fellow, all right take it, but don't stay long because your parents will say it's we that uphold you.' So I touch a little and put it back because I still feel shamed. So next evening after I play organ I stop by the shop and she say, 'I know what you want. See it there? Take it.' And from that she never stop me, and finally I was the streamline player of guitar in Cahuita. Nobody teach me to play.

There was a man in Hone Creek named Mr. Lewellen, used to play clarinet. He always encourage me to take up the clarinet because he said I was born for music. But I didn't do nothing with the clarinet until years later. By then Mr. Lew start to go blind, but he bought a clarinet, special for me, give it over to me and said, 'Don't depend on me to teach you because I'm sick. But I know you will learn to play clarinet.' I start practice, me alone, in October. And that same December I play for the Christmas Dance by Mr. Palmer clubhouse.

Somebody must be told Mr. Lewellen that they heard me play clarinet that night, because on New Year's Day my wife call me and say, 'Here's Mr. Lew to see you.' Mr. Lew said, 'I heard you played for dance Christmas night, but I came because I have to hear for myself. Now, play something.' And I started to play. Him laugh and laugh and say, 'I tell you I know that you going to be a clarinetist.'

But when I playing I notice him look at me a funny way, and when him look I see him kick back and him laugh laugh laugh. Him say, 'But tell me something. How you hold that clarinet?' I said, 'I hold it this way.' He say, 'But how you find that B-flat note?' I say, 'Well, I take this little finger and touch so.' He said he never hear that from he was born. So he take the clarinet and he show me hold it *this* way.

They make another dance after the Christmas and Calvin Maxwell, he played the trumpet, he said, 'You know now since Mr. Lew show you to hold the clarinet the right way, you can improve.' So I started to play the way Mr. Lew show me, but you know, I was backward again because I had my way good. And a fellow named Ben Scott said, 'I going to tell you. When you just started you were doing better. You're backing down now.'

After a while a friend of mine bring me a big shot of liquor and say, 'Take a warm-up, man.' And I say to Calvin, 'I going to play my old-time way, man.' So when I started to play again the way I was accustomed to play, the man Ben Scott say, 'Oh, I knows what. You did want a warm-up, man. Why you never tell me you did want a warm-up? Now you're playing good, man.'"

Calvin Maxwell joined Mr. Gavitt with his trumpet, and two locally famous calypso singers known as Oyé and Rogie played guitar and tumba. The factory fanciness of the trumpet and the clarinet were balanced by the homemade craftsmanship of the tumbas. These were fashioned by Daniel McLeod, who "put some varnish on and painted it green with red scallops between, and it was pretty, I tell you!" Mr. Gavitt describes the making of the tumbas:

"Daniel McLeod made them. He used trumpet tree, took his own time with a long chisel and made a good tumba. From that bird they call pelican, we call it 'Old Joe,' he take the craw and make the drum skin. You set the skin over a metal ring and band it down. We call that 'hot-head' tumba because we use it with string to tighten. And whenever it is getting slack you wet the skin a little and you catch up some fire and hold it over and it start to shrink up, tighten. Those tumbas were about a foot across, about two and a half feet long. I use several different skins on it. I use quash[1] skin, goat skin, and the pelican craw."

Occasionally a bit of the old-time bush band do-it-yourself spirit would rise again in Mr. Gavitt's band. He tells of one night when Sylvester Plummer's brother, "Soji," delighted dancers with a bush bass:

> "One day we were practicing, and Soji came and said, 'I'm going get a bass and come join the band.' So he go down to Cahuita Point and cut a bamboo and he came home and say, 'I going to play with you all tonight.' And we laughed. But when we started to play the night for dance, we see this man come in with this long bamboo and as we play we hear this 'Whoo-Whoo' and everybody wonder what it was. And when he bid goodnight we sorry that he was gone because it was well done! I don't know how he manage it, but it sound like a bass. It was well done, man." [2]

During the 1960s, when transistor radios became popular along the Talamanca Coast (and everywhere else in the world) and jukeboxes were installed at the Lam, Tabash, and Solón shops, few local musicians competed against the new electronic sounds. It takes an electric guitar to compete against a jukebox, and it wasn't until 1976 that the young men who formed the Buda Band were ready for the challenge. Roberto Kirlew, the "Buda" of the band, came up with an electric guitar, piecing the rest of his band together with a borrowed bass, tumba, and amplifier. Plugging in to any generator they could find, the "Buda boys" added a flute and a variety of percussion instruments to their collection, and they were on their way. As the money from their Saturday night dances in Cahuita shops rolled in, they replaced borrowed equipment with instruments of their own, and that's where they are today, playing a repertoire of Latin American salsa, Jamaican reggae, and a few calypso and North American songs that reflect the cultural mix of modern Cahuita.

---

[1] Local English name for several different species of the raccoon family.

[2] Mr. Gavitt's original calypsos have been recorded by Folkways Records ("Calypsos of Costa Rica") and by the Costa Rican Ministry of Culture. They are also performed and recorded by the popular Costa Rican band, Cantoamerica.

## Celebrations

Until the advent of tourism in the Seventies, the coastal communities celebrated their Christmas and Easter Monday holidays pretty much as they always had. The Spanish school initiated observance of the Fifteenth of September celebration for Central American Independence, Juan Santamaría Day, and religious holidays of the Catholic Church. For Easter Monday, if a horse race wasn't organized, it was a baseball game or picnic or dance. Delroy Fennell tells of another Easter Monday custom he remembers from his boyhood in Cahuita during the Fifties:

> "On Easter Monday we had this game where from people's house you take off their flowers pot, their pack saddle, their shovel, their old boots, their chair what they sit in on the porch, their horse, whatever they had around their home, and we carry it and put it right on the main shop in town. You come in the night and carry everything off and put it at Tabash shop, right on the porch there. Monday morning you could go out and see everything spread out there. Even sheets, wet clothes from the line. And people would go out there and laugh and have a big fun with it.
>
> Now Holy Week is tourist season in Cahuita. Thousands of people come in, and they all bring their tape-decks and radios and rum and they make crowds on the beach and in the bars, and the people from here are just thinking to make a little money selling food and doing business. And plenty commercial people come in from Turrialba and Limón and San José to do business, and they're the ones that makes the most money."

Mr. Clinton Bennett reflects on the recent decline in community celebrations in Old Harbour (Puerto Viejo):

> "Teacher Cranston and another old man, Mr. Roper, always organized the holiday celebrations in Puerto Viejo. They got the people ready, taught the songs they would sing, prepared the programs and trained the children to recite. Mr. Roper died, and later Teacher Cranston, something happened to him and he just lost interest in life and he wasn't the same.
>
> So since the Fifties we haven't had those celebrations. It's such a shame. We're really missing something. And I often think how strange it is that now, when everything is easy—transportation, communication—we don't do the things that we did before, when conditions were so difficult.
>
> I remember the last time we celebrated Easter Monday, Mr. Eddie's father made a *carreta* [ox cart]. He cut down a big fig tree

and made the wheels from the buttress wood, cut the wheels out of two solid pieces of wood. Imagine the work he put into that, just so some children could ride around in the cart! Now, anything you want, you send to Limón for it, but in those times everything was work and the people were happy to work, to make all kinds of sacrifices, just to celebrate a holiday and see the people happy.

Now that spirit has died out. I don't think we will see those things again, ever, because now everybody sits at night and watches television. If they want to dance, they go to the disco, they don't make a dance for the community. Now everything is business instead of community."

For the past three decades, Limón's October Carnival has drawn boat loads, mule-car loads, train loads, and now bus loads of coastal people in to the provincial capital for its calypso celebration, a pure Caribbean tradition. Selven Bryant says the Limón Carnival is an offspring of the Colón Carnival in Panama. Contract laborers from Limón who enjoyed the Colón festival during the years of World War II started the Limón version in the late 1940s, he says. The Carnival, which began with competing groups of local calypso singers, has become a tourist attraction in recent years. Expensive salsa bands from Puerto Rico have replaced the original Calypsonians from Limón and Siquirres and Cahuita, who sang for their own enjoyment and the pleasure of their neighbors. What was once a cultural celebration has become a commercial opportunity. "Everything change up, you see, everything change," says Cyril Gray, who worries now about theft and violence in streets full of strangers during Carnival Week.

## The Government Establishes a Presence

Involvement of the agencies and ministries of the Costa Rican government on the Talamanca Coast began with the establishment of police headquarters in Old Harbour and Cahuita as early as 1900. Modern delegation offices and jails of the Rural Guard now serve Old Harbour, Cahuita, Hone Creek, and Bribri, but the judges still serve multiple functions as mailmen and civil clerks in addition to their police duties.

The Ministry of Public Education gained a presence on the coast in the 1920s, through the establishment of public primary schools in Cahuita and Old Harbour. During the first administration of president José Figueres (1953-1958), dozens of new schools were opened in the Talamanca region. Alphaeus Buchanan recalls: "The first thing the Figueres government did, and for me it was something great, was to fortify the educational system in the Atlantic Zone. They started sending teachers even to the most remote areas of Talamanca, especially into the Indian villages high up in the mountains, and after the teachers came in they sent the materials to build schools. I don't know how many schools they build in the 1950s, but it was plenty of them."

The most recent accomplishment of the coastal people in cooperation with the Ministry of Education was the 1973 founding of the *Instituto de Capacitación Técnica de Talamanca*, a four-year agricultural and technical high school serving the region at El Cruce. The high school has been occupying an abandoned grain warehouse that lacks most facilities of educational institutions, even running water, electricity, and sanitary facilities. Its students and their parents are campaigning for a new building.

The Ministry of Public Works and Transportation became involved in the area with the construction of the road, beginning in 1953. The municipal government, from its offices in Bribri, now coordinates relations with appropriate ministries to serve the transportation needs of Talamanca.

The Ministry of Health made its first appearance in Talamanca enforcing its nationwide anti-malaria campaign, beginning in 1957. Workers in the National Service for the Eradication of Malaria (SNEM) tacked up posters on houses along the Limón-Penshurst railroad and on every shop front, warning: CHILLS AND FEVER? IT MIGHT BE MALARIA. Teams of SNEM employees, toting tanks of DDT spray powder, moved from house to house with their mandate: spray everything, inside and outside.

The objective of the malaria eradication program, which successfully eliminated the disease in the lower Talamanca region by 1976, was to kill the malaria-carrying *Anopheles* mosquito when it rested on DDT-coated surfaces. Since the Afro-Caribbean people rarely suffered from malaria, due to a genetic resistance to the disease, the eradication program was not really for their benefit but for the more susceptible hispanic population. The program had the effect of making life on the coast more comfortable for people of European origin, resulting in an increasing inflow of Spanish-speaking settlers.

The SNEM sprayers were hated for their forceful tactics and for the white mess they left behind them. Mrs. Elmy Brown, of Cahuita, says the SNEM men sometimes said they were spraying to rid the houses of cockroaches and flies, but the house pests seemed to thrive on the DDT. Small animals, kittens and puppies, took sick when they licked the powder. Scrubbed walls and freshly waxed and polished floors disappeared under the dreary white coating. Finally, when reports showed no cases of malaria in the coastal communities, the in-town spraying stopped in 1976.

In early 1975 the Ministry of Health sent to the Talamanca region two Rural Health workers, whose basic nursing services and advice on matters of sanitation and nutrition were well received. The region's first public health dentist arrived in 1976, followed by a doctor in 1977. In cooperation with the Ministry of Health, a nutrition committee in Cahuita is in the process of constructing the area's first Education and Nutrition Center, and a Red Cross committee is raising funds for an ambulance.

In a largely agricultural area like Talamanca, the farmers naturally look for technical assistance to improve their crop production. The Ministry of Agriculture established an extension office in Cahuita in 1969 to serve the area's farmers and cattle raisers. Mr. Ivan Watson, of Cahuita, says the first agents that occupied the office had a nursery from which they sold farmers cocoa plants, black pepper plants, and seeds. "I don't know what really happened," Mr. Watson says, "but they were all fired. There were rumors that they were selling the plants too dear, I don't know. But technical assistance is necessary, because whatever you see being done in Cahuita, we did it just from natural ideas of our own, without any technical assistance. And then that first group taught us how to spray, and then we found that we had more product, for true. So I think it's very necessary."

Having had their initial experience with the extension office turn sour, the farmers have wondered if the Ministry of Agriculture can really do much to help them. Several agents have come who have known nothing at all about cocoa. The current agent, Juan Carlos Valverde Conejo, has plans to prepare workshops for cocoa farmers to inform them of recent developments in cocoa production research, to offer direct technical assistance to farmers, and to plant a demonstration plot of cocoa to exhibit modern methods. Señor Valverde also intends to encourage and instruct farmers in corn production and cattle raising.

The *Consejo Nacional de Produccion* (National Production Council) showed a brief interest in providing services to the Talamanca region. They built the building that the high school now occupies at El Cruce, designing it as a dryer and storage unit for basic grains: rice, beans, corn. But shortly after the building was erected, Mr. Watson says, "they just abandoned it and went away, and the people who were planting those grains had to find another way to sell their products."

The future of cocoa farming on the Talamanca Coast is an issue of concern to many local farmers. Mr. Watson says, "Around the area of Puerto Viejo and Cahuita, cocoa will forever be the main crop because you see the land is in the hands of small farmers. Over in the Sixaola region where the land is in the company hands it's something different, but here, if a company should come in now and try to buy out Cahuita, I'm not going to sell my farm. All these small farmers, no one is going to want to make any sacrifice with the farm. The money leave you quick, but you will always have the farm."

But Arnold Hanbelamt wonders if the young men of Talamanca will be content to carry on the farming life of their fathers. He says:

> "The cocoa has a future, but not with these old farmers nor their children. Some of the children might participate, like those Buchanan children, but I think the people from the Central Plateau might be coming down, having interest in cocoa. You know, they have interest in any way they can make a living, so I think in the near future they will be doing most of the cocoa farming this side. Most of the Jamaican people won't be farmers in ten years' time.
>
> If you want these children to keep on with farming, first thing, you have to start from school. If you teach them agriculture from school, whichever one of them really likes it, they will take to it from school. But if they doesn't see much about it as they're growing, they will always look at farming as something inferior as they always used to. Most of the colored women don't like farming. They always like their children to be working in an office, maybe carpenter or mechanic or something. But they always say, 'I don't want you to be like your daddy, all day long going off to the woods. Look, it's raining, and he got to go see the farm.'"

Mr. Sorrows echoes Mr. Hanbelamt's concern:

> "There are a lot of farmers who have a lot of children here, and they're all drifted out. They have a better privilege for education, and the moment they become educated they don't want to stay here anymore. They want to go out to the United States, or to San José. They have given up here. The moment for instance, the people who owns farms, the moment they die, their children sell out the farms. There are a lot of places now that are sold out to foreign people because these young people don't want the farm.
>
> Every foreigner that comes here knows what land means, while we never did know the value of land. We have it, but we don't know the real value of it. And these people are who let us know what is the value of land. Until now our children haven't seen the value."

## The Cahuita National Park

The issue of land and its value is the most serious matter confronting the people of the Talamanca Coast today. The through-road, connecting Talamanca directly with Limón since 1976, has opened the doors to land-hungry people from Costa Rica's Central Valley and from all over the world. Until the road was completed, the difficulties of the local population in getting out of the region also prevented the outsiders from getting in. The road, which represents to the coastal people a final reward for generations of struggle, runs two ways, ushering in a steady stream of strangers with money and plans. They want to buy, with dollars and colones, the land that the Afro-Caribbean settlers made beautiful through one hundred and fifty years of labor, care, and perseverance.

The decision to sell or not to sell has been a matter of individual choice until this year, when the National Parks Service began sending out surveyors to evaluate the farms occupying space within the boundaries of the Cahuita National Monument. At this moment (May 1977) the people of the Talamanca Coast are in a turmoil over the proposal before the Legislative Assembly in San José to establish the area as a National Park. The current proposal would force the farmers who cultivate land between Suárez Creek and Hone Creek (see map, p. 214) to sell out their property to the Park Service or pay an annual concession to harvest their crops. The united protest of the people against forced government acquisition of their farms moved the President, Daniel Oduber, to assign a commission to study the issue and make its recommendations directly to him. The commission is currently at work.

Guillermo Canessa, administrator of the proposed Park, says the Cahuita National Monument was established by Executive Decree 1236-A in 1970. Plans for the area became confused in the following years when authority over the area passed from the National Park Service to JAPDEVA (Atlantic Zone Port Authority) and back to the Parks Service again. In public meetings throughout these years the coastal farmers and fishermen heard many different versions of regulations that would apply to the area. First they were told they could continue to catch fish for local consumption; then they were told spear guns were prohibited on the reef. How can one dive for lobster among barracuda and sharks without a spear gun?, they asked. Coconut cultivators were told once to stop chopping the underbrush in their coconut walks; later they were reprimanded for failing to keep the area clean. The confusion, according to Alphaeus Buchanan, led to an open forum meeting in 1975 at which the Parks Service agreed to work with the Municipal Board to write legislation for the Park that both the Park

Service and the local population would support. Mr. Buchanan continues the story:

> "We worked on it twice in Bribri with the Municipal Board along with the men from *Parques Nacionales,* and we had a lawyer from the IFAM [Institute for Assistance to Municipalities] that was giving us counsel. But when the Parks men were to come back with the final results so that we could have it in black and white and approve it by the Municipal Board for them to take back to Congress, they didn't return. They had everything hidden from us until this last moment when they came and said, 'Show us your documents. We're going to take your land.'"

Speaking for himself as a landholder, and for his neighbors in Cahuita and Hone Creek, Mr. Buchanan explains the coastal people's position on the National Park:

> "What we want is that we can remain on our properties, and those who want to sell will sell to the State. We don't want the people to sell either to anybody else. This law is to protect us from something that we can't see yet, that is coming up ahead of all of us.
>
> Personally, I want a special law on the reef area because it's good for everybody. I don't want to see our people sell it for any tourist complex in the future. Because we know that if tourism take over the area, that's the end of our boys and girls. Look at Acapulco. You know what it brings: venereal diseases, crime, prostitution, drugs. They tell us we will make more out of the tourist than we are making out of the farms. But we are not interested in money. We are not money-craving. We want to live as we are.
>
> We are more concerned than anybody else about preserving the area, because it's our farms. That's what they don't realize, that those lovely coconut groves that they see along the beaches are our farms, something built by our people. They call it 'natural resources,' and it is natural resources, but it's our farms! If the government is really concerned about protecting the area, there is nobody more capable of preserving and protecting it than those who preserved and protected it for more than a hundred years. They can come and enjoy it with us as long as they respect our rights and our property. We are not stopping anybody from enjoying it. We never did. We have taken so many of them into our homes, have treated them so nicely, and now some of them are giving us the knife in the back. But to take away what is ours? No, no, no, no. We have to keep our farms.
>
> If they were intelligent they would realize that you can't function a park in an area where people are going to be hostile. If they take away our rights, the people are going to be hostile,

and the tourists are not going to want to come, and the park is not going to be effective.

I'm optimistic. I believe the government is going to give us a fair deal. The President said when we met with him that he would never hurt a farmer. I don't think he would be so cruel to take back those words. We believe that our integrity will be respected, and the government is going to be pleased with us because we're going to be the first ones to keep this place protected."

Another Cahuitan, Arnold Hanbelamt, supports what Mr. Buchanan says about keeping industry and tourism out of the area. For environmental reasons, Mr. Hanbelamt supports the philosophy of a protected Park:

> "The same thing that they did with the Everglades in Florida they would do here. Even part of the reefs would be used up, because they fill in land and build on it for tourist resort and recreation areas, artificial lakes for fun and such. But because we never had good communication and transportation in here till now, this never permit many foreigners coming in to make much of an offer. Although maybe two foreign companies I think tried to buy plots down where National Park is now, but they didn't get their projects for tourist resort through. That was before the National Park made claims on these lands.
>
> The creeks that empty out in these marsh lands down at the point, they provide lots of the feed for the fishes that live in the sea. Say, for instance, the small shrimps and crayfishes and so on wash out by the creek mouths. The smaller fishes come and feed upon them. It's the chain of life. So these marshes produce food for all the living species in the sea. It's part of the food chain. And if all these lands were cut down and dumped up, well, the fishes will go farther down, the reef will be almost destroyed because everything goes where they can get where to live from. So we wouldn't be having marshlands, we'd be having towns that empty out their waste in the sea. Big industry might bring lots of money, but in the long run it brings lots of destruction, too."

What does the Parks Service have in mind for its Cahuita National Park? Guillermo Canessa gives an explanation for the establishment of the Park and a description of the facilities that he envisions in it:

> "There is not just one reason for the Park in Cahuita; there are many reasons. The coral reef is the best in Costa Rica. This will be our only marine park and will offer students an opportunity to learn about marine biology and ecology. The beaches provide a

natural recreation area. The animal and plant life of the land areas deserve study and protection. And there is historical significance in the area as well, the shipwrecks on the reef, for example.

The cocoa farms and coconut walks in the Park area don't harm the reef in any way, but many other activities do. We'll need to protect the land area because anything that drains from these lands through the rivers and creeks to the sea affects the life in the sea. Cattle pastures, for instance, must be limited in the area for this reason, and the wildlife must be protected from hunters.

We want to provide a park for education and recreation. We want to build a museum where students from all over the country can come to study exhibits, watch films and slides, so that they can appreciate what they see in the Park. Throughout the area we'll have signs pointing out everything of biological or historical interest. What we hope to provide is an open-air classroom.

At the entrance to the Park in Cahuita, we'll have concessions for refreshments and souvenirs. People in Cahuita will have the opportunity to manage these concessions, so it will be a benefit to the local economy. Men who are fishermen now will be able to take Park visitors out to see the reef on guided tours. They'll be able to fish for local consumption, but to protect the reef we will have to prohibit commercial fishing.

The main recreation area will be at Puerto Vargas where we're starting to set up camping and trailer facilities. We'll be able to accommodate large and small groups with sanitation facilities and drinking water, and somebody from Cahuita will get a concession to operate a grocery store for the campers.

The Park can serve the community of Cahuita in many ways. We can participate in any kind of community improvement project, like waste disposal, for instance. We can work with committees to improve all the social services. The Park will be a great educational benefit to the school children, too."

The issue of the Cahuita National Park will probably be resolved this year. However it is resolved, it will greatly influence the future development of the Talamanca Coast.


Responding to the Changes

Several organizations are working in the communities of Talamanca to help the people respond in an organized and effective way to all the changes they are experiencing. The first is a government agency, DINADECO (National Directorate for Community Development), which set up an office in Cahuita in 1975. DINADECO offers partial financing and administrative aid to local development associations which are constituted according to DINADECO regulations. Association boards, elected by community members, are functioning now in Cahuita, Hone Creek, Old Harbour, Bordón, and Manzanillo.

Miss Irma Morgan, the DINADECO promotor working with these Talamanca associations, says her job is to help the board members put through whatever programs they consider valuable to their communities. In Cahuita the Association is working to establish an *estanco*, a government store where nationally produced goods are sold at wholesale prices through the National Production Council. During Semana Santa, 1977, the Association solicited donations from visiting tourists for the ambulance that it is hoping to purchase this year to serve the Talamanca region.

The second organization which is involved directly with the people of Talamanca communities is *Lenguaje Total* (Total Language), a privately financed group working in Costa Rica in conjunction with the Ministry of Public Education. *Lenguaje Total* is a philosophy as well as an organization, based on the idea that effective action of any kind is dependent on effective communication. Three *Lenguaje Total* team members have been working under the leadership of Talamanca director Delroy Barton to expose the communities to all different forms of communication techniques, personal and technological. In weekly meetings community groups have been experimenting with everything from role-playing skits to videotape film-making in an effort to discover how the use of communication techniques can help them solve their problems. In May 1977, a group of high school students carried to San José a videotape showing the seriously inadequate facilities of their high school at El Cruce. They had made the film themselves, adhering to the *Lenguaje Total* concept that effective communication, in this case visual as well as audio, would help them achieve their goals.

A community organization that is new on the Talamanca Coast but upholds the oldest traditions and values of the Afro-Caribbean people is the Jamaican Burial Scheme Society. Founded in Jamaica in 1901 by Andrew Duffus Mowatt, the Burial Scheme provides funeral, health, and social security benefits to members who pay a minimum monthly fee. Branch 134 of the Burial Scheme Society has been functioning in Limón since 1934, according to its president, Mr. Standford Barton.

In 1976 the people of Cahuita formed a "social," a neophyte society under the parentage of the Limón Branch. In addition to providing specific benefits to its members, the Burial Scheme offers a forum for discussion of community and individual problems and concerns. It supports the Protestant Christian religious values of its members and strengthens group identity among the English-speaking people of Afro-Caribbean origin. To raise funds for the Cahuita "social," members staged a wonderful "Old-Fashioned Night" in February 1977, delighting their audience with old-time songs, comedies, and dancing. In a community that is experiencing rapid growth and change, the Jamaican Burial Scheme Society provides a form of cultural continuity that is clearly important to its members.

Another avenue through which the people of Cahuita are expressing their concerns and their values is theater. The director of the Cahuita elementary school, Mr. Claudio Reid Brown, is a promotor for the National Theater Company. In 1976 Mr. Reid supervised the construction of the school's all-purpose room, a roofed basketball court with a spacious wooden stage. The *Grupo Artístico de Talamanca*, under Mr. Reid's direction, gave two original stage performances during 1976, entertaining their mixed Spanish and English audience with a series of short comic dramas. One of Mr. Reid's special skills is orchestrating dramas that are instructive as well as funny, demonstrating social issues and cultural conflicts that are humorous because they are truthful. The actors in the Talamanca Theater Group focus on local situations, slipping back and forth between English and Spanish, often highlighting their humor with misunderstandings based on linguistic confusion. Cahuita residents are looking forward to the 1977 production, "*Hablamos al Estilo de mi País*" ("Let's Talk in the Style of my Country"), which will confront social issues of the Talamanca Coast more directly than ever, Mr. Reid promises.

Which of the good things from Cahuita's past are still a part of the daily experience of Old Smith's descendants and their newer neighbors? No one wants to go back to homemade shoes and rawa ranches. But what of homemade music? What of Easter Monday? What of community picnics and Anansi stories? Are these old-fashioned too, soon to be forgotten?

So many of the hardships of the past have now been eliminated by roads and telephones and political organization, but what of the new problems that come tagged on to the conveniences? Mr. Alphaeus Buchanan remembers that Hugh C. Lobit, the Third Secretary of the American Embassy who was so helpful to the people of the coast during the 1960's, wrote him a letter once saying, "Now that you are fighting, the time will come when you will have roads, telephone, and everything else that you are fighting for now. Then you can sit at ease." But Mr. Buchanan says, "Mr. Lobit is dead and gone, and I'm not at ease because now is when we have to be fighting most of all. We have everything as he predicted. But now we have to fight to protect our community, our property, our way of life."

Dennis Glick

Mr. David Dandy entertains children in Cahuita.

# 14. The Future: Contemplations and Preparations

What will the future bring? This story of the Talamanca Coast closes with thoughts from its residents, young and old, relative newcomers and great-grand children of the original turtle fishermen and coconut cultivators who founded these communities along a barren coast one hundred and fifty years ago.

Mr. Leslie "Sorrows" Williams, Cahuita farmer, father, and shop owner, was born in Jamaica in 1913 and has lived in Cahuita since 1929. He says:

> "According to my outlook of the future, there is no future here for the real Cahuiteños because the older people are going out and the younger people are not sufficiently responsible. They are taking no kind of responsibility for the betterment of the future here. Really, this place is growing, and it is going to be a wonderful city in the future. But the children of those that built this place are not going to enjoy the future here because they have kept themselves out.
>
> If you notice, for example, in Cahuita they haven't got a shoemaker shop, a hardware store, a cabinet shop. Haven't got nothing here. And all who's taking interest here are the people from outside. But our young people should be taking part. They should be more in politics where they can run the Municipality and help in the community. Because it's only politics can help to build the progress of the community.
>
> There are a lot of people here who have died already and leave a lot of property, and it disappear out of their hands. The children sell it out. So if those children or grandchildren come here now they are dead strangers. They have nothing here. The people who built Cahuita, their future generations will have no holdings here."

Mr. David Buchanan was born in Cahuita in 1923. Two of his daughters are studying nursing in Mexico, and one son is helping Mr. Buchanan in the family's cocoa farms. Of the future Mr. Buchanan says:

> "I was reading tonight in this magazine, *The Sentinel*, and I see an article called, 'Alarming Growth.' It says, 'According to the Latin American Demographic Center, the population of Latin America increased from 126 million in 1940 to 278 million in

Paula Palmer

Mr. David Buchanan and his wife Eva.

1970, more than double… Experts predict that in the year 2000 … the total population of Latin America will be 645 million. The question we must answer is, How will Latin America clothe, shelter, educate, employ, and above all feed this great mass of human beings?'

So I've been thinking, we can't do anything to plant because you have a certain group that will steal everything you plant. You can't get no social justice because if they steal you there is no authority here you can go to. So when I read it I say, well, all we have to do is if we are alive that time, decide to die of hunger. Because naturally there is land, but there are boys around who steal everything you plant.

So the future of Cahuita, unless you can change parents, it will be very dark. The most of us parents we don't tell our children the right way to live. We don't insist as the parents in the past used to do. So now the boys here don't want to work. And unless they have education they are not going to be able to occupy positions, because nobody is going to employ you and you uneducated. What we need now to improve the future of Cahuita are more discipline in the home and education. Since vice in this country has increased, sometimes even the home influence has very little power.

The change is going to distress those of us who live all these years here a lot. For me, the Americans don't distress you so much when they come to your place. Who distress you more is the native Costa Ricans, because an American will come and if he take your coconut and you talk to him, if he has education he realize that he has done something wrong because in his country he can't do it. And if he come here and he do it by chance and you talk to him he generally say, 'Okay, sir.' But the natives, some of them are abusive. They want to do as they like with you. Some of them are from rich parentage, and wherever they go they think they are boss. They doesn't respect what you have. They come with a jeep and they take the coconut and go with them.

So that is our future: destruction."

Mr. Noel McLeod, age 31, works as marketing manager for workmen's compensation at the National Insurance Institute in San José five days a week. On weekends and holidays he drives from the capital to his farm near Cahuita, his birthplace, where he is producing cocoa, plantains, and cattle. Mr. McLeod is one of the few young people from the Talamanca Coast who is using his advanced education and work experience to make a future for himself in his native province. These are some of his thoughts about Cahuita's future:

"As far as I can see, Cahuita isn't ours anymore. There are too many people from outside. Everybody wants to take over everything. Too many government agencies. At first we used to get things done by ourselves. Now it's all government agencies. I think the government is interfering too much in our private lives. The people in our community aren't prepared for the kind of things the government is trying to push on us. For example, they say, 'You need this,' and they try to push it on to you. They don't allow us to do things from our own conviction, to say what we need. That's why many of the government programs don't survive, because they don't have the necessary help from the community.

You see, the people are very skeptical about the government because the government has been meddling a lot with us. And we don't want to be pushed around. For example, tourism. I know hotel is good business, but I'm not going to build a hotel in Cahuita because we don't want the tourist business. We want our own way of life. We just have to ignore government projects until they're tired of being ignored, and then they'll back out. The government is promoting tourism in the Atlantic Zone, but they haven't made any studies. They haven't come to talk to the people, to hear what the people have to say. They just sit at a desk in San José, make their project and push it on to us. You don't see anyone from ICT [Costa Rican Tourist Institute] in Cahuita making a survey. They just sit at a desk with a map and make their plans. But for a tourist set up, they need land. I am one who have been promoting the idea of not selling.

The problem for the young people here is that the older heads like to hold on tight to their farms. They won't release in time. They think the kids aren't prepared. And they grow the kids up with the idea that they aren't self-sufficient, that they can't do anything without Daddy. When a boy is still young a father should say, 'I ain't giving you this thing yet, but you can manage it.' And release the kid, give him a chance to do something on his own, don't try to impose on him, dictate to him. Let him learn about farming so he can manage it.

About three years ago I brought the Minister of Labor to the zone, and I told him that I think it's a need to set up some kind of industry so the mothers and the girls can work in the daytime while the fathers and boys are on the farm, and at night they could afford to go to school or something. They could raise their economic level. We could make a cooperative to make cocoa into bars of chocolate like they do in San José, and the ladies could do that work. But the government wants the people to be dependent on the government. They don't want the people to be independent. So they haven't done anything about it.

But Limón will always be different from the rest of Costa Rica. As a matter of culture I think we shall stick to our English language. I think in Limón they should give classes in English to people who want it, of course not forgetting Spanish as the language of our country. But we need to continue the English as a matter of culture and of international communication. Costa Rica should be proud that they have a group of Costa Ricans that speak English. But as a matter of time I think the Protestant churches will go. The grandchildren will drop away from it, and at the end I think it will be all Catholic, as a matter of convenience, not conviction. The people started baptizing their children Catholic in the 1950s, and it worked. It went easier for them in schools and employment.

But there are certain things that will last out as long as there is a Negro in Limón. For instance, this clandestine lottery, selling what they call 'chances.' As long as there are two Negroes, there will be chances. One will sell, and the other will buy. Because it's a part of the Negro. Like dancing. Like the Nine Nights. It's not that the people believe the idea of the Nine Night anymore, but it's a tradition that won't die out among the Negroes. As long as there are Negroes in Limón, they will be keeping Nine Nights for the dead."

Mr. Ervin Grant was born in Cahuita in 1942. While several of his brothers have pursued business and professional careers in Limón, Mr. Grant has stayed in Cahuita managing the family farm. Since the completion of the road between Cahuita and Limón, he has devoted a greater portion of his time to local trucking services. He and his brothers together are in the process of building a number of tourist cabins on their beach property. Of Cahuita's future Mr. Grant says:

"According to my experience in the time we've been living here, the progress of Cahuita is going bit by bit. We can't expect a big change right right now. I feel it will take another ten years to see Cahuita as a town. It's actually a town now, but it need a lot of things like sewage pipes. From when I was working in the Municipality I've been thinking if the government could just spend a little money and put in a sewage system, that would help the town a whole lot.

All during the years from when I was a little boy the people of Cahuita depend only on cocoa. In some years the crop is good, but the price is low. In other years you have a good price but low crops. I would suggest that the cocoa growers begin to do other business, especially now that tourism is coming. Around tourists there can be a lot of business, restaurants, cabins, and small industries. Away from that the farmers could have a few cows and not just depend on cocoa same way.

I have a lot of plans. I want to build at least two or three more cabins over there for the tourist business. Cahuita is not prepared for tourism. We have no good hotels, good accommodations, swimming pools, lights and sidewalks on the streets. But it needs money from the government for the place to improve. With more people living here we could get better schools and a college [high school]. The future of Cahuita depends on population. With a bigger population more business can come in. I am one hundred percent with the National Park because a few years from now this will all be town, and still we will have Cahuita Point as in the older days. That would be pretty. That would be nice."

Miss Mavis (Tyndal) Iglesias, age 34, is an active member of a number of Cahuita committees. Here she talks about the future of her hometown:

"In ten years' time Cahuita will be something to talk about and something to see. Things will be more advanced. The population will be growing, we'll have stores, buildings, drugstores, houses will be all around. Oh, a lot of things will be going on. We will have the road right through to Panama, and things will be going and coming like that. And I guess the streets will be paved and so forth. I feel proud about it. I feel very good. One day I will sit and tell my children what Cahuita was twenty, thirty years before. Well, you will have a lot of things not as before, because first time you could sleep quietly and everything was just smooth. But now, the more populated the place gets, the more you have to fix your house secure to bar against the many different things that can happen.

I went to San José five years when I came out of school here. I worked and studied up there and came back. You have a lot of them that went to school with me in Cahuita that left and never came back. Some go to the United States, some are in Panama, and some I don't know where they gone, but they never come back to Cahuita. It's just one or two of my classmates that are here with me. The rest, they are all about. You see, the place here don't have no stores where they can get a job or anything, and that's why they have to leave.

For my own daughter, I would want to send her out to San José for advanced studies. I wouldn't like her to stay right here because the high school in Talamanca is mostly for boys in agriculture. It just suit for boys. Unless if they build a real high school here. But if not, I prefer for her to go to San José to take her education, and then maybe she can come back and get a job whether here or in Limón.

For myself I would like to stay in Cahuita, have my home right here. But Cahuita needs more opportunities for work. The Municipality have a certain amount of land here. They could build fabrics [factories]. They could make stores. They could make hotels so that the women and young men could have jobs."

Mr. Irad Clarke was born in Cahuita in 1951. He attended English and Spanish primary schools in Cahuita, then continued his studies at the high school in Siquirres. After several semesters of agronomy studies at the University in San José, Mr. Clarke returned to his family farm in Cahuita. He has been active in many local community development projects, teaching agriculture classes for a brief time at Talamanca's high school. Mr. Clarke says he would like to return to his teaching post to help prepare Talamanca's young people to develop their rural economy. These are some of Mr. Clarke's thoughts about the future:

"I believe that the base of the future is the people, and any changes in the future depends on the people. I wouldn't like it to continue as right now. We need better attention to the province and to the people here, which is something the same people have to develop because there isn't any interest from anywhere else to do it.

The economy is the first thing we should attend to. We need to establish a more independent economy. The people should produce more of their own food. We have enough land. We can produce our own clothes, take care of our own needs. The problem is that all the earnings or the gainings here are always going out to other people, nothing stays here. And this way our people would stay in the same situation forever. The people of this zone should participate in economic development so that some of the money would stay in the area. They can develop more of their own projects to satisfy their own needs. That's the way I look at it.

For instance, look at eggs. People have enough land here to produce corn and other nutrients for growing chickens. And instead of paying one colón for an egg that is coming from somewhere else, that money could be staying right here. We could have a small chicken market where people could buy eggs and chicken meat.

And fish. There's the big Atlantic Ocean right over there. We could have fish for the time that the fishermen can't go to sea. We could preserve it in bottles, or dry fish, and have it here for the people, and the money stays right here. Seeing that the cocoa cooperative went to pieces some of the people won't have much confidence that we can do it. But if four or five people join together and start something and keep it running in a simple way, I think it would make it. Especially with the young people. The young people are frustrated and I don't blame them. But I think we should start things here on our own if we want to get anywhere.

San José has got all our money. All our wealth goes to San José, and we have to go begging them for something when we want it. I'm convinced that this situation should change. We shouldn't be anymore beggars. Because we are people who work, and we work very hard for nothing. All our economy is going to San José. That's the thing that has me worried. I've seen my parents and my grandparents working all their lives for nothing, and I'm not going to do the same thing. I'm not against working, but I'm going to work for something, not for nothing. Some of the young people won't work, they won't do anything because they haven't seen anything from their parents and grandparents, and it seems stupid to be working so hard for nothing. And I agree with them. If you're going to work you have to know you are working for something.

We can observe how economics affects all different aspects of life, for instance, culturally and socially. You have some people say that we live in a democratic country and everybody has equal rights and the same opportunities. But you can see that most of this saying is not true in practice. If you don't have money you can't have an adequate preparation. That's why I say economy is the base of development. What good is it to get a college [high school] in the area if the people are so poor that their children have to work on the farm and can't study?

We have the so-called college which is supposed to be an agricultural high school. To start, we don't have a decent farm. The land there is no good for agricultural purpose. And second, the college don't own the land, so at any moment the owner can come and say, 'I want my place,' so you can't develop any serious project on the land because it's not secure. We have no laboratory where you can do soil testing. You're going to talk about types of cows that are the best for producing milk, and the students haven't seen in all their lives one of these cows. We don't have the equipment to give the students any practice.

The Ministry of Education sends teachers from the other parts of the country which are not interested in taking care of the interests of the community. That's a problem. We need teachers from our own communities in the future. We need our own teachers, our own doctors and engineers from this zone. We need our own young people to go out and study and come back to improve the zone. But some, when they go out, they feel integrated to the other society and they don't return. I think the educational process has a lot to do with it, because in the history of the country our Atlantic Zone is not mentioned as a place of importance, as a place of value. But I would like to say that we shouldn't wait that somebody from somewhere else has to come and tell us how valuable our place is. We can see for ourselves. We can feel for ourselves. At least I feel it; I know it.

There are young people who grew up in Cahuita who are nurses and teachers and business professionals but in San José and the States. Only a few come back to Limón. But at least from the college in Siquirres I have *compañeros* who have been studying in Honduras. They are agronomists, and they are right back in Siquirres teaching. And they are not planning to leave Siquirres. And this year I have the next *compañero* which will be a doctor, and he says he is coming back here. He wants to work here with his people. So it's one by one, but it's a start. I'm proud of that situation."

Mr. Selven Bryant has lived the farming life in Old Harbour for all of his sixty years. He has great faith in the earth as a provider for the future, but can people be depended upon to use the earth wisely and justly? Mr. Bryant shares his thoughts:

"I have the idea that in the future to come we might have to leave this coast. The government have the first fifty meter in from the sea that they call *Zona Turística* [Tourist Zone] and the next hundred and fifty meter is for the Municipality. You get no title for that land, don't mind how long you been there. So the government has two hundred meter from the sea in, and they can just do what they feel, can dispossess you of it. So that not looking so good to me for the future. We don't know what will happen in a couple years to come. They may come and pay you, and you just have to leave. They may want to sell to some rich people that want to make a tourist zone. If they want the place, not even a title do you any good.

The best thing for a poor man is the earth. That's the best thing. You plant one grain of corn, you not going get just one grain. You have plenty land to work. And you have lots of facility now. In my days we never did have any. Now the bank will lend you money to plant, to raise animal, to buy wire, make fence. So it's no trouble now, but what happen is the younger generation don't want to work. In Old Harbour you don't see a young man in his twenties have even two or three hectares of cocoa that he plant himself. And that's the best way for a poor man, the earth. Check all them millionaire and see where the riches come from, see where it start from. It start from the earth.

Now is the time that everybody should be holding on to a piece of land. Nobody looking about that. After a while people going to come from outside and develop the place, and people who live here are not going to have any land. We have it now, and the young people don't want. When they want it they find it going to be too late. All the land will be taken up from outside people. You don't see no black man 'round here chop bush, and without that the farm will ruin. These young boys, they don't want anyone to see them with a machete to them side. If they even go to work in the farm they leave the machete hide in the bush.

In this country, too, you have a lot of color question. You have too much Spaniard that have the same education, maybe less than the colored ones, but them is who get the jobs. The Limón people now are getting down on that hard. Because you have all those ICE. You have good electrician in Limón, and still the majority of the ICE men coming from San José, Guanacaste, Puntarenas, Heredia and all about. And you born and grow in Limón and have good education, and you can't get a job.

And very few people can leave Limón, go to San José and get a job. Very few. What helping the colored people to get work in San José is through the English, because the majority of those office there looking for English-speaking people. But anytime the Spaniard develop in the English you wouldn't see the colored people working there again. It's just a color question. Them say we don't have color question in Costa Rica, but they have it here plenty. They say one thing, but it not so."

The people of Manzanillo and Grape Point are pinning their hopes for the future on one prayed-for event: the completion of the road from Old Harbour south to the Panama border at Sixaola. In Cahuita and Old Harbour the people are already worrying about problems that have arisen since their communities have been connected directly with Limón by road: tourism, land speculation, theft, government interference. But the folks of Grape Point and Manzanillo look forward to the benefits they expect from land transportation: easier marketing and better prices for their farm products, and "livelier" times in their communities.

Mr. Samuel Hansell, who has lived in Manzanillo for seventy-four years, says:

"There's plenty future in Manzanillo if the road goes through, but away from that there is nothing. They start the road year before last and they say they would finish last year, but they stop.

If the road put through it would be uplifting for the whole coast. If the road don't put through, Manzanillo will remain just as you see it. They not so interested in putting the road through. If there were more Spaniard here I feel they would be more interested. But how this place is mostly colored people, they not so interested. I had good faith in it when they start. The last tidings I get from Old Harbour, they say they to start work on it again this same year. I hope so myself.

I'm the oldest liver in Manzanillo. I come here 1903 when I was three years old, and I'm right here till now. And I'd like to see that road put through, take even a few trips out, up and down, before I gone."

Mr. Hermenegildo "Minin" Hudson spent many of his seventy-one years on the sea. Still, he hopes to see the day when Manzanillo's boats go out of business, replaced by safe and certain land transportation:

"The future of this coast will be very very poor through education. The young set today, after they get a good learning, they don't want to hear nothing of agriculture. Each one is looking for a job to get money easy without work. Consequently, after we older ones disappear, there will be a very hard time in the new world.

The greatest thing in the world is thinking, and the wickedest thing in the world is power. The worst sickness in the world is hungry. And the young set prefer to die outside in the city than to return to the country to cultivate. Right now there is a scarcity of provisions: rice, beans, and so forth. A few around here plant a little provision, but not enough.

If the road put through it will be a great success for farmers, because we will get a better price for our produce. We lose around thirty percent. For instance, coconut in Puerto Viejo go from seventy cents up to eighty cents for one, and here the most you get is fifty cents because of the transportation trouble.

We meet it very hard when we have weather. In December gone, the sea come up right under these house here. God was on our side that no accident happen that time. Nobody could leave out here that time through the weather, high sea. You have twenty-two creeks to cross from here to Puerto Viejo, and of the twenty-two, three is very dangerous. I can handle a boat on the sea up to now, but what of the others? So we would be very glad to see the road put through."

Mrs. Aurellita Hudson came from Bluefields in 1949 to make her home in Manzanillo. She worries now about her daughters: what kind of life can they look forward to in Manzanillo? Or will they have to find new homes in which to unravel their futures?

"I have hopes that the road will come through. If it wasn't for me, maybe my daughters would like to go someplace else. But being that I am here and sick, they like to stay around with me. But I have hopes that the place will come better, especially if the road come through. When the road comes, if it does, the place may be a little different with stealing and so on, but even so it will be better for us, for we will be able to go out whenever we like. We may have a little more problem, but it will be a good for us. I have lots of friends that would like to come look for me, but no

273

way for them to come, especially when the sea is rough and they afraid for the boat.

Sometimes I have good hopes, and sometimes I feel we will just sink. If the place don't come better, my daughters will have to go out and look for better, for their own betterment. I don't know what will happen. If it go on like this, they will have to go out."

This history of the Talamanca Coast began with the stories of Mr. Augustus Mason of Old Harbour and Mr. Selles Johnson of Cahuita. It closes with their responses to the question, 'What do you think the future will bring?'

Born in Jamaica, Mr. Mason was brought to Old Harbour by his godparents at the age of seven. There he hunted and traded with Indians until he acquired property, which he converted to coconut walks, cocoa, and banana farms. Always ready to experiment, to gamble on the future, Mr. Mason built a plane base before there was any use for it and imported a truck before there was a road to run it on. During the last two decades he has managed a trucking business, a lumber mill, a general store, and a restaurant in Old Harbour. He has recently constructed a number of new houses for rent. Having watched and participated in seven decades of changes in his community, Mr. Mason, now seventy-three, is characteristically optimistic about the future, and uncharacteristically brief:

"Well, you can see and you can hear. There is a great future in Old Harbour. Plenty of things will happen. I can't tell you, but there is a lot of improvement coming for the future."

Mr. Johnson is Cahuita's oldest native son. In his childhood he helped his grandfather build ranches, plant coconuts, and raise cows. As a young man he enjoyed fishing and hunting, cricket, horse racing and quadrille dancing, but his greatest love was for the sea. For forty years he sailed the Caribbean coast, returning finally to build a home in Cahuita and tend to his coconut walk on Cahuita Point. The crop that sustained the first generation of farmers on the Talamanca Coast provides Mr. Johnson's livelihood today. At the age of eighty-three, Mr. Johnson gives his outlook for the future:

"Right now I'm worried about the future. They're destroying the property of mine. For the coconut, I'm not getting nothing again like before. The people destroy a part, the monkeys destroy a next part, the squirrels destroy a next part. In about two years now if we don't put a stoppage to the monkeys we won't have any coconut. You can't kill no animal out there now through this Park business. They say it prohibit to run them off. I don't know about the snake. They don't tell us nothing about that one, but no monkey, no squirrel, no *pizote*, nor the two-foot monkey, and he do more. You know who I mean?

I'm not against the tourist coming in, but they should be a little more respectful. Look. We from here can't go to San José and do that, go on their coffee farm. They come here and they go through my coconut farm and steal my crop, climb the trees. The beach is theirs. They can go and bathe, nobody will disturb them. But how they think they can take what they want from my farm?

I planted an amount of those coconut trees, I get an amount from the grandparents them, and I buy a little too. And if I depend on the coconut to live, I don't live. I'm too old now to go to sea fishing. I don't used to beg, so I don't beg. Before I always get ten thousand coconut a month. Now if I even get seven hundred I think I get plenty. The cost of living is high. From just the coconut all those years I save enough money to build this house, and the coconut was cheap that time. Now I meeting it hard. Very hard.

It's sixty-five years I own those properties. If they would pay me what I want for it I would quit here and go somewhere else, go to Colombia and live there. All my life I live here. You think I want to leave? No man. But I got to live. And I can't live from the coconut again. I told them in a meeting the other day I never beg, from birth I never used to beg, and I'm not begging. Before I beg I die. And it looks most like it going for that."

# *Postscripts*

(January 1979)

During the twenty months between the time this book was written and its publication, the appearance of the Talamanca Coast has changed a bit. Cement houses have replaced some of the old Jamaican-style wooden homes; more vehicles come and go, and the buses are more crowded than before; the mountain ridge that parallels the coast bears some scars of deforestation. But the greater change is in the conversation of the people. Having achieved through years of struggle a measure of prosperity and convenience, they are reeling with the news that the coast may not belong to them at all. And they are organizing themselves as a united cantón to influence the course of the coast's development.

## The Beach Front Law

The Costa Rican Tourist Institute (ICT) has designated four beachfront "tourist zones" between Tuba Creek and Manzanillo and plans to extend their boundaries to include most beach property in the cantón. Within established tourist zones priority is given for commercial facilities (hotels, cabins, restaurants, souvenir shops); private residence is limited, and industry is prohibited. A Beachfront Law (*Ley sobre la Zona Marítimo Terrestre*, No. 6023, passed March 2, 1977) spells out regulations for all Costa Rican property within 200 meters of the sea. According to the law, the first 50 meters of beach land is for public use; no private ownership is recognized within this zone. The next 150 meters inland is under the supervision of the municipal government; concessions may be purchased on an annual basis for residence, business and farm management.

While the Talamanca Coast was cut off from the Costa Rican interior—until the Estrella River bridge was built—no attempt was made to enforce these laws or inform the coastal people of their precarious hold on beachfront houses and coconut walks. Now, as the Tourist Institute is preparing a National Plan for Tourism, coastal farmers are learning that they have no right to the fruit of the coconut palms planted by their fathers and grandfathers, and that their homes may be razed at any time in favor of tourist bungalows and camping facilities. Farmers between Puerto Viejo and Manzanillo who have eagerly assisted in surveying the roadway in anticipation of the day they can market their coconuts and cocoa by truck, now feel sickened by the understanding that when the road is completed those crops may no longer be theirs to sell.

Defense Committees in Cahuita, Puerto Viejo, and Manzanillo are coordinating efforts with the Municipality to protect long-time coastal residents and to rescue the coconut industry. While Tourist Institute officials recognize the delicacy of property expropriation, they are pressed by fast-growing national and international tourism to move quickly and aggressively to prepare the coast for visitors.

Mr. Alphaeus Buchanan, Cahuita: "If they take away our rights the people are going to be hostile, and the tourists are not going to want to come. We want to live as we are. We have to keep our farms."

A Tourist Institute planner: "We don't want the people to be against us. We hope they'll stay to work in the restaurants and hotels."


The Cocles Indian Reservation

On August 20, 1977, President Daniel Oduber signed Executive Decree No. 7267-G, establishing the Cocles Indian Reservation within the cantón of Talamanca (see map, chapter 13). Under the regulations of the Indian Law (Ley Indígena, No. 6172) all private property in the hands of non-Indians within a declared reservation will be expropriated. The government's Land and Colonization Institute (ITCO) will assess the value of the property and pay the owners in cash or relocate them on land outside the reservation. Because the 3538-hectare Cocles Reservation extends to the sea along a three-kilometer stretch south of Puerto Viejo, it includes the cocoa farms of a number of Afro-Caribbean families that have lived there more than a hundred years.

Puerto Viejo's Paul Rodman expresses the concern of the community about the reservation, established without consultation with the coastal people: "We have never had problems between black people and Indian people here before. And now the government is coming in and it is the government that is causing a problem between us. They are taking away land from poor black people to give to poor Indian people. But there is País S.A. [a company that controls the old United Fruit Company holdings] with all that land along the Sixaola River, and you don't see the government taking anything away from them. It looks like the government wants to start a problem here."

As funds become available the expropriation within the Cocles Reservation will be initiated. But a staff member of CONAI (National Commission for Indian Affairs) says special consideration may be given to families who have a long history of living on the Talamanca Coast.

## COOPETALAMANCA R.L.

On December 17, 1978, cocoa farmers from all of Talamanca gathered in Cahuita to celebrate the legal founding of COOPETALAMANCA R.L., an "agricultural and multiple services" cooperative, established according to national regulations. The top priority of the cooperative is to get the highest possible sale price for Talamanca cocoa by improving the quality of the crop and increasing production. The elected members of the administrative board are determined to provide for coop members services that they say national ministries and agencies have failed to provide: legal assistance in defending property rights and gaining title to farmland, technical assistance in improving agricultural production of cocoa and other crops, and administrative assistance for disabled and aged farmers. Members view the cooperative as a legally-constituted power base from which they can launch endeavors of many kinds in the interest of the cantón as a whole. "It's a bright day," said Mr. Selven Bryant of Puerto Viejo at the inaugural meeting. "I really did say the farmers here is not united, but I glad to see I was wrong. Now you see we starting up again. We getting strong."

The coast lost one of its most energetic leaders in December 1977 when Mr. Augustus Mason died. My hope, in his memory, is that the love he felt for Talamanca, his home, will be born again and again in the children of the coast, that the land and the sea will be treasured by them as by their forefathers, and that they will match the beauty and bounty of their home with their care.

P.R.P.

# Glossary

abaca (*Musa textilis*). The fiber obtained from the leafstalk of a banana plant native to the Philippines. Also known as Manila hemp, the plant was cultivated in Limón province by the United Fruit Company during World War II.

ackee (*Blighia sapida*, Spanish: *seso vegetal*). Native to Africa, ackee was carried to the New World by British colonists. Its spongy, yellow fruit, encased in three-inch pods, is poisonous until the pods open. When boiled the fruit resembles scrambled eggs. A favorite Jamaican dish is ackee sautéed with salted codfish.

apoo (*Iriartea gigantea*, Spanish: *chonta*). A tall palm whose extraordinarily hard wood is planed to fashion bows and arrows, harpoons, etc. The growing tip of the apoo is an edible vegetable, known as *palmito dulce* in Spanish.

bar. Local term for the mouth of a river, as in "Sixaola bar."

barbecue. Local English word for the wooden dryers constructed by coastal farmers to dry cocoa beans and coconut meat (copra) in the sun. The wooden planks slide under zinc roofs to protect the products from rain. Barbecues can be seen in nearly every yard on the Talamanca coast.

breadfruit (*Artocarpus communis*, Spanish: *fruta de pan*). A tall tree with shiny, deep-lobed green leaves that produces cantaloupe-sized fruits. The white flesh inside a tough green skin is eaten boiled, baked, or fried, most often roasted over an open fire. It can also be grated and dried to make flour.

calabash (*Crescentia cujete*, Spanish: *calabazo*). A tropical tree which produces gourds that can be dried and cut into a variety of shapes for use as bowls, bottles, etc. Almost every dugout canoe on the Talamanca coast carries a calabash or two for bailing water.

cantón. Costa Rica is divided politically into provinces, which are subdivided into *cantones*. Each *cantón* is governed by an elected Municipal Board (*Municipalidad*).

caway (*Pterocarpus officinalis*, Spanish: *sangrillo, sangregao*). Local English word for the tree called *cawi* by the Miskito Indians, who are said to have named Cahuita Point for the caways that grow there. The Spanish name recognizes the tree's bloodred sap.

cocoa (*Theobroma cacao*, Spanish: *cacao*). The beans of the cocoa tree, fermented, dried, and ground, produce chocolate. Indigenous to Central America, cocoa was harvested by pre-Columbian Indians who cherished it to the extent of using the beans as currency. Since 1950 cocoa has been the major cash crop of the Talamanca coast.

college. Local English word for the equivalent of North American junior high and high school, derived from the Spanish word *colegio*.

colón. Costa Rican currency. The colón is divided into one hundred *céntimos*, called "cents" by English-speaking people of the coast.

deputy. Local English word for an elected member of Costa Rica's Legislative Assembly, derived from the Spanish term *diputado*.

fresco. Taken from the Spanish word *refresco*, meaning natural or bottled soft drink, "fresco" has been adopted by the English-speaking people of the coast as part of local English vocabulary.

gibnut (*Agouti paca*, Spanish: *tepezcuintle*). Local English word for the paca, a large, spotted rodent whose meat provides a favorite meal for coastal hunters.

gig. Local English word for homemade wooden spinning tops.

hectare. Metric measure equal to 10,000 square meters, or 2.471 acres. An average cocoa farm on the Talamanca coast measures about five hectares.

kankibo wis (*Thoracocarpus bissectus*; Spanish: *bejuco del hombre*). A strong, durable vine that coastal settlers used in place of nails for house construction, as clothesline, and as rope. Also known as "iron wis."

Miskito Indians (Spanish: *Mosquito*). The Carib Indians, indigenous to the Caribbean coast of Nicaragua, intermarried with African slave survivors of a 1641 shipwreck to produce the Miskito tribe.

mountain cow (*Tapirus bairdii*, Spanish: *danta*). A Central American tapir.

palmito. The growing tip of several varieties of palm trees (including rawa, apoo, and pejiballe), which can be boiled or roasted as a vegetable.

pejiballe (*Bactris utilis*, English: *peach palm*). The lemon-sized fruits of the pejiballe palm grow in clusters of about fifty at the base of the palm's crown. The starchy fruits are boiled with salt and eaten as a rich and filling snack. English-speaking people of the Talamanca coast pronounce the Spanish word "picky-BY-ah."

pine. Local English word for pineapple.

quadrille. A square dance of French origin performed by four couples. The quadrille became popular in England during the colonial period and was taken up with enthusiasm in the West Indies. Afro-Caribbean quadrille dancers in Limón today dress formally (women in long evening dresses, men in matching jackets and bow ties) and memorize the steps to the dances, having no "caller" to remind them of the sequence.

ranch. Local English word for a thatch-roofed shelter or dwelling, derived from the Spanish *rancho*.

rawa (*Socrates durissima*, Spanish: *maquengue*). A tall palm (25 meters or more) whose bark provided early coastal people with building material. The heart (growing tip) of the rawa is edible as *palmito amargo* or bitter palm heart.

sandbox tree (*Hura crepitans*, Spanish: *javillo*). A large tree, common in coastal lowlands, from which the Jamaican immigrants make dugout canoes. Its poisonous, milky sap is used medicinally on open sores but contact with the eye can cause blindness.

sea cow (*Trichechus manatus*). The manatee, a large sea mammal with flippers, feeds on shore and river grasses.

sea grape (*Coccoloba uvifera*, Spanish: *uva del mar*). Ranging from shrub size to tree height, the plant grows wild along Caribbean beaches, producing clusters of dark blue single-seed grapes. When sea grapes are in season most coastal children can be found in the tree boughs, shaking down the fruits for their companions to retrieve in the surf below.

silico (*Raphia taedigera*, Spanish: *yolillo*). A common swamp palm whose leaves were used by the early settlers of the Talamanca Coast to make pin-thatch roofs.

sina (*Tayassu tajacu*, Spanish: *saino*). The collared peccary. It is distinguished from the white-lipped peccary (wari) by its markings, its smaller size, and its scent gland, which secretes an odoriferous liquid.

sorrel (Spanish: *Rosa de Jamaica*). A relative of the hibiscus, sorrel was imported to the Caribbean from tropical Asia. The bright red bud-shaped flowers are boiled with ginger for a favorite Christmas drink or dried as a tea.

trumpet tree (*Cecropia obtusifolia*, Spanish: *guarumo*). A hollow tree, common on the Atlantic coast, usually infested with ants. Inner fibers of the trunk can be used as rope, and the leaves can be dried and smoked as a tobacco substitute.

tuno (*Poulsenia armata*, Spanish: *mastate*). A tree whose bark the Indians of Talamanca used to make clothing, hammocks, mosquito nets, and blankets. Although factory clothing has now replaced tuno skirts, the Bribri Indians still use tuno bark to make saddle blankets and bags.

wari (*Tayassu pecari*, Spanish: *chancho de monte, cariblanco*). The big, fierce white-lipped peccary runs in large packs, foraging in heavily forested areas.

wild pine (*Aechmea magdelanae*, Spanish: *pita*). Coastal people correctly relate this plant to the pineapple although it bears no edible fruit and its leaves grow as long as ten feet. The Indians of Talamanca use the leaf fibers to make fine thread.

wis. Local English word for vine or liana.

yam (Spanish: *ñame*). The Caribbean yam is a large tuber, commonly weighing up to fifty pounds. Prepared by boiling or frying, it is a staple in soups and stews.

yuca. Also known as cassava and manioc, the plant produces long pink-sheathed tubers, edible boiled and fried. People of the Talamanca Coast grate and dry the tuber to produce starch and to make puddings. The young leaves, cooked, are also edible.

# Selected Bibliography

Acuña Ortega, Victor H. *La huelga bananera de 1934*. San José: CENAP/CEPAS, 1984.

Anglin Edwards de Scott, Joyce. "Anancy in Limón." Thesis, Universidad de Costa Rica, 1981.

Appiah, Peggy. *Ananse the Spider: Tales from an Ashanti Village*. New York: Harper, Row and Wilson, 1966.

Barrantes, Claudio, María Eugenia Bozzoli, Gloria Mayorga, Paula Palmer and Juanita Segundo Sánchez. "El sendero de Cuabre: UkábLe." *Herencia* (Universidad de Costa Rica), 2 (1990): 65-74.

Bienert, Sharon. *Rundown and Other Recipes from the Caribbean Coast of Costa Rica*. San José: Sal Press, 1983.

Bourgois, Philippe. *Ethnicity at Work: Divided Labor on a Central American Banana Plantation*. Baltimore: The Johns Hopkins University Press, 1989.

Bovallius, Carl. *Viaje por Centroamérica, 1881-1883*. Managua: Fondo de Promoción Cultural, Banco de América, 1977.

Boza, Mario A. and Rolando Mendoza. *The National Parks of Costa Rica*. Madrid: INCAFO, S.A., 1981.

Bozzoli de Wille, María Eugenia. *El Nacimiento y la Muerte entre los Bribris*. San José: Editorial Universidad de Costa Rica, 1979.

Carr, Archie. *So Excellent a Fishe: A Natural History of Sea Turtles*. New York: Anchor Press/Doubleday, 1973.

_____. *The Windward Road*. Tallahassee: University Presses of Florida, 1979.

Casey Gaspar, Jeffrey. *Limón 1880-1940: Un estudio de la industria bananera en Costa Rica*. San José: Editorial Costa Rica, 1979.

Cronon, E. David. *Black Moses: The Story of Marcus Garvey and the Universal Negro Improvement Association*. Madison: University of Wisconsin Press, 1969.

Duncan, Quince. *Los Cuentos del Hermano Araña*. San José: Editorial Territorio, 1975.

Duncan, Quince and Carlos Meléndez. *El Negro en Costa Rica*. San José: Editorial Costa Rica, 1981.

Duncan, Quince and Lorein Powell. *Teoría y Práctica del Racismo*. San José: Editorial DEI, 1988.

Duke, James A. *Isthmian Ethnobotanical Dictionary*. Fulton, Maryland, 1972.

Fallas, Carlos Luis. *Mamita Yunai*. San José: Lehmann Editors, 1978.

Fernández Guardia, Ricardo. *Reseña histórica de Talamanca*. San José: Editorial UNED, 1969.

Gabb, William. *Talamanca: El espacio y los hombres*. San José: Imprenta Nacional, 1981.

Glesne, Corrine and Paula Palmer. "Coastal Talamanca: A Cultural and Ecological Guide." San José: Asociación Talamanqueña de Eco-turismo y Conservación, 1993.

Hill, Carole E. "Local Health Knowledge and Universal Primary Care: A Behavioral Case from Costa Rica." *Medical Anthropology* 9 (1985):11-23.

_____. "Traditional Mental Disorders in a Developing West Indian Community in Costa Rica." *Anthropology Quarterly* 51 (1986): 1-14.

Instituto de Fomento y Asesoría Municipal. *Información básica de la Municipalidad de Talamanca*. San José: IFAM, 1990.

Janzen, Daniel, ed. *Costa Rican Natural History*. Chicago: University of Chicago Press, 1983.

Joseph, Dolores. *Tres Relatos del Caribe Costarricense*. San José: Ministerio de Cultura, Juventud y Deportes, 1985.

Kepner Jr., Charles David and Jay Henry Soothill. *The Banana Empire: A Case Study in Economic Imperialism*. New York: Vanguard Press, 1935.

Koch, Charles Walter. *Ethnicity and Livelihoods: a Social Geography of Costa Rica's Atlantic Zone*. Ann Arbor: University Microfilms International, 1981.

_____. "Jamaican Blacks and their Descendants in Costa Rica." *Social and Economic Studies* 26, 3 (1977): 339-361.

Lefever, Harry. *Turtle Bogue: Afrocaribbean Life and Culture in a Costa Rican Village*. Selinsgrove: Susquehanna University Press, 1992.

Lemistre Pujol, Annie and Miriam Mayela Acosta Vega. *Monografía histórica de la provincia de Limón*. San José: Editorial Ministerio de Educación Pública, 1983.

Lindo Bennett, E. "La actividad cacaotera en Costa Rica." Thesis, Universidad de Costa Rica.

Macune Jr., Charles W. *The Building of the Atlantic Railroad of Costa Rica, 1821-1891*. Thesis, George Washington University, 1963.

Municipalidad de Limón. *Luchas y esperanzas: 100 años de historia doble e inconclusa del Cantón de Limón*. San José: Uruk Editores, S.A., 1992.

Nietschmann, Bernard. 1976. *Memorias de Arrecife Tortuga: historia natural y económica de las tortugas en el Caribe de América Central.* Managua. Fondo de Promoción Cultural, Banco de América.

Olien, Michael D. *The Negro in Costa Rica: The Ethnohistory of an Ethnic Minority in a Complex Society.* Ph.D. diss., University of Oregon, 1967.

Palmer, Paula. "Self-history and self-identity in Talamanca, Costa Rica." *Grassroots Development* (Winter 1982/Spring 1983): 27-34.

_____. *"Wa'apin man": La historia de la costa talamanqueña de Costa Rica, según sus protagonistas.* San José: Instituto del Libro, Ministerio de Cultura, Juventud y Deportes, 1986.

_____, ed. *Nuestra Talamanca Ayer y Hoy.* San José: Ministerio de Educación Pública, 1983.

Palmer, Paula, Juanita Sánchez and Gloria Mayorga. *Taking Care of Sibö's Gifts: An Environmental Treatise from Costa Rica's KéköLdi Indigenous Reserve.* San José: Asociación de Desarrollo Integral de la Reserva Indígena Cocles/KéköLdi, 1991.

Palmer, Paula, Juanita Sánchez and Gloria Mayorga. *Vías de extinción/Vías de supervivencia: Testimonios del pueblo indígena de la Reserva KéköLdi, Costa Rica.* San José: Editorial Universidad de Costa Rica, 1992.

Proyecto investigación, difusión y promoción de las diferentes manifestaciones culturales de la provincia de Limón. *El carnaval limonense.* San José: Ministerio de Cultura, Juventud y Deportes, 1984.

_____. *Cuentos tradicionales afrolimonenses.* San José: Editorial Ministerio de Educación Pública, 1985.

_____. *Remedios caseros y comidas tradicionales.* San José: Editorial Ministerio de Educación Pública, 1984.

Purcell, Trevor. *Conformity and Dissention; Social Inequality, Values and Mobility among West Indian Migrants in Limón, Costa Rica.* Ph.D. diss., Johns Hopkins University, 1982.

Quesada Camacho, Juan Rafael. "Algunos aspectos de la historia económica del cacao en Costa Rica: 1880-1930." *Revista de historia* (Universidad Nacional de Costa Rica) 5 and 6 (1977).

Reid, Carlos. *Memorias de un criollo bocatoreño.* Panama City, Panama: Asociación Panameña de Antropología, 1980.

Ruiz, María Teresa. *Racismo: algo más que discriminación.* San José: Editorial DEI, 1988.

Salazar Salvatierra, Rodrigo. *Instrumentos musicales afrolimonenses (estudio organológico)*. San José: Editorial Ministerio de Educación Pública, 1984.

_____. *La música popular afrocostarricense*. San José: Editorial Ministerio de Cultura, Juventud y Deportes, 1984.

Sánchez Vindas, Pablo Enrique. *Florula del Parque Nacional Cahuita*. San José: Editorial Universidad Estatal a Distancia, 1983.

Sarkis, Alia and Victor Campos. *Curanderismo tradicional del Costarricense*. San José: Editorial Costa Rica, 1978.

Servicios de Parques Nacionales. "Plan de Manejo, Parque Nacional Cahuita." San José, 1983.

Sherlock, Philip M. *Anansi the Spider Man*. New York: Thomas Y. Crowell Company, 1954.

Stewart, Watt. Keith and Costa Rica. Albuquerque: University of New Mexico Press, 1964.

Sunshine, Catherine. *The Caribbean: Survival, Struggle and Sovereignty*. Boston: EPICA/South End Press, 1985.

# About the Author

Paula Palmer arrived in Costa Rica in 1974 with a background in journalism and educational program development in the United States. When she learned that the people of Cahuita wanted to revive their tradition of Caribbean English education, she volunteered to help design a program of studies. She served as director of the Cahuita English School for three years with support from the Peace Corps.

To create culturally appropriate reading material for her students, Paula began tape-recording and mimeographing the life stories of the coast's oldest residents. Encouraged by the people of Cahuita, she organized the stories into a comprehensive folk-history—"What Happen"—first published in 1979. Seven years later she published an expanded, updated edition in Spanish (*"Wa'apin man": La historia de la costa talamanqueña de Costa Rica, según sus protagonistas*).

As director of an oral history project at the Colegio de Talamanca (1980-1983), Paula assisted her students in publishing a magazine, *Nuestra Talamanca Ayer y Hoy*, which was later reprinted by the Ministry of Education as a textbook. With two Bribri (indigenous) women she co-authored *Taking Care of Sibö's Gifts: An Environmental Treatise from Costa Rica's KéköLdi Indigenous Reserve* (1991) and *Vías de extinción/Vías de supervivencia: Testimonios del pueblo indígena de la Reserva KéköLdi*, Costa Rica (1992).

Paula Palmer holds a Master's degreee in sociology from Michigan State University. Since 1996 she has been executive director of Global Response, an international network for environmental action and education, based in Boulder, Colorado.